'This is an outstanding history and a genuinely compelling read. It's about the lost opportunity, in a time of relative affluence in public spending on prisons and probation, to provide a decent prison service and a more effective management of offenders. It's about the inconsistency and lack of strategy from Ministers – often from the same party – who changed too frequently and were generally disinterested in carrying through the initiatives of their predecessors. And it evidences an unwillingness of Number 10·to maintain any sort of strategic grip or direction. It's a product of meticulous research and painstaking interviews and fact checking. It's the best thing I've read on criminal justice in this period. I recommend it most warmly.' – **Sir Martin James Narey DL**, *advisor to the British Government, and a former civil servant and charity executive, UK*

'This is an impressively detailed (and depressing) insight into the impact of the "churn" of political leadership on criminal justice policy and practice. The authors have been amazingly successful in persuading the "movers and shakers" of criminal justice policy in recent decades to speak candidly about what they did and didn't do – it is particularly rare to see the senior judges speaking so frankly. The book is an eye-opener into the impact that the individual can have – thereby revealing many missed opportunities and false steps.' – **Nicola Padfield**, *Professor of Criminal and Penal Justice, University of Cambridge, UK*

'This excellent book should be read by all who care about what has happened to our prison and probation services over the last 30 years and should be a compulsory case study for anyone involved in public policy making. It provides a compelling analysis of what has gone wrong and calls

for a non-partisan approach to put things right. This is long overdue and deserves a full and honest response from our politicians and policy makers.'
– **Michael Spurr**, *Former CEO of HMPPS, UK*

'This outstanding book takes us behind the scenes in the theatre of criminal justice policy. A series of penetrating interviews with politicians, judges and public servants shows how a mixture of short-termism, amateurism, populism and indifference to evidence have damaged the prisons and the probation service. In half a century of involvement with criminal justice I have seen many changes which made little sense at the time. This book shows how and why they happened, and how things might be done better. Everyone who cares about the future of prisons and probation services should read it.' – **Peter Raynor**, *PhD, FRSA, FAcS, Emeritus Research Professor in Criminology and Criminal Justice, Swansea University, UK*

'The roll call of politicians, senior civil servants and judges who agreed to be interviewed for this work is extraordinary. Their candour, and the skill with which those accounts have been compared, provide a unique insight into a tumultuous 30 years in prison and probation affairs. If ignorance of the past dooms us to repeat it, then this book provides an antidote.' – **Peter Dawson**, *Director of the Prison Reform Trust, UK*

'An American tourist was part of a group being shown round Westminster Abbey. When they stopped in front of a plaque which read, "Here lies a politician and an honest man", the visitor observed laconically:

> "I didn't know you were allowed to bury two people in the same grave."

The authors of this important book have convincingly explained their choice of title in their prologue; and the repetition by this reviewer of an old (and feeble) joke should not detract from the value of their overriding theme: access in their own words to the explanations provided by those politicians responsible for the creation and implementation of the policies adopted during the last 30 years for the development of the criminal justice system, laid alongside the equally revealing comments of those senior officials whom they authorised to deliver those policies during the same period.

The drumbeat to those oral explanations is provided in Chapter 6: the near unanimity of view, from each of those occupying the position of Lord Chief Justice during the 30 year span, that policies selected for implementation by the politicians were doomed from the start; those tasked with their implementation were presented with an impossible task; and the inevitable conclusion that what was properly identified as a shambles in penal policy at the time of the Woolf report in 1991 has, over the succeeding 30 years, developed into an omni-shambles.

The initial doubling of the prison population, coupled with the decimation of the funding necessary to support that explosion of incarcerated numbers, requires no elaboration. This important work throws a shaft of light on how we have managed to end up in this situation.

With charm, and one suspects persistence, the authors have allowed politicians from either side of the political divide to expose themselves to a critical analysis of how they equip themselves to undertake the role (all admitted that they failed the elementary test of prior knowledge, or even an induction from a predecessor). Some have stood in a penitential white sheet; while the majority have moved on to other responsibilities, heedless of the wreckage strewn on the battlefield which they have left behind.

The officials responsible for the application of these policies have watched the developing train crash with stupefied horror, as they failed to apply the brakes to a locomotive out of control.

The authors provide a menu of their own suggestions for reform which those bold, brave and wise enough to introduce would do well to ponder. Perhaps the most important lesson to be learned is that identified by Lord Woolf in his lecture to the Prison Reform Trust, 25 years after the Strangeways riot: "Let's take the politics out of prison.'" – **His Honour Judge John Samuels**, *QC, UK*

THE HONEST POLITICIAN'S GUIDE TO PRISONS AND PROBATION

Through a comprehensive analysis of legislative and organisational changes and interviews with all the key players, *The Honest Politician's Guide to Prisons and Probation* provides an authoritative account of the crisis which has gradually engulfed the prison and probation services since 1991. Setting out the nature and extent of the crisis, King and Willmott show how the Woolf agenda was overridden in a process of political churn, through explorations of the Conservative government until 1997, New Labour from 1997 to 2010 and the Coalition and Conservative governments since 2010. Uniquely, interviews with all surviving Home Secretaries and Justice Secretaries of the period include insightful and candid reflections upon their time in office, and how they saw the future. Views from both inside and outside the prisons and probation services are also explored, based on interviews with the Director Generals of the Prison Service and of the new National Probation Service, Chief Inspectors of Prisons and Probation and the four most recent Lord Chief Justices, including Lord Woolf himself. Concluding by drawing on this collective wisdom, King and Willmott set out what is needed for an effective and sustainable future. It is essential reading not just for those in Westminster but also for practitioners in criminal justice, advocacy organisations, thinktanks and scholars and students in Criminology, Criminal Justice, British Politics and Public Policy.

Roy D. King is Emeritus Professor, Wales, and Honorary Senior Research Fellow at the Cambridge Institute of Criminology, UK.

Lucy Willmott is Teaching and Research Associate at the Cambridge Institute of Criminology, UK.

THE HONEST POLITICIAN'S GUIDE TO PRISONS AND PROBATION

Roy D. King and Lucy Willmott

Routledge
Taylor & Francis Group

LONDON AND NEW YORK

First published 2022
by Routledge
2 Park Square, Milton Park, Abingdon, Oxon OX14 4RN

and by Routledge
605 Third Avenue, New York, NY 10158

Routledge is an imprint of the Taylor & Francis Group, an informa business

British Library Cataloguing-in-Publication Data
A catalogue record for this book is available from the British Library

Library of Congress Cataloging-in-Publication Data
Names: King, Roy D., author. | Willmott, Lucy, author.
Title: The honest politician's guide to prisons and probation /
Roy D. King and Lucy Willmott.
Description: Abingdon, Oxon ; New York, NY : Routledge, [2022] |
Includes bibliographical references and index. |
Identifiers: LCCN 2021032268 (print) | LCCN 2021032269 (ebook)
| ISBN 9781032063263 (hbk) | ISBN 9780367773069 (pbk) |
ISBN 9781003201748 (ebk)
Subjects: LCSH: Prisons--History--20th century. | Probation--
History--20th century. | Prisons--History--21st century. |
Probation--History--21st century. | Prisoners. | Criminal justice,
Administration of.
Classification: LCC HV8501 .K56 2022 (print) | LCC HV8501 (ebook)
| DDC 364.6--dc23
LC record available at https://lccn.loc.gov/2021032268
LC ebook record available at https://lccn.loc.gov/2021032269

ISBN: 9781032063263 (hbk)
ISBN: 9780367773069 (pbk)
ISBN: 9781003201748 (ebk)

DOI: 10.4324/9781003201748

Typeset in Bembo
by Deanta Global Publishing Services, Chennai, India

This book is dedicated to
Meg
and to the memory of
Norval Morris and Gordon Hawkins
whose work inspired it

CONTENTS

TABLES

ACKNOWLEDGEMENTS

This book could not have been written without the contributions of many others and we wish to place on record our grateful thanks to them. First and foremost are the many people who agreed to be interviewed in the interest of trying to elucidate the evolution of policy in regard to prisons and probation: the Home Secretaries, Justice Secretaries and Junior Ministers, the Lord Chief Justices, and the Chief Inspectors and Directors of Prisons and Probation as well as various influential report writers. They all played a part in this 30-year journey of turbulence and change and generously shared their experiences with us.

We owe a special debt to our colleagues, Alison Liebling and Ben Crewe, with whom we shared our ideas at the very earliest stages, and we hope that we have not trespassed on areas of their own actual, or potential, research.

As our research began we decided to seek further background on the politics relating to prisons from Peter Dawson, and probation from Peter Raynor. We soon found that we also needed to seek advice on legal matters from Nicola Padfield and on problem solving courts from John Samuels. Their advice was invaluable. We sent them a copy of the 2nd draft of the manuscript and received many comments which helped enormously to improve our text.

We found it a difficult history to pin down and we had to go back to several of our interviewees, some of them several times, in order to clarify things that we had not been able to cover in the original interviews. Their responses had greatly added to our understanding of what was going on, and so we sent copies of the manuscript to Richard Tilt, Martin Narey, Phil Wheatley, Roger Hill and Michael Spurr in an attempt to eliminate any remaining errors. We owe them a deep debt of gratitude, for being so patient with us in trying to get the record as accurate as we could.

With so much help from others we sincerely hope we have not omitted anyone from our list of creditors. If we have we hope we will be forgiven. Needless to say the responsibility for all remaining errors is ours alone.

We cannot end without a word of thanks to Loraine Gelsthorpe, Director of the Institute of Criminology, both for her general support for the project and for finding sufficient funds from tight budgets to cover the cost of transcribing our many and lengthy interviews. Most of the transcriptions were carried out with exemplary skill by Louise Radok.

Finally, Lucy would like to say thank you to Roy, for inviting me on this journey of discovery with you, and to my students and colleagues for being a constant source of inspiration and information. Above all she wishes to say thank you, Dad, for trusting me to try to make a difference, and sharing my sitting and thinking space; Mam for spurring me to action and little sis for being my sounding board throughout this project. And to my wonderful husband for taking care of me and our girls; and to my girls for being so kind, funny and insightful throughout this difficult year.

RDK and LW
9 May 2021

PROLOGUE

Welcome to *The Honest Politician's Guide to Prisons and Probation*. When we submitted this title and a synopsis to our publishers some of the academic reviewers, whom they asked for opinions as to its merits, raised doubts – even complaints – as to the title. We made no apologies for 'borrowing' part of the title from the justly famous book by the late Norval Morris and Gordon Hawkins *The Honest Politician's Guide to Crime Control* published by Chicago University Press in 1970.

The two books could scarcely be more different. Morris and Hawkins cast their gaze across a broad spectrum of legal and other matters related to 'crime control', and the cure for crime which they offered to essentially generic 'politicians' assumed no limits to resources. Our book is much more limited in scope, focussing on a thirty year period during which prisons and probation in England and Wales were reduced to a level of crisis never previously seen –although there had been a difficult history of what might be thought of as mini crises, which in some degree had been, or were being overcome. The politicians who were in charge during this decline are very real – and we interviewed most of them to try to discover what went wrong and why in the hope of suggesting ways to restore the situation and prevent it from happening again. But we also wanted to pay homage to two illustrious criminologists, many of whose ideas have in a real sense inspired our thinking. Besides, although one of us was not yet born when their book was published the other is old enough to have met them both at conferences during an impressionable stage of his career and when they were at their peak. He has reason to believe that they would have welcomed the idea of this book. The Australian Morris, did his PhD, and then briefly taught, at the London School of Economics before moving to Chicago and Berkeley. Hawkins was born in London, graduated from the University of Wales, but then abandoned his PhD in Oxford to work as an Assistant Governor at Maidstone prison and then became the Assistant Director of the Prison Service Staff College at

DOI: 10.4324/9781003201748-1

Wakefield. Morris and Hawkins died in different continents and on opposite sides of the world eight days apart in February 2004. Separately and together they had railed against criminal justice policies conjured up by populist politicians without regard to the evidence. Our commissioning editor, Lydia de Cruz, deserves credit, and our gratitude, for standing by us, and our title, and for seeing the book through to publication.

Like Morris and Hawkins we have the intelligent general reader in mind as part of our target audience. There can hardly be any of them unaware that our prison and probation services have faced recurrent crises, over such periods of time, that they are now looked on as the norm. Our book attempts to show how that has come about and what might be done about it. Whilst our work has been the product of research, which has taken much longer than we had anticipated, this is not a research monograph in any usual sense. We have tried to keep it clear of footnotes and end notes on the ground that if something is important enough to mention it should be in the main text. We have made no attempt to review the great wealth of literature which represents the state of our knowledge on the topics we address not just because to do it properly would have taken us way over our word limits, but also because it would have diverted us from our main task. Nevertheless, we hope that what we report here will be of interest to our academic colleagues, and that they will forgive us for taking their work for granted as well as for any mistaken assumptions we may have made. We think it should be a useful source for students in the field. Some references have been essential but we have kept them to a minimum.

But we also seek to reach several target groups who have influenced, or have been influenced by, what has happened to prisons and probation over the last thirty years and are concerned about what should happen in future. First among them are our current and future politicians who are, or one day might be, involved in developing legislation concerning sentencing policy and the organisation of the prisons and probation services, including those who might find themselves on relevant select committees. Secondly, all those whose daily work is, at any level, in or around the prisons and probation services from Directors General to front line staff, the Inspectorates, members of the Parole Board and members of prison Independent Monitoring Boards as well as all those involved in the many charitable foundations interested in penal and criminal justice reform. Thirdly, magistrates and judges who rely on the reports of probation officers, and whose sentences might take greater account of funding considerations, and whose courts might be organised in somewhat different ways. Last, but by no means least, we hope it might capture the attention (and consciences) of the editors of national newspapers and perhaps influence them to resist the temptation to present their reporting of crimes and punishment in terms of sensational headlines. In a civilised society we have a right to expect responsible reporting with due regard to the facts from our journalists. They would better serve the public and victims of crime by making it clear as to what it is reasonable to expect from any criminal justice system.

One of the persistent problems which beset democratic politics - at least in Britain – is the remarkable speed at which Secretaries of State and Junior Ministers are moved from post to post. Although this probably affects all or most Departments of State there are arguably very strong grounds for thinking this is far more consequential for departments which have large scale commitments to operational matters – such as prisons and probation – within their mandate. There were sixteen Home Secretaries, and later Justice Secretaries, during the 30 year span of our research. They spent an average time in post of just 22 months. Most had little prior experience of the field. Even more remarkably, none had received a serious briefing, let alone a detailed hand-over package, from their predecessor - and none passed one on to their successor. Sometimes they had an instruction, or a nod and a wink from the Prime Minister, to move in a tougher or more liberal direction. Some prime ministers – Blair and Cameron particularly - took a closer interest in these matters than others. Within those limits Ministers were left to develop things more or less as they saw fit, often based on ideas that they thought had worked in their previous department, regardless of whether these were appropriate for their new one. Several distrusted their civil servants and were reluctant to accept their advice which might not agree with their own views. In any case civil servants were no longer quite the custodians of departmental history and culture that once they were because they too had become liable to be moved from department to department more frequently. Some Ministers relied on their own Special Advisors, even in a few cases having them present at our interviews, but their advice would likely not be based on any operational experience or understanding. We would stress that this did not apply to every Secretary of State – Ken Clarke, for example, in some but not all respects, being an honourable exception who very nearly managed to make things work - but it applied to enough to make it more or less the norm. Junior Ministers tended to be closer to the ground on operational matters and intriguingly some developed a longer lasting interest in their brief – which they maintained well after they had left office. This was despite the fact that few had found the prospect of the office appealing when it was first offered to them. But they too were destined to move upwards if they were ambitious and successful, or sideways or downwards if they were not.

We called this the 'politics of churn' – though we stake no claim to have invented the expression which was already in common use. In fact several of our key politicians across the political divide recognised the problems of the absence of collective memory, and the lack of continuity that resulted. David Blunkett, for example, told us that the 'Home Office has very little collective memory so you're never clear whether you're talking to people who have a clue as to what's happened in the past.' Andrew Selous, referring to departmental collective memory, said 'I'm not sure it's there at all .. what's been tried … if it hasn't worked, why?'. David Lidington, lamented that 'there is no process anywhere, in any department, for ... formal handover and … induction by your predecessor.' Ken Clarke told us that he didn't 'jog back' or 'interfere with my successors' once he had moved on.

Likewise, Michael Gove, speaking of his successor, Liz Truss said 'I don't think I can fairly mark her homework' But although they recognised the problem they mostly thought it was an insoluble one. Yet for those responsible for delivering the operations, like Michael Spurr, the result was 'you end up having to work through a whole load of stuff time and again that eventually often gets you back to the same place you were before.' Instead of continuity of policy what remains central to Ministers is the spectre of events. Kenneth Baker told us that 'Strangeways was a disgrace ... I was determined as a Home Secretary I was never going to let that happen again'. We hope this book will help to devise a better way.

One central proposition which Morris and Hawkins regarded as axiomatic has turned out fifty years later to have been overtaken by events. In 1970, in their prefatory note (p ix), they wrote:

> 'Crime is man's second fear. The cataclysm of war is the first. Crime, not disease, is the second; it has a quality of aggression, generative of fear, which disease lacks'.

That was long, long before the WHO declared COVID-19 to be a global pandemic. If the shadow of Brexit hung over the political landscape throughout the currency of our research – several of our interviews were interrupted by our politician having to leave to answer the division bell - the fears of the latest coronavirus pandemic had become the number two fear if not the number one - at least in large parts of the world. The pandemic eventually put a stop to our fieldwork with arranged interviews having to be cancelled and future plans put on hold. It quickly became apparent that we would need to add an Epilogue to our story, but with new strains of the virus being identified, apparently spreading more quickly and perhaps with more lethal force, that has had to be constructed on the basis of secondary sources.

Plan of this book

In Chapter 1 we offer a brief summary of the crisis and describe the origins, aims and methods of research. Given the apparent lack of understanding by ministers and their political advisers of the nature and history of prisons and probation we provide a thumbnail sketch of the differences between the work involved for those services. The chapter ends with a short account of how the two services have developed, in the case of prisons it is a story that can be told in terms of struggles to overcome a series of mini crises. Those readers who are familiar with such matters (and some may be more familiar with them than we are) should move straight on to the next chapter.

The next four chapters deal with developments in policy and organisational changes to prisons and probation under successive governments. Chapter 2 relates to the Conservative Government from the time of the Woolf Report on the riots at Strangeways and elsewhere up to the General Election in 1997. Chapter 3 discusses the New Labour policies from 1997 to 2010. In Chapter 4 we follow the changes introduced by the Coalition Government and in Chapter 5 those of the subsequent Conservative Government up to the general election of 2019. Each of those chapters is divided into two main sections. The first records the views of the politicians about the policies for which they were responsible and the second the views of the Directors of prisons, and where appropriate of probation, who had to carry them out. In both sections we quote extensively from our interviews as well as other sources.

In Chapter 6 we present what emerged from our discussions with the four most recently retired Lord Chief Justices.

Chapter 7 is devoted to our conclusions.

1

RESEARCHING THE CRISIS IN PRISONS AND PROBATION

Crisis? What crisis?

Politicians are reluctant to admit that there is a crisis until it is too late to do very much about it. That proposition has been exemplified in the twists and turns of the government's continuing response to the COVID-19 pandemic but it seems to have been embedded in British politics for quite some time. Jeremy Hunt, during his long tenure as Health Minister, and despite the ever-growing waiting lists for surgery, the cancelled appointments – sometimes for the second or third time, the numbers of doctors leaving general practice, the massive shortfalls in the numbers of nurses, the crowds at A and E departments with patients left on gurneys in corridors, proclaimed in his interview with Emily Maitlis on 3 January 2018, 'I think a crisis is when you have adverse circumstances and you don't have a plan to deal with those challenges and that is not the case, in fact, it is the opposite.' Just how inadequate those plans were became clear when the government's first, but still belated, and continuing response to the COVID-19 pandemic has been to panic about it overwhelming such an ill-prepared National Health Service (NHS). Although the funding for the NHS was notionally protected from George Osborne's protracted policy of austerity, in reality it was already unable to meet the demands upon its services.

Chris Grayling, when Secretary of State for Justice, had already established such a pose in a Radio 4 interview on the *Today* programme on 19 August 2014, by which time the Ministry of Justice (MoJ) was feeling the full force of major cuts to its budget. When faced with questions about prison staff shortages and rising levels of self-harm and serious assaults, he said

DOI: 10.4324/9781003201748-2

'There are pressures which we're facing but there's not a crisis. We're meeting those challenges, we're recruiting those staff but I'm absolutely clear – there is not a crisis in our prisons'.

It took successive reports from first Nick Hardwick, then Chief Inspector of Prisons, who was promptly given to understand for his troubles that his contract would not be renewed, and then from his successor Peter Clarke and perhaps especially Glenys Stacey as Chief Inspector of Probation, for it to become impossible for Ministers to deny that there was indeed a deep crisis in both prisons and probation and that something must be done. In prisons and probation, the decline happened under a constant churn of Ministers, here today and gone tomorrow, many of them determined like Robert Buckland, at the time of writing the latest in the line, 'to do it my way'. Too many of his predecessors did it their way, but the prospect of a short time in office in which to make one's mark does not make for coherent joined up policies. Some of the initial responses to the crises by Michael Gove and Liz Truss, for example, seemed only to place yet more unrealistic demands on beleaguered services. As yet, although there have been important efforts to stop the rot, there is still no coherent plan for a more stable future for prisons and probation based upon realistic assessments of what those services can achieve within the criminal justice system. This was more puzzling because 30 years ago there was a broad consensus about the way ahead – at least for prisons – as academics, penal reformers, civil servants and politicians were as one in endorsing the recommendations of Lord Justice Woolf's Report into the trauma of the riot and roof top protest at Strangeways prison in Manchester in April 1990. We discuss the Woolf Report in Chapter 2 but our story seeks to unravel the journey from Lord Woolf's Report to where we are today.

The origins, aims and methods of our research

When we first started to think about this research late in 2017, we had no cause for optimism. We had looked helplessly on at the seemingly endless demands for tougher sentencing which had more than doubled our prison population since the time of the Woolf Report, from around 40,000 to 85,000, and shifted the probation services from having a core focus on community-based professional case work to public protection and enforcement of a growing multiplicity of conditions attached to supervision in the community. We had watched the prisons and probation services being pulled this way and that as re-organisation was piled upon re-organisation and initiative upon initiative. And we had seen our students on the Master's course in Penology at Cambridge, who mostly aspired to senior management roles in prisons or probation, struggling to make sense of, and cope with, those changes. Like Dame Glenys Stacey, we had been at a total loss to understand how such important public services had been deliberately pushed through contradictory policy decisions into these dire straits. By early 2018, it had become clear, for the first time, that there was a Secretary of State, David Gauke and a Junior Minister, Rory Stewart, who publicly acknowledged that there was a crisis, and were prepared to begin to address it – albeit in very small ways. They have already now departed the scene and it may well turn out to be much too little and much too late to repair the damage. But in our view, it would not be sufficient to restore these services to a healthier state – there has to be some way to prevent a relapse and to develop a coherent plan for the future, based on evidence and best practice of what it is reasonable to expect, and which cannot be wilfully undone.

It is easy, with hindsight, to present one's methodology as a neat and well thought out predetermined scheme. In practice, things are often rather different and in a very real sense, this research – like Topsy, in Harriet Beecher Stowe's *Uncle Tom's Cabin* – 'just growed'. As prisons researchers coming from a sociological and social psychological background, we had considerable experience of analysing the everyday life and culture of prison staff and prisoners, and the evaluation of particular programmes. Although we had initially intended to focus on how changes in policy had affected prisons, it quickly became clear that it made no sense to study them in isolation from probation which meant that we had to do some further research to catch up on an area with which were insufficiently familiar. Similarly, it soon became apparent that we needed to take a still wider approach through examining sentencing policies and exploring the constitutional relationships between the Executive and the Judiciary. Fortunately, there was much expertise in and around the Institute of Criminology on these matters and from time to time we sought the advice of our colleagues. We also had to dip our toes into the more accessible reaches of the political science literature.

In the process of analysing our assembled materials, we found the framework offered by Pollitt (2013) useful. In a review of 40 years of new public management, Pollitt found four recurring situations regarding policy reforms:

i.   Where fundamental problems are said to exist without systematic evidence to support the claim
ii. Where reforms are introduced without any clear vision of the intended destination, or markers along the way
iii. Where there are no serious costings of the development despite being advocated on the basis of efficiency savings
iv. Without any serious plans for evaluation

In our analysis we found examples of all of the above and more, including:

v.   Promising ideas piloted by one Minister and not followed up by the next
vi. The existence of acknowledged areas of good practice but which are allowed to remain as isolated examples

vii. The revisiting of old ideas as though they are newly minted

viii. The belief that it is always possible to do more for less

In their brilliantly entertaining exposure of *The Blunders of our Governments*, Anthony King and Ivor Crewe (2013) devoted only four or five of their 450 or so pages to blunders in relation to prisons or probation. They first singled out (pp 190–2) the disastrously expensive failures in developing IT systems intended initially to integrate data to serve the courts in England Wales (Libra) and later to facilitate the *end to end management* of offenders (C-NOMIS) for the National Offender Management Service (NOMS), both introduced under New Labour. Their second example concerned the changes to the probation service under Grayling's Transforming Rehabilitation (although they never named the Minister concerned) which they concluded 'could in time turn out to have been a serious blunder' (pp 421–2). They also mentioned, but only *en passant*, the possible abolition of HM Inspector of Prisons under the coalition government's 'bonfire of the quangos' (pp 403–4).

King and Crewe's criteria for inclusion were deliberately free of value judgements and simply limited to whether or not policies delivered (or could have delivered) what was intended. Some of their listed human errors which gave rise to the blunders – cultural disconnect, group think, prejudice and pragmatism, operational disconnect and panic and spin – also figured strongly in our study. So too did some of their examples of system failures – musical chairs, Ministers as activists, lack of accountability, a peripheral parliament, asymmetries of expertise and deficits of deliberation. Like King and Crewe, we have tried to keep our account neutral in that we are even-handed in our critique of governments of all persuasions and we hold no pre-judged preference for public or private provision, but instead concentrate on what seems to us have been the consequences of individual policies as they became clear. Although we never intended this book to be a contribution to an understanding of the wider political process, as our appreciation of the way in which policies in regard to prisons and probation deepened, we began to understand that what has happened in criminal justice may have far wider implications.

The first aim of our project was to try to understand better how we got into this situation, and to do that we wanted to talk to the Ministers who had been responsible for those policy decisions and organisational changes to explore where they got their ideas or advice from, what they had intended should happen as a result and, where necessary, to confront them with what the consequences appeared to be. In exploring those consequences, we also needed to talk to those responsible for managing, and for inspecting, the prison and probation services at the relevant times. To get a better grasp of some of the legal and constitutional issues surrounding criminal justice, we decided to try to talk to senior members of the judiciary. Lastly, we had been aware that there were a number of important reports which had varying degrees of influence on the development of policy or organisational reforms and we resolved to try to interview the authors.

Our second aim was to try to formulate a set of arrangements for the future of the prison and probation services which would incorporate sufficient checks and balances to ensure that they had a well-resourced capacity to carry out the reasonable duties required of them, and with legal safeguards to protect them from the slings and arrows of outrageous fortune, if not for things for which they could be reasonably held to account. We hoped we might find sufficient areas of agreement both within and across parties to work towards such a basis for the future.

The basic bedrock for our research was the creation of what became a comprehensive archive on the development of policy, painstakingly and systematically undertaken by Lucy Willmott through an analysis of parliamentary debates as reported in Hansard. Most of the quotations in our account, unless otherwise acknowledged, are taken either from those debates or directly from our interviews.

We were confident from the outset that the Directors of Prisons would agree to be interviewed because we knew most of them personally either through earlier research or their links with the Institute of Criminology. We also felt sure that the Directors of Probation and Her Majesty's Chief Inspectors would be more than willing to help. But we had no idea what response we would get from politicians. And because we could not be sure of that, there seemed no point in drawing up a detailed proposal and submitting it to the usual research funding bodies. Accordingly, we started tentatively to test the water by writing to a few MPs whom we thought might be willing to help and when they did, we carefully transcribed our first few interviews ourselves. That was a novel, painful and time-consuming business best left to experts in that particular art. When it eventually became clear that we would get a substantial number of interviews, we sought two small grants from the Institute of Criminology which covered some of the travel expenses for one of us, and the cost of transcribing the remainder of our interviews respectively. Apart from that, the project has been self-funded.

In our initial letters to politicians, we explained who we were, what we hoped to do and why. Looking back, our early letters to politicians were rather apologetic probably reflecting the fact that we had been advised by friends and colleagues that we had a rather small chance of success. But we nevertheless hoped that our Cambridge credentials might hold some sway – several of our interviewees had been undergraduates at Cambridge – and we tried to put Ministers at ease by explaining how we wished to give them the opportunity to explain their policies and answer their critics. Gradually, as one or two Ministers signed up, we became more confident and were able to cite the names of people who had already participated by way of encouraging others to join us. This seemed to work. Ministers who had turned us down initially or failed to reply, finally responded when we were able to explain that they were among the few, and eventually the only one, for whose views we would have to rely on secondary sources. In the end, we managed to interview all 16 surviving Home Secretaries or Secretaries of State for Justice from 1990 to the end of 2019: in chronological order of holding office, Kenneth Baker, Kenneth Clarke (as Home Secretary), Michael Howard, Jack Straw (as Home Secretary), David Blunkett, Charles Clarke, John Reid, Charlie Falconer, Jack Straw (as Lord Chancellor), Ken Clarke (as Lord Chancellor), Chris Grayling, Michael Gove, Liz Truss, David Lidington and David Gauke. David Waddington who had been Home Secretary at the time of Strangeways had died before our research began. We also interviewed nine of their junior ministers: Peter Lloyd, Anne Widdecombe, Joyce Quin, Beverly Hughes, Hilary Benn, David Hanson, Crispin Blunt, Andrew Selous and Rory Stewart. That in the end we were successful in getting so many to participate was largely down to our sheer persistence – in some cases it took four letters and emails and many months before we got agreement. Even so, a further five Junior Ministers – Paul Boeteng, Patricia Scotland, Jeremy Wright, Michael Forsyth and Sam Gyimah either refused or did not respond to any of our entreaties. The process took far longer than we would have liked. Unfortunately, three influential Junior Ministers – Angela Rumbold, Gareth Williams and Paul Goggins – had died well before the start of our project. And sadly, we failed to identify from the government websites that three other Junior Ministers – Fiona McTaggart, Gerry Sutcliffe and Maria Eagle – had responsibilities for prisons or probation. We regret very much that we never tried to contact them, and we learned too late that they had done important and interesting work.

As we expected, all of the Directors General of prisons or Chief Executives of the NOMS – Joe Pilling, Derek Lewis, Richard Tilt, Martin Narey, Phil Wheatley and Michael Spurr – needed no persuasion from us and all readily agreed to be interviewed. We were less successful on the probation front failing to make contact with either Eithne Wallis or Steve Murphy, the first two of the three Directors of the National Probation Service (NPS), although their time in office was well covered by both Martin Narey and Phil Wheatley. The third and longest serving Director of Probation until that post was abolished was Roger Hill who later had experience with one of the Community Rehabilitation Companies (Sodexo) and he was very happy to participate. When the probation service was again represented at the national director level, we also interviewed Sonia Crozier (now Flynn).

All of the Chief Inspectors of Prisons and Probation whom we approached agreed to be interviewed: David Ramsbotham, Anne Owers, Nick Hardwick and Peter Clarke for prisons and Rod Morgan and Glenys Stacey for probation. It was a matter of regret that, when faced with the need to keep the book down to a manageable length, we took the decision not to provide the Inspectorates their separate section. We did so, however, in the knowledge that they alone among our interviewees had a well-established route for expressing their views in their regular and easily accessible reports. We approached three writers of important and influential reports: Keith Bradley on mentally disordered prisoners, Jean Corston on women in prison and Patrick Carter whose first report led to the creation of NOMS and whose second had resort to proposals for the so-called Titan prisons. In addition to persons we have acknowledged in our preface to whom we spoke in sometimes lengthy orientation discussions at the outset of our research, we also approached Alan Beith, a long-time member of the Justice Committee, Gemma Buckland, researcher for the Justice Committee, Andrea Albutt, Chair of the Prison Governors' Association and Richard Burgon, then the Shadow Justice Secretary. All agreed to be interviewed.

Finally, we were delighted to find that the four most recent former Lord Chief Justices – Lords Woolf, Philips, Judge and Thomas – all responded positively to our invitations, metaphorically, if not quite literally, by return of post. Three planned interviews were overtaken by the restrictions imposed by the COVID-19 pandemic and at the onset of the first lockdown, there remained a number of people we had planned to interview but hadn't yet asked.

All of our interviews, except one, were carried out jointly. For each interview, we did a search of publicly available sources to ensure that we had a relevant factual basis around which to construct an interview which meant that all interviews necessarily differed in substantive content. Interviews took place in whatever setting was most convenient for our respondents: they included private homes, the House of Lords, Portcullis House, MoJ, DEFRA, hotel foyers, clubs and business premises as well as the Institute of Criminology in Cambridge. Two were conducted by telephone.

We structured the interviews around the most important topics and attempted to make the interview a more or less coherent conversation. Our approach was not inquisitorial because we wanted to give our interviewees the opportunity to tell us how things were from their point of view. For our politicians we explored their prior experience of the field, what they thought they brought to the office, the extent to which there was continuity with their predecessors and successors and their relations with other stakeholders before giving them free rein to tell us what they had done and why they had done it and what they thought the effects were. Only in the latter part of each interview did we seek to explore alternatives which might have been followed and occasionally we found ourselves drawn into a vigorous argument. Our interviews with those responsible for the management and operations of prisons and probation were structured much more around the impact of policies on the services for which they were responsible, as well as their diagnosis of what had gone wrong and how it could be put right. When we talked to the writers of reports, we concentrated on how far and how effectively their recommendations were implemented and why they thought that was the case. Our conversations with the most senior Judges covered sentencing policy and sentencing guidelines, the issues surrounding the changing role of the Lord Chancellor and the establishment of the MoJ, as well as constitutional issues around judicial independence and the need for liaison with the executive branch. Our interviews with Inspectors were concerned with their relations with those whom they inspected and with Ministers, how they saw their role and their independence, as well as their findings from inspections.

We indicated in advance that we would wish to record the interviews but would be happy to agree a protocol with each interviewee as to what was on or off the record which might vary from everything was on the record, with the transcript protecting both parties, to everything was off the record unless it was already in the public domain. In fact, only John Reid adopted the latter stance and indeed declined to be recorded. Once we had scrambled to find pen and paper, we settled for relying on scribbled notes to jog our memories. The majority of our respondents opted to tell us within the interview itself what was on and what was off the record usually when what they had said might hurt someone's feelings. We agreed to work within those protocols. In the event, however, and before we embarked on our final draft, we asked every respondent for whom we could find a current mailing or email address, whether they would like to see a copy of the transcript of their interview and if so whether there was anything they might wish to modify. This was mainly because we recognised that in a conversation there are understandings that go beyond the spoken word and that unless one has quite exceptional skills the spoken word is likely to be less precise or well considered than the written word. Since the last thing we wished to do was to misrepresent our respondents we wanted them to have the opportunity to clarify what they had said. We explained that, like Hansard, we would eliminate 'ums' and 'ers', and sometimes when we returned to topics several times in the course of the interview, we might link these together, signifying the linkage by a series of dots between passages. By far, the majority of our respondents stood by what they had said subject to the minor elimination of infelicities of expression. Michael Howard asked us not to link passages from different sections of the interview and we agreed to that.

Our longest interview amounted to about five hours of recording over a morning and afternoon session; our shortest was done by telephone and lasted about half an hour. Most were of about 90 minutes duration. It would have saved a lot of time fitting the jigsaw together had it been possible to interview respondents in chronological order of their time in office but our imperative was to grab whatever interviews we could when we could. We recognise that it was difficult for some of our interviewees to search for memories of events long past. However, all of our interviews turned out to be cordial occasions, with interviewees seeming to enjoy the opportunity for reflection and agreeing that the research was a timely endeavour. We are very grateful to them all.

One of our most striking impressions as our research proceeded was how little many of the politicians knew about the history of the prison or probation service. Some started with a *tabula rasa* and seemed to formulate plans on the hoof. Some worked on the ideas developed with their own trusted political advisers. Some sought to apply policies they had applied in previous ministries which they thought had been successful, regardless of whether they were appropriate in the new setting. Some simply carried out what was dictated by their one-size-fits-all political ideology. One or two even claimed to have listened to the advice of their civil servants. Almost all had an eye to what No 10 was thinking and what yesterday's headlines had brought and what tomorrow's might bring. But none had a deep appreciation of the history of the services or a coherent view of the future that built upon the past. On reflection, a major omission of our research was that we were unable to include career civil servants on the policy side, as distinct from the operational side, of the Home Office or the MoJ. However, we got the impression that it was common for senior civil servants to move from department to department more frequently than used to be the case and so they may no longer be the carriers of that history that once they were. We have also moved into an era when politicians increasingly seek to place their own political advisers into influential civil service posts – a few had their special adviser present during the course of our interview. Yet, politicians ignorant of history may be doomed to repeat it. We, therefore, set out below a quick sketch of how the work of prison staff and probation officers are very different from one another, and a brief history of the challenges the prison and probation services had faced before our main story begins. It is our contention that the MoJ now seems to be unique in that it has *direct control over two large operational services and its own civil service workforce.* Shifts of policy and changes in organisational structure within the MoJ are likely to be far more consequential than they would be in other government departments without such operational responsibilities. Those with longer memories and who are familiar with those two services can proceed straight to Chapter 2.

The nature of prison and probation work

This is not the place to review the literature on prisons and probation, and we make no attempt to do so. While it is invidious to pick and choose, newcomers to the field might like to look at the work of, say, Alison Liebling (2004) and Ben Crewe (2011) as an introduction to the highest quality research on prisons in this country and Loraine Gelsthorpe and Rod Morgan (2007) and Peter Raynor (2012) for probation listed at the end of this chapter. But pick up almost any two books – one on prisons and one on probation and it will be clear they are as different as chalk and cheese. It is likely that the book on prisons will have been written by an academic, though there have been occasional contributions by practitioners, and that the book on probation will have been written by an ex-practitioner turned academic, though there are some written by academics without such experience.

Much of the literature on prisons relates to either case studies of different types of establishment, or to particular categories of prisoners – women, young offenders or high security risk prisoners for example – and different categories of staff – governors or uniformed officers. In one sense, a prison is a prison is a prison – for they inevitably have much in common. But the fascination for researchers is that they are all different, with their own social or moral 'climate' and distinctive staff and prisoner cultures. In every prison there is a relatively small, but usually, at least until recently, still substantial, group of staff for whom the prison is a place of work. They are outnumbered by a much larger group of prisoners, for the most part held against their will, and for whom it is – for want of a better term – their home. For staff it is a means of making a living and they

can leave at any time but they are also charged with a multiplicity of tasks – from vigilance about security, through the maintenance of good order and discipline, to helping prisoners prepare for release. For the other group, it is a place they cannot leave, and where they have little control over events which affect them either inside or outside the prison, and they have to find a way of making their existence a life they can live. Between them they have to make and remake their world day after day – and for many prisoners the number of those days has increased exponentially. Both staff and most prisoners have a vested interest in a sustainable and stable pattern of order – but there will probably always be some for whom those informal norms do not apply. Staff somehow have to provide for all the basic necessities – 'three hots and a cot' in American prison terminology – in addition to supervising exercise, visits, showers and the provision of education, work and a variety of programmes – in a timetabling jigsaw which has to be matched to staff shift systems and allow for holidays, sickness and other contingencies. It doesn't take much to upset this order and annoying upsets occur from time to time in even the best-run establishments. Staff are charged with making good or 'right' relations with prisoners in a double-edged way – through good relationships it is possible to develop 'dynamic security' or the provision of the intelligence that trouble may be on the horizon. But through good relationships staff can help prisoners through their sentence and to prepare for release. It is a delicate balance which can be difficult to maintain – relationships that become too close can jeopardise security and officers may become targets for corruption.

None of those prisons can exist in isolation from one another – although there may be scope for developing some genuinely locally based prisons serving their local communities. Short of that happening, they have to be part of a system which comprises prisons of different security levels to deal with the perceived security risks of prisoners, and prisons for adult males and females, and for young offenders. The system has to deal with prisoners in different legal categories – prisoners awaiting trial, those convicted but awaiting sentence and those already sentenced – and there are bound to be occasions when it is necessary to move prisoners from one prison to another in a complex puzzle which becomes worse the more crowded the system. The vast majority of prisoners come from disadvantaged backgrounds, have low educational attainments and often poor physical or mental health. Many are addicted to drugs, and there are powerful forces both inside and outside the prison which benefit from their trade. New psychoactive substances have to some degree replaced, heroin and crack cocaine, which in turn had supplanted the once ubiquitous cannabis – and there are ever more ingenious ways of getting them into prisons.

By contrast, traditionally – and in an idealised world which we hope doesn't descend into caricature – probation work has been quite different. In essence, it has involved a close relationship with the *courts* to whom the probation services have long provided pre-sentence reports to assist with court disposals, and with the local *community* in which the offender would serve their community sentence or to which they would return after release from custody. Once the supervision of offenders had been assigned to the probation service, one-to-one relationships between individual probation officers and their probationer clients prevailed. Each probation officer would deal serially with a number of probationers who together constitute her case load, allocating different amounts of time to each in accordance with their diagnosed needs and perceived problems. Unsurprisingly, much of the literature focuses on different forms of 'case work' between probation officers and their clients, and on the nature of probation as a profession in which the role was encapsulated in the phrase as 'advise, assist and befriend'. Those she supervises may have been placed on community orders of one kind or another, or else may have been released from custody on parole licence or other forms of post-release supervision. But whereas the prison officer is involved with prisoners day in day out, possibly for years, the work of the probation officer is always based on an intermittent one-to-one relationship for relatively short periods of time. Sometimes, but increasingly rarely, they may meet clients at their home, or at approved premises, but more often at the local probation office. Sometimes, increasingly so, contact may be by telephone. The aim is one of providing support and assistance of various kinds which may include allocation to treatment or other programmes. But there has always been an element of control in the relationship with the possibility of reporting someone for the breach of conditions which could lead to a return to, or the imposition of, custody and the emphasis on that has increased dramatically in recent years. What they share with prison officers is that there has to be balance between support and control. Traditionally and culturally, prison officers may lean more towards control and probation officers towards assistance and support.

What is clear is that the two services – prisons and probation – have little in common except that they share the same clients at different stages in their careers. So little, in fact, that it is hard to see why so much attention has been given to pushing the two services together in the same organisational framework. Although there is an obvious need for liaison between the two services, the natural place for probation is based in the communities where their clients reside – their natural bedfellow traditionally being the courts.

A little pre-history

Prisons

In post-war Britain, the first Criminal Justice Act (CJA) 1948, did away with the remaining vestiges of 19th-century policies on sentencing by abolishing penal servitude, hard labour and the lash. It also introduced new sentences – detention centres and attendance centres and corrective training to sit alongside Borstal and probation as measures intended to reform the future behaviour of offenders. The prison population had been stable in the interwar years at around 10,000–12,000. The 1959 White Paper, *Penal Practice in a Changing Society* (Cmnd 645), recognised that reported crime had increased substantially and that the prison population was steadily rising, but there was some degree of optimism and the CJA 1961 which followed it encouraged the use of Borstal Training at the expense of imprisonment. It was hoped that the establishment of the Institute of Criminology in Cambridge and the Home Office Research Unit would establish the causes of crime, and uncover ways that would help to rehabilitate offenders and bring down both the rate of crime and the numbers in prison.

In February 1963, then Home Secretary, Henry Brooke, announced that the Prison Commission was to be formally merged into the Home Office as the Prison Department, alongside the Probation Department, the Children's Department and the Criminal Division. In the House of Commons debate on 12 March, Brooke drew attention to the rise in the prison population which then stood at over 30,000 and in spite of a planned building programme, he regretted that 'we cannot build more prisons as fast as people during a crime wave commit crimes'. As a result, there were too many prisoners housed three to a cell built for one and too few prisoners had work because of the lack of workshop spaces. On the brighter side, he reported an increase in male prison officers from 4,200 in 1956 to over 6,000 in 1963 but he recognised that still more officers were needed. In many respects, the dissolution of the Prison Commission made little difference, because the Commissioners and their staff were already civil servants based in the Home Office. Brooke argued that:

> 'If the Prison Commission did not exist as a separate statutory body I cannot believe that we would now create a distinct agency organisation of that kind to run the prisons. It would be contrary to all modern thought'.

Some 30 years later, however, that was more or less what happened: the prison service was reinvented as a Next Steps Agency at arms-length from the Home Office only to face a further 30 years of chop and change in relation to that status.

The most famous Commissioner, Sir Alexander Paterson, was committed to the rehabilitative ideal and grappled with what he regarded as the central paradox of imprisonment – that one cannot 'train men for freedom in conditions of captivity'. He developed the notion of open prisons by establishing a prison farm attached to the closed prison at Wakefield and he pressed the case for providing productive work for prisoners. Neither the Criminal Justice Acts of 1948 and 1961 had provided a comprehensive statement of the aims of the penal system and it was hoped this might be remedied by the setting up of a Royal Commission in 1964 – but after three years it produced only volumes of evidence and never a report. Nevertheless, in 1964, Rule 6 of the of the 1949 Prison Rules, which stated that 'The purpose of training and treatment of convicted prisoners shall be to establish in them the will to lead a good and useful life on discharge, and to fit them to do so', was only slightly modified when it was promoted to Rule 1 (S.I. 1964, 388).

As the 1960s progressed, the optimism gradually diminished and by the 1970s had turned to disillusion as politicians, many criminologists and some professionals, lost faith in the 'rehabilitative ideal'. Despite this, the CJA 1967 introduced a number of important new policies introducing suspended sentences and discretionary parole for those serving 18 months or more between the one-third and two-thirds point of their sentence to be decided by an independent Parole Board. Although the Home Secretary continued to make the decisions on life sentence prisoners, and the Board was exceedingly cautious, its work was predicated in part on the assumption that prisoners reached a peak in their response to custody at which point release under the supervision of, and with assistance from, a probation officer was preferable to a gradual deterioration in custody. By this time, however, the prison system had been rocked by the first of five inter-related major problems which beset the service over the next quarter century four of which constituted crises in their own right. We summarise each of them below.

Escapes

Until the beginning of the 1960s, security had not been an issue although a plan for a small high security prison on the Isle of Wight to cope with a new class of criminal was in the pipeline. With the dramatic escapes of train robbers Charles Wilson and Ronnie Biggs, the prison service developed the notorious Special Wings as a temporary stop-gap response. However, the escape of the spy George Blake in 1966 who was serving the longest fixed term sentence of 42 years, left Roy Jenkins little choice but to commission an external inquiry, undertaken by Lord Mountbatten (Home Office, 1966). He delivered a rare example of an external report which was rapid (two months), precisely focused on the issues and well informed by consultation within the service. He offered a parsimonious solution; categorise prisoners in terms of their security risk, and *concentrate* the highest-risk prisoners (Category As) in a single high security prison, and build another if and when it was needed. This was broadly in line with the evolving policy of the Prison Department. It would have left other areas of activity untouched. However, his proposed design for the prison, and fears that such a concentration of prisoners might be a powder keg of control problems, so outraged the liberal establishment of the day that Jenkins felt obliged to refer the matter to the Advisory Council on the Penal System (ACPS) where it was considered by a subcommittee chaired by Professor Radzinowicz (the founding Director of the Cambridge Institute of Criminology). Just over a year later, it recommended that instead of concentrating high-risk prisoners they should be *dispersed* among lower security risk prisoners, in several high security prisons where they could experience a 'relaxed regime within a secure perimeter' (ACPS, 1968). It also called for an increase in the coefficient of security throughout the estate. It was an expensive solution destined to become ever more expensive. However, the report seriously misunderstood the relationship between security and control problems and the ways in which prisoners react to the conditions of their confinement. Above all, it was mistakenly thought to be in line with the policy of the US Federal Bureau of Prisons following the closure of Alcatraz. Far from diluting the problems of control, the dispersal prisons became the locus of major riots. And the policy led to many more prisoners being held in high security than was necessary. Robert Carr's first response to the riots was to have more of the same – to dilute the problem further by having even more dispersal prisons. The policy was nearly reversed by the May Committee (Home Office, 1979) and was roundly condemned as a costly mistake by the Control Review Committee (Home Office, 1984a). But it was left to Lord Woolf (Home Office, 1991) in the wake of the Strangeways riot to call for security to be brought back into balance with a sense of justice, fairness and humanity.

Riots

Whilst both staff and prisoners have a clear common interest in a safe and orderly environment, it is a balance that depends for its legitimacy upon trust and pro-cedural fairness. It did not take long for that to break down in most (though not all) dispersal prisons and rioting prisoners plagued the dispersal system throughout the 1970s and 1980s. It was the Control Review Committee (Home Office, 1984a) which laid the foundations for a more lasting solution. By then, the Committee had reviewed riots or major disturbances in five of the dispersal prisons: in Albany (1972 and 1983), Gartree (1972 and 1978), Hull (1976 and 1979), Parkhurst (1969 and 1979) and Wormwood Scrubs (1979 and 1983). The authors had come to accept research evidence that security and control problems could be analysed separately and required different solutions. Working closely with its Research and Advisory Group, comprising Professors Anthony Bottoms, John Gunn and Roy King, the Committee set out a basis for understanding that control problems stemmed as much from the way prisons were run as from inherently troublesome prisoners, and developed a strategy for dealing with the most intractable prisoners through designing small units that recognised, and were adapted to, their needs. Until then, the service resorted to transferring the most troublesome prisoners from one segregation unit to another. The original units were tentative and had limited impact, but the philosophy was established and the units were later reorganised, following an internal report by Michael Spurr (later to become Director General) into a system of Close Supervision Centres (CSCs). The early days of the CSCs were marked by stand-offs between prisoners on 'dirty protest' and officers 'suited up' in what the Press loved to call riot gear. Although the CSCs certainly had their critics, they eventually settled down into a well-managed and parsimoniously used system, subject to a degree of external monitoring, whereby the staff felt confident enough to open up pris-oners' cells in their 'shirtsleeves'.

Industrial relations

The third major crisis concerned *industrial relations*. The prison service was tra-ditionally staffed by hourly paid prison officers who were represented by the Prison Officers Association (POA) . It was also a service heavily dependent upon overtime working especially in regard to escorting prisoners to and from the courts. The crises over escapes and riots and the publicity that was accorded them gave the POA the opportunity to claim that virtually everything had implications for staff safety and the manning levels required to ensure that safety was maintained. Over the 1970s, the POA became more and more confrontational with local branches often at odds with their national executive and it soon became apparent that there were far more instances of industrial action by staff than there were protests by prisoners. During 1978, there were no fewer than 114 separate actions in 60 different establishments leading the Press to pose the question: *Who governs our prisons?*

The Home Secretary, Merlyn Rees, set up an inquiry under Mr Justice May (Home Office, 1979). Much of May's report was inevitably concerned with arcane matters such as the use of 'continuous duty credits' and other so-called 'Spanish practices' operated by the POA. He came up with no solutions to the industrial relations problems which were simply put back to the Home Office to deal with. However, Mr Justice May did leave one enduring legacy – the establishment of a genuinely independent Inspectorate of Prisons. After seven years of hard negotiating, the Prison Department thrashed out arrangements to turn uniformed officers into members of a salaried professional service. This was done by buying out the overtime arrangements in the package known as Fresh Start which was announced in Parliament by Douglas Hurd. This certainly did not solve the industrial problems as we shall see but it was a big step in the right direction.

Regimes

The fourth major problem was something that had received very little publicity but was nonetheless a dangerous and largely hidden crisis, namely the *deterioration of prison regimes*. This gradually, but insidiously, came about as part of a complex interaction with the other three problems: the raising of the coefficient of security across the estate, the anxiety about losing control and the industrial actions by staff, all contributed to the development of more restricted regimes which were increasingly accepted as normal. The May Committee acknowledged that in the crowded local prisons little more could be done than to offer 'humane containment' whilst still holding to the idea of 'rehabilitation' in the training prisons which were kept free from crowding. King and Morgan (1981) argued that whilst 'humane containment' was a perfectly legitimate aim, it was far from actually being achieved. Bottoms (1990) argued that something more than humane containment was needed to motivate and inspire prison staff. Nearly 40 years on, and despite major improvements under the 'decency agenda' encouraged by successive Directors of Prisons, we are still not able to provide humane regimes in many of our prisons, though admittedly the prison service faces different and far more complex problems now than it did then.

The first of many potential benefits which it was claimed would flow from Fresh Start was the enhancement of regimes for prisoners, paid for out of savings from the elimination of the Spanish practices. If it happened it would not be before time but it didn't. Research by King and McDermott (1989) published the year before the Strangeways riot, demonstrated that in five prisons, representative of all types of establishment for adult males, prisoners spent far longer locked in cells in 1987 than had their counterparts in five similarly representative prisons in 1970. Time spent locked in cells had knock-on consequences, of course, for access to education, work and other purposeful activities which had all declined. Follow-up research demonstrated that very little discernible benefit had flowed from Fresh Start into improved regimes. The findings provided something of a wake-up call for the prison service, but turning juggernauts around does not happen quickly. The stage was set for the events at Strangeways the following year. The riots at Strangeways and other prisons in 1990 had nothing to do with the inherent problems in the high security dispersal prisons but derived directly from the squalid conditions in which prisoners were housed, especially in the large Victorian local prisons, and what prisoners rightly perceived as legitimacy deficits in the way in which they were treated – though they didn't use such highfalutin language.

Management and organisation

The fifth major problem concerned not so much who governed prisons – governors or the POA – but *how* the prison *system* was managed. This was more like a grumbling appendix than a crisis requiring surgery – but it was to become a serious issue during the period covered by our research. Henry Brooke may have thought that no one would have invented an arrangement like the Prison Commission in 1963 but few were happy about the Home Office Prison Department which was run by career civil servants, including the former Commissioners, with no actual first-hand experience of running prisons. An internal management review in 1968 enabled governors to be seconded to posts in headquarters, and established an internal Chief Inspector of Prisons who became a member of the Prisons Board, alongside three Controllers of Personnel, Operational Administration and Planning and Development respectively, as well as the Director of Prison Medical Services. The English prison service was then divided into four regions – North, Midlands, South West and South East although responsibilities were distributed in confusing ways, including those for recruitment, manning and posting as well financial matters being handled by the Principal Establishment Officer and Principal Finance Officer in the Home Office, rather than the prison service itself.

Mr Justice May recommended that the Prison Service should have a clear corporate identity but concluded that it should remain within the Home Office. He recommended that the membership of the Prisons Board be increased, establishing a new post of Deputy Director General, and new directorates at headquarters including two non-executive Directors, in addition to the four Regional Directors. In 1984, a new framework of accountability was put in place under Circular Instruction 55/84 making governors directly accountable to the Regional Directors as their line managers. But there remained an enduring sense on the part of governors and staff in prisons that headquarters staff were remote and had little understanding of what it was like to run a prison. Staff at Headquarters tended to regard prison governors rather like maverick captains of ships at sea elusively beyond their reach, but nevertheless issued Circular Instructions and Standing Orders as if the word was father to the deed. Morale was generally pretty low.

The idea of 'hiving off' some areas of civil service work to separate agencies had been recommended in the Fulton Report (1968) to give clearer leadership and lines of accountability. Fulton proposed that newly created agencies should 'carry out the executive functions of Government within a policy and resources framework set up by a department' (para. 19). The framework 'sets out the policy, the budget, specific targets and the results to be achieved' and 'how politically sensitive issues are to be dealt with.' The agency management would 'be held rigorously to account for the results they achieve' (para. 20) in operationalising the framework. Parliamentary accountability would be visible through the Chief Executive answering parliamentary questions on operational matters, and public accountability would be through the publication of the framework document and an annual report on accounts and performance targets. In return, power and responsibility for all operational matters was to be delegated to an autonomous agency board 'as free as possible to manage within that framework' (para. 21), progressively moving towards the most delegated model of management possible. Fulton argued that whilst agencies should operate 'outside the day to day control of Ministers and the scrutiny of Parliament ... Ministers would retain power to give them directions when necessary' (para. 188) but also recognised that 'much new policy ... springs from practical experience in its operation. Any complete separation of policy-making from execution could therefore be harmful' (para. 190). He noted that for some areas of executive function, complete separation should not be problematic but for 'more sensitive matters' there needed to be further consideration of parliamentary and constitutional issues. There was limited take up of Fulton's proposals. Civil service unions rejected it on grounds that it would limit career prospects to within agencies.

Twenty years later, the Ibbs Report (1988) picked up these ideas and was more wide-reaching in its ambition. According to Peter Hennessy, as cited in the House of Commons Research Paper 97/4, Ibbs envisaged:

> 'A real devolution of power over budgets, manpower, pay, hiring and firing to executive agencies ...;
>
> A change in the British constitution, by law if necessary, to quash the fiction that ministers can be genuinely responsible for everything done by officials in their name'.

(p 10)

It was thought that overburdened Ministers would be relieved of onerous operational tasks and, as with the prevailing wind of the time, efficiencies would be made through applying private sector practices to public sector services. However, Henessey concluded that 'The salesmanship failed. The Ibbs report was sat upon for months and then diluted ... when it appeared it was instantly clear that the Treasury power was intact' and that the 'constitutional changes in ministerial responsibility were out.' In his memoirs, Nigel Lawson (1992) reiterated the need to maintain ministerial responsibility and control over expenditure, which was a result of a negotiation between No.10 and the Treasury. In reaching this compromise agency status was second best to privatisation, requiring the chief executive and board of any agency to adhere to strict targets and monitoring from the Treasury.

Probation

Probation was very much less in the spotlight than prisons during the post-war period and in large part its worst problems began after the Strangeways riot. Its humble beginnings go back to much the same time that the Prison Commission was established when Frederick Rainer, a member of the Church of England Temperance Society (CETS), encouraged the Society to appoint two 'missionaries' to Southwark court to reclaim drunkards and prevent them from returning to crime. What became known as the London Police Courts Mission (LPCM) worked with magistrates to discharge offenders who were required to keep in touch with, and accept guidance from, their missionaries. In 1886, this process was made available to other courts but the most significant legislation came in 1907 when the Probation of Offenders Act made missionaries 'officers of the court' and allowed courts to discharge offenders who entered into recognisances of between one and three years under the supervision of a person named in the 'probation order' – i.e. a 'probation officer'. Paragraph 28 of the 1909 Departmental Committee of the Home Office made the official position clear:

> 'It is a system in which rules are comparatively unimportant, and that personality is everything. The probation officer must be a picked man or woman, endowed not only with intelligence and zeal, but, in a high degree, with sympathy, tact and firmness. On his or her individuality the success or failure of the system depends. Probation is what the officer makes it'.

Gradually, the initial emphasis on attendance at church and pledging abstinence from alcohol under the CETS gave way to the development of a broader concept of probation work involving requirements that offenders without suitable accommodation reside in approved lodgings and the tasks of the probation officer expanded to include giving help in such matters as obtaining employment and support in family relationships. In 1938, the legal formula of 'entering into a recognisance' was replaced by 'consent to probation' which emphasised the essentially voluntary nature of the relationship – even though there may have been compelling pressures for offenders not to withhold their consent. The formula whereby probation officers were enjoined 'to advise, assist and befriend' their 'clients', which dates from the Probation of Offenders Act 1907, was restated under the CJA 1948.

After-care

The aftercare of offenders discharged from prisons had its origins in the hands of philanthropic bodies forming a patchwork of discharged prisoners aid societies organised around their local prison or prisons. The local justices originally were able to contribute £2 for each prisoner towards their expenses on discharge although this charge was later transferred to the Prison Commission. When the Commission took over in 1878, there were some 29 aid societies and in less than a decade that number had grown to 63. After-care was essentially voluntary but prisoners were provided with information about the local society and how to contact them. In 1933, the various aid societies formed themselves into the National Association of Discharged Prisoners Aid Societies (NADPAS) which in 1966 was to form the basis of the National Association for the Care and Resettlement of Offenders (NACRO) – the largest criminal justice charity by far. The aid societies, initially at least, were just that: they provided financial assistance and practical support but it was the police who were responsible for monitoring the behaviour of prisoners after release.

There were some categories of prisoners for whom some form of aftercare was not voluntary but compulsorily built into the sentence. The introduction of Borstal Training for young offenders came to follow a pattern of two years of training in custody followed, on the recommendation of the Visiting Magistrates, by release on licence supervised by an agent of the Borstal Association, a semi-official body which was funded partly by voluntary subscriptions and partly from public funds. In a prescient phrase, Sir Lionel Fox (1934), then a Prison Commissioner and the official chronicler of the prison and borstal system, noted that the agent acted first of all as 'friend and adviser then as policeman' (p 193) – bad reports could lead to revocation of licence, arrest and return to Borstal. This was later to become a major tension in the role of what came to be called probation and aftercare officers: were they supposed to be social workers assisting in the rehabilitation of offenders or law enforcement officers monitoring their post-sentence behaviour? Prisoners in what were then called the convict prisons were outside the brief of the aid societies and in 1910, Churchill, then Home Secretary, founded the Central Association for the Aid of Discharged Convicts which was wholly financed from public funds and this body, as with the Borstal Association, took over the responsibility of supervision of offenders to ensure they did not re-offend from the police. The Association for the Aid of Discharged Convicts later became the Central After Care Association (CACA) and came to share offices with NADPAS.

In 1963, a seminal report was published by the Advisory Council on the Treatment of Offenders (ACTO) shortly before that august body was disbanded. *The Organisation of After-Care* (ACTO, 1963) recommended that the Probation Service should become the lead after care agency – to be called The Probation and After-Care Service – thus removing this work from NADPAS. However, the report had a dissenting appendix by Leon Radzinowicz who feared that the aftercare element in probation work would be overshadowed by higher priority work for the courts. One can see here, perhaps, the first articulated tension between different facets of the probation role which is still in evidence today. In 1984, a paper on *Probation Service in England and Wales: Statement of National Objectives and Priorities* (Home Office 1984b) made it clear that the main job of the Probation Service was to enable the courts to pass non-custodial sentences, and to provide the reports and credible supervision which would encourage them to do so. Voluntary aftercare was no longer to be given any priority and received only resources that were left over from other core tasks. The report represented the first attempt by central government to tell local probation services what they should be doing. The report quickly became known by its initials SNOP.

Welfare in prisons

The welfare of prisoners whilst in custody was initially largely limited to concerns about their moral welfare during the early years of the Prison Commission and each prison had a Prison Chaplain from the established church and Catholic priests and Ministers from non-conformist churches were brought in as deemed necessary. In 1922, the Prison Visitors scheme, which had been started in women's prisons some years earlier, was extended to male prisons. These lay visitors were invited to serve by the Commissioners on the recommendation of governors, and were allocated to prisoners who might benefit from discussions with, and moral support from, someone from the outside world. They were appointed on a renewable 12 monthly basis but could only visit the prisoner to whom they had been allocated, although they were able to conduct their visits in their prisoner's cell. In 1931 there were 557 male and 85 female prison visitors.

Under the Statutory Rules of the CJA 1948 Welfare Officers were formally recognised in prisons as officers of the local discharged prisoners aid societies with responsibilities to sit on reception boards and identify the welfare needs of prisoners and to enlist their cooperation in the arrangements for their eventual release. Prisoners could apply to see the Welfare Officer at any time and without prison officers present. But a few years later, the Prison Commission was under pressure from the Howard League and the Magistrates' Association, to consider the employment of trained social welfare officers to have oversight of a prisoner's external relations during sentence and prepare for resettlement on discharge, but the idea was not popular in all circles. However, the Advisory Council (ACTO, 1963) endorsed the idea of appointing specialist social workers and in January

1966 the first probation officers were seconded to work in prisons and the existing 'welfare officers' were incorporated into the probation service. By this time, professional training was mostly provided through a specialist probation option within the Diploma in Social Work offered in many universities although there was also a route to the profession via courses provided by the Home Office at Rainer House in London.

The introduction of the probation service into the prison system was not universally welcomed either by prison officers or, somewhat more surprisingly, by probation officers. In 1963, the POA had responded to the ACTO Report, which had suggested a supporting role for prison officers, with an argument that prison officers should be directly involved in prisoners' welfare as a way of enhancing their role beyond their purely custodial 'turnkey' functions and offering a potentially better career structure for uniformed staff. Rank and file members, however, were always ambivalent; some welcomed the idea of becoming more professional whilst others feared it would not sit well with their disciplinary function. Whilst many Chief Officers of probation saw the development as a better way of achieving what they called 'through care' others on the ground found it difficult to negotiate a role which enabled them to pursue case work with individuals when bogged down with requests for phone calls, visits and the like. Through the 1970s, there were a number of experiments to explore the effectiveness of Social Work in Prisons (SWIP) with prison officers being designated as 'personal officers' and using their inevitably closer relationship with prisoners to assist the welfare officers in their tasks in a variety of ways. But with disillusion setting in about the effectiveness of 'treatment' and the 'rehabilitative ideal', the practical difficulties often proved insuperable: prisoners complained they never saw 'their personal officer' (if, indeed, they knew who that was) because staff shift systems and duty rosters not to mention sickness and annual leave often made that almost impossible. By 1981, the National Association of Probation Officers had become committed to a policy of withdrawal from prisons. Nevertheless, by the time our main story opens with the riots at Strangeways and elsewhere, the Woolf Report endorsed the idea of personal officers providing an enhanced role for prison officers and argued for greatly improved training. Rather oddly, it appeared to make no mention of the role of probation officers in prisons.

The stage is now set.

References

ACTO (1963) *The Organisation of Aftercare*, Report of the Advisory Council on the Treatment of Offenders, London: HMSO.
ACPS (1968) *The Regime for Long-Term Prisoners in Conditions of Maximum Security* (Radzinowicz Report), Advisory Council on the Penal System, London: HMSO.
Bottoms, A. E. (1990) The aims of imprisonment. In *Justice, Guilt and Forgiveness in the Penal System*, Edinburgh University Centre for Theology and Public Issues, Paper No. 18.

Crewe, B. (2011) Depth, weight, tightness: Revisiting the pains imprisonment, *Punishment and Society*, 13(5), 509–29.

Fox, L. W. (1934) *The Modern English Prison*, London: Routledge and Sons.

Fulton Report (1968) *The Civil Service*, Report of the Committee 1966–68, Volume 1 Cmnd 3638, London: HMSO.

Gelsthorpe, L. and Morgan, R. (2007) (Eds.) *Handbook of Probation*, London: Willan Publishing.

Home Office (1979) *Report of the Committee of Inquiry into the UK Prison Services* (May Report) Cmnd 7673, London: HMSO.

Home Office (1984a) *Managing the Long-Term Prison System* (Control Review Committee Report) Home Office, London: HMSO.

Home Office (1984b) *Probation Service in England and Wales: Statement of National Objectives and Priorities*, London: Home Office.

House of Commons (1997) *The Accountability Debate: Next Steps Agencies*, Research Paper 97/4, 24th January 1997, House of Commons Library.

The Ibbs Report (1988) *Improving Management in Government: The Next Steps*. A Report to the Prime Minister, London: HMSO.

King, A. and Crewe, I. (2013) *The Blunders of Our Governments*, London: Oneworld Publications.

King, R. D. and Morgan, R. (1981) *The Future of the Prison System*, Farnborough: Gower Press.

King, R. D. and McDermott, K. (1989) British prisons 1970-1987: The Ever-deepening crisis, *British Journal of Criminology*, 29(2), 107–28.

Lawson, N. (1992) *The View from No 11: Memoirs of a Tory Radical*, London: Bantam Books.

Liebling, A.; assisted by Arnold, H. (2004) *Prisons and their Moral Performance: A Study of Values, Quality and Prison Life*, Oxford: Clarendon Studies in Criminology, Oxford University Press.

Pollitt, C. (2013) 40 years of public management reform in UK Central Government – promises, promises, *Policy and Politics*, 41(4), 465–80.

Raynor, P. (2012) Community penalties, probation, and offender management. In Maguire, M., Morgan, R. and Reiner, R. (Eds) *The Oxford Handbook of Criminology* (5th Edition),Oxford, OUP, 928–54.

Stowe, H. B. (1852) *Uncle Tom's Cabin*, Boston & Cleveland: J.P. Jewett.

2

THE CONSERVATIVE GOVERNMENT 1990–1997

Introduction

Our story starts in 1990. Conservative governments had been in office since 1979 under Margaret Thatcher who won two further elections in 1983 and1987. Crime, as measured by the then British Crime Survey (BCS) had risen steadily at roughly 3.5 times the rate of police-recorded crimes since the early 1980s. In 1990 the BCS estimated the total number of crimes at around 14 million a year compared to the 4 million recorded by the police. The prison service was still run by career civil servants in the Prison Department at the Home Office although prison governor grades were seconded to headquarters in various capacities, the most senior among them being designated Deputy Director General (DDG). Although often referred to as the Head of the Operational Service, according to Martin Narey, the DDG played only a minor role in policy discussions. The prison population stood at around 45,000 having fallen from a peak of 50,000 in 1988. The system was overcrowded compared to its certified normal accommodation (CNA), and in the absence of integral sanitation, especially in the large local prisons and some older training prisons, buckets were provided at night for prisoners to use, which were 'slopped out' in a degrading morning ritual. A planned building programme for 20 new prisons was nearly half way through with eight completed. If the fall in the prison population continued the Prison Department anticipated that the numbers of prisoners and the certified accommodation could be brought into balance in two or three years.

A Probation Department had been established in the Home Office in 1938 and had introduced, or approved, training schemes for probation officers, but probation remained a locally organised service managed by some 54 probation committees, comprised mainly of magistrates, to whom the local Chief Probation Officers were accountable. It had a history of growing professionalism which

DOI: 10.4324/9781003201748-3

embraced a social case work approach as it sought to 'advise, assist and befriend' its clients. Its professional pride, however, had been damaged by concerns as to its effectiveness at rehabilitating offenders, especially as a result of what came to be called the 'Nothing Works' literature. In fact what that research actually showed was that 'nothing works much better than anything else' – in other words every-thing worked to some degree – the task was to unpick what did and didn't work and for whom. It had begun to regain confidence with the emergence of a finer grained approach under the 'What Works' movement.

By far the most significant event at the start of the period was the riot at HMP Manchester (hereafter referred to as Strangeways by which it was gener-ally known) although there were also serious disturbances at five other establish-ments. Together these prompted the Inquiry by Lord Woolf (1991, Cm 1456).

In Table 2.1 we list the main protagonists in the unfolding events of the time – the Secretaries of State and Junior Ministers responsible for prisons and proba-tion policy, the Directors of the Prison Service (there were no national directors for probation at this time) together with some key legislation and organisational changes. Part One of this chapter discusses developments during the period of office of each Home Secretary based largely on our interviews. Part Two is based upon our interviews with the successive Directors of the Prison Service. It was not possible for us to provide the same kind of commentary for probation at this time because as yet there was no national service. There were some national bodies – the Association of Chief Probation Officers and the Central Council of Probation Committees – but we did not locate any national representatives to interview.

Part one: The politicians

David Waddington (October 1989–November 1990)

By the time the protesting prisoners took to the roof of Strangeways in April 1990 David Waddington had been in post as Home Secretary for six months. He had been appointed by Margaret Thatcher when she moved Douglas Hurd to the Foreign Office and was, according to Kenneth Baker, 'delighted to have a right-winger at the Home Office'. David Waddington died shortly before our research began. His obituarist, Dennis Kavanagh writing in the *Independent* (25.02.17) declared that Waddington was particularly concerned that 'the Home Office still bore the liberal imprint of Roy Jenkins's tenure' (1965–67) and which Willie Whitelaw, Leon Brittan and Douglas Hurd had done little to change. He was reputedly the last pro-hanging Home Secretary or Justice Secretary (although Priti Patel previously held such views), and he introduced the first change of policy from his predecessor who had been working on a major Criminal Justice Bill since 1987.

Hurd had consulted widely before publishing the Green Paper, *Punishment, Custody and the Community* (Cm 434, 1988). In a speech to the Magistrates'

TABLE 2.1 Conservative Ministers, Directors of Service, Key Legislation, Department and Service Reorganisation 1990–1997

Year/month (general election in bold)	Home Secretary	Key legislation for prisons & probation	Prisons Minister	Director General of Her Majesty's Prison Service (HMPS)/ CEO of HMPS agency	Director of the National Probation Service (NPS)	CEO of the National Offender Management Service (NOMS)/ NOMS agency/ Her Majesty's Probation & Prison Service (HMPPS) agency	Department and Service Reorganisation
1990 Jan	David Waddington (D)	**Criminal Justice Act (CJA) 1991** new 'Just deserts' sentencing framework for the punishment to fit the crime and prison to be reserved for the most serious offenders; probation expanded and rebranded as punishment to increase use of community sentencing; backbench amendment to permit the privatization of all prisons.	David Mellor	Chris Train (D)	N/A	N/A	N/A
1990 Jul			John Patten		1990-1997 Probation is a local not a national service run by 54 local committees funded 20% locally and 80% nationally.	1990-1997 Prison & probation services are not managed together at this time.	1990-1997 Prison & probation services are in the Home Office throughout this period.
1990 Dec	Kenneth Baker		Angela Rumbold (D)				
1991 Jan				Joe Pilling			
1992 Apr	Kenneth Clarke		Peter Lloyd				
1993 Apr		**Criminal Justice Act 1993** starts to reverse the new sentencing framework following murder of James Bulger, Blair's 'tough on crime, tough on the causes of crime' & Major's 'society needs to condemn a little more & understand a little less'.		Derek Lewis			**1st HMPS Next Steps Agency** to establish operational autonomy with its 1st Chief Exec replacing the position of Director General on the Prison Board. The only CEO recruited independently from the private sector.
1993 May	Michael Howard						
1994 Jul			Michael Forsyth				
1995 Jul			Ann Widdecombe				
1995 Oct				Richard Tilt			
1997		**Criminal (Sentences) Act 1997** introduces automatic life sentences, minimum mandatory sentences & extends licenses, further reversing the CJA 1991.					

Association, he told them that in 'making the punishment fit the crime' this did not just

> 'mean that serious crimes need to be dealt with severely. It also means that the punishment should not be any more severe than the crime warrants (just) because of offences for which he has already been dealt with. Nor does he deserve to be sent to prison, if the current offence does not call for it, simply because he has previously been given non-custodial sentences'.

The late David Faulkner, Deputy Secretary at the Home Office at the time, and a former Director of Operational Policy in the Prison Department, had worked extensively with Hurd, deftly crafting the concept of 'principled sentencing' to fit within the Thatcherite environment of the day. It was intended to reduce the use of imprisonment on the one hand, and enhance the role of probation on the other, as well as to restore an effective system of fines, to be called 'unit fines' which would be linked to the ability to pay. After his retirement in 1992, he became a Research Fellow at the Oxford Centre for Criminological Research, but unfortunately, he no longer answered any of the email addresses we had for him. He died in November 2020. As far as the probation service was concerned these ideas involved some partly cosmetic rebranding as punishment in the community in order to realise the aim of decarceration. This fitted well enough with the Statement of National Objectives and Priorities in 1984 which had stated that the role of the probation service was to provide *alternatives* to custody, and probation's leaders liked the idea of moving to centre stage.

It fell to Waddington to introduce a revised White Paper, *Crime, Justice and Protecting the Public* (Cm 965) in February 1990 with a noticeably different tone signalling the start of a shift in the rhetoric – and soon the reality – of probation work from one of support to one of law enforcement, but much of Hurd's work survived. Under the rubric of 'just deserts' it emphasised proportionality in a *twin track* approach whereby custodial sentences were to be restricted unless the offence was so serious that no other sentence would do. Tougher community sentences combined with probation would be available for less serious offences, including the new system of unit fines. The probation service was to be given a wider role which included mandatory written pre-sentence reports to the courts designed to increase the use of community sentences. It had been anticipated that the proposals could lead to a net reduction in the prison population by perhaps as many as 4,500. However, Waddington's insistence that prisoners should serve at least half of their sentence rather than a third before becoming eligible for parole undermined those expectations. Waddington also opposed the unit fine system although that survived, and was duly passed into law, albeit not for long.

The Strangeways riot came out of the blue, both for Waddington and for the prison service, which was massively under-prepared for such a large-scale event and it exposed confused lines of authority and communication. Waddington quickly commissioned the Woolf Inquiry and encouraged his officials to give evidence. Whilst Phil Wheatley told us that it would be inconceivable for a minister to stop officials from giving evidence in such circumstances, Peter Dawson, now Director of the Prison Reform Trust but then one of those officials, thought it 'very strange' to be given permission to give evidence 'in public.' He recalled giving evidence that Boards of Visitors (now Independent Monitoring Boards) should no longer have any disciplinary role in prisons which became a recommendation of Lord Woolf and has since come into force. Waddington nevertheless stoutly defended the statement in the White Paper that prison 'can be an expensive way of making bad people worse' (Cm 965, p 6) – a phrase bearing the hallmarks of David Faulkner's drafting.

Woolf's report (Cm 1456, 1991) was published three months after Waddington left office but it is appropriate to discuss it here. The report came in two parts, the first dealing with the local circumstances of the riots at Strangeways and elsewhere and what lessons could be learned from the way they were handled. Here Woolf was concerned that Christopher Train, the Director General, an administrative civil servant who had overseen *Fresh Start*, was barely visible during the riot because he saw his role as primarily about policy and giving advice to Ministers. Management of the Strangeways incident, by common agreement, was left to the Deputy Director General, Brian Emes. The details of what went wrong in managing the situation need not concern us here although Waddington was clearly angry and frustrated that he had allowed civil servants to persuade him not to end the crisis through the use of force. He had come into office with a distrust of civil servants reminiscent of Jim Hacker's fear of Sir Humphrey Appleby in 'Yes, Minister', the 1980s sit-com. According to Kavanagh, Waddington felt that civil servants 'regarded ministers as birds of passage, coming and going while they endured'.

The second part of Woolf's report, conducted with Stephen Tumim, then HM Chief Inspector of Prisons, offered a blueprint for the future prevention of disturbances. It brought officials, academics, prison reform organisations and even prisoners into a consultation process like no other, including many public seminars. Together with their expert assessors, Gordon Lakes, Rod Morgan and Mary Tuck, they managed to bring about a consensus that most thought constituted a watershed from which there could be no turning back. Indeed David Ramsbotham, who succeeded Tumim as Chief Inspector, wrote that the Woolf Report was 'one of the greatest penal documents of all time' (Ramsbotham, 2003, p 73).

Woolf wrote that 'one principal thread … draws together all our proposals and recommendations. It is that the Prison Service must set security, control and justice in prisons at the right level and it must provide the right balance between them' (para 1.148).

His agenda for action was centred on 12 recommendations set out in para 1.167

    i. Closer co-operation between different parts of the Criminal Justice System
   ii. More visible leadership by the Director General to be publicly accountable as operational head of the Service
  iii. Increased delegation of responsibility to Governors of establishments
  iv. An enhanced role for prison officers
   v. A compact setting out prisoners' legitimate expectations and responsibilities
  vi. A national system of Accredited Standards to become, in time, legally enforceable
 vii. A new Prison Rule that no prison should hold more prisoners than is provided for in its certified normal accommodation
viii. A Ministerial commitment to provide access to sanitation no later than 1996
  ix. Location in community prisons to provide better links with families through visits and home leaves
   x. Division of existing prisons into smaller and more manageable units
  xi. A separate statement of purpose and more appropriate conditions for remand prisoners
 xii. Improved standards of justice through giving reasons for decisions, better grievance and disciplinary procedures removing Boards of Visitors from their adjudicatory role and creating a means of access to a Complaints Adjudicator

Lord Woolf was critical of the many organisational changes that the prison service had undergone over the previous 20 years, which had led to a basic split between field staff and headquarters whereby the latter was seen as 'more interested in reorganisation than the men and women who make up the Service' (Cm 1456, para 12.3). The most recent review of the organisation and location of management above the establishment level had been announced by Douglas Hurd on 3 February 1989 and its report was published on 10 August, a couple of months before Waddington took office. This report had also identified the gulf between HQ policymakers and operationally focused prison managers – something which most of our interviewees from the prison service confirmed – and its recommendations were, in part, aimed at dealing with that issue. After a short period of consultation, during which the Prison Governors' Association argued strongly for delay until the report on Strangeways was published, Waddington accepted the main recommendations which were designed to make the prison service 'a more managed organisation.' Henceforth, the Prisons Board would comprise the Director General and two non-executive Directors, plus the Directors of Buildings and Services, the Prison Medical Service, Personnel and Finance, Inmate Administration, Custody, and Inmate programmes. The last three of these would have both policy and operational responsibilities, but between them and the establishments themselves, there would be 14 Area Managers (later increased to 15) each of whom would be responsible for approximately nine prisons. The posts of Deputy Director General and the Regional Directors were to be abolished. It was also announced that the headquarters was to be relocated to the Midlands and that consideration was being given as to whether and, if so, when the prison service should become a Next Steps Agency, Waddington introduced the reorganisation in September 1990, five months before the Woolf Report was published. In the circumstances, Woolf took the view that it would be unwise to comment on the changes until they had bedded down although he expressed the hope that suitable candidates for Director General would be found from those who had direct operational knowledge of how prisons worked. That would help to give the Director General a much clearer voice as the head of the service and help bridge the distrust which had built up between establishments and headquarters. But Woolf also concluded that 'the one thing which is not needed is more change to the structure of management within the Service' (para 12.6).

Understandably, given his terms of reference, Woolf had little to say about probation, although he welcomed the evidence of the Central Council of Probation Committees which complained that the prison service seemed unable 'to recognise the potential of the Probation Service to make an effective contribution in working with prisoners' (para 10.31). Woolf also pointed to the need to 'further the development of through-care' (para 10.33) and spoke favourably about the evidence of the Association of Chief Officers of Probation concerning Bail Information Schemes (paras 10.88–91).

In 1988 Hurd had become persuaded that the private sector could exert pressure on an intransigent Prison Officers Association (POA) which stood in the way of desirable changes through its control over prison staff, and published a Green Paper on Private Sector Involvement in the Remand System. On the basis of unspecified research about the cost effectiveness of contracting out, Waddington invited competitive tenders for court escort services and the operation of a new remand centre – The Wolds – asserting that this 'will make a valuable contribution, raise standards and improve efficiency' (Hansard, HC 11.07.90). But it was the Strangeways riot which effectively ended his career and it became a fate that subsequent Home Secretaries were determined to avoid at all costs. Martin Narey, at that time Private Secretary to Lord Ferrers in the Home Office, told us that the general view at the time was that Waddington had been out of his depth in such a large ministerial role. When John Major became Prime Minister Waddington was replaced by Kenneth Baker and offered the role of Leader of the House of Commons, which he turned down in favour of a peerage and the Leadership of the House of Lords. Narey recalled that Major came to the Lords and sat on the steps of the throne for Waddington's maiden speech as an unusual act of support. In 1992 he became Governor of Bermuda from where he retired in 1997.

Kenneth Baker (November 1990–April 1992)

We interviewed Lord Baker in his office at the Baker-Dearing Educational Trust in Millbank, just a short walk from Parliament. Baker had been a Chief

Executive of a public company before he was elected to Parliament and he considered himself to be both 'a businessman and a politician'. He regretted that today most MPs were *only* career politicians. There were now so few lawyers in the Commons, he told us, 'that it was very hard to find people to serve as Attorney General or Solicitor General'. There were also too few people with business experience. Not surprisingly he was an advocate for privatisation, the seeds for which had been sown by his predecessors. He stressed in our interview 'that private prisons were necessary because the prison system was so dominated by the Prison Officers Association' and he was evidently pleased that 'the first private prison – the Wolds – opened on my watch'.

He thought questions about prior experience preparing one for office were irrelevant pointing out that 'Cameron, Osborne, Blair and Brown had all come to office with no experience of running anything'. He also thought that Ministers claiming prior experience of prisons in their constituency had often visited only to 'watch the prisoners put on a play or something.' He disarmingly claimed he had visited more prisons than most Home Secretaries in part because racing and the Tote also came under the Home Office portfolio and he was able to visit a prison in the morning and go racing in the afternoon. He similarly did not think our concern about the frequency with which Ministers were moved on was particularly important – and no more problematic for the Home Office than other government departments. He argued that it was the norm and not much could be done about it.

In his memoirs, he had written that no 'Home Secretary enters that great office with a long agenda of things to be done' (Baker, 1993, p 425). Nevertheless, early on, he commissioned Dr John Reed to review the services for mentally ill offenders. Although Reed's report was not published during Baker's time in office it must have been painfully clear that prison was no place to remand offenders for psychiatric assessment, and that large numbers of prisoners had multiple mental health problems which prison conditions were more likely to exacerbate than alleviate. But in large part, Baker inherited things from his predecessors – both Waddington and Hurd – and was content to carry them forward more or less in their original form – something of a rarity among Home Secretaries.

The first part of his inheritance was the legacy of the Strangeways riots.

> 'Strangeways was a disgrace. The really big mistake was made before they put it to Waddington that they should not use violence in any way shape or form to deal with it'.

He was one of many Home Secretaries to tell us that 'I was never going to allow that to happen again'. But he quickly moved on to express his wholehearted support for the Woolf Report which he thought was 'outstandingly good'. 'I accepted virtually everything that was said and implemented it as soon as I could.' Not everything was implemented, of course, but it was probably the last occasion when there was non-partisan agreement around a major criminal justice issue:

there was a sense that, as far as prisons were concerned, things could only get better. When the Woolf Report was published with its 12 recommendations and 204 proposals, he welcomed it with the words 'Lord Justice Woolf emphasises that we need to balance security and control with justice and I wholly endorse that view.' But presumably with a nod to the right-wing press he added, 'Prisons should be places that are austere but decent' (Hansard, HC 25.2.91) whereas Woolf had emphasised the need for treating prisoners fairly and taking account of what he called their 'legitimate expectations.' A little over six months later he introduced the White Paper *Custody, Care and Justice* which enabled him to describe himself with some justification in our interview as 'the last of the liberal Home Secretaries … because after me it was "Prison Works" and the ambition of all the other Home Secretaries was to be tougher than their predecessors'. On reflection, he partially exempted Ken Clarke from that group.

Baker began the process of implementation with a determination to end 'slopping out' even more quickly than had been proposed by Woolf, as well as moving to increase the hours spent in constructive regime activities and reforming the complaints procedures. The creation of a code of standards was more problematic – both for Ministers and civil servants because of the complexity of the system and the fear of creating hostages to fortune and providing a rod for one's own back. As Peter Dawson told us 'it was conveniently shelved' in *Custody Care and Justice*. Richard Tilt told us that senior managers continued 'to argue long and hard' for a code of standards 'but were always blocked by the Treasury'. Baker was also sympathetic to the idea of clustering prisons in areas of high population – but the exigencies of coping with changes in the prison population were always likely to override the development of Woolf's community prisons unless there was to be a massive investment to facilitate the restructuring of the estate. It was not long before it became clear that there was no overall timetable for the completion of the programme and no commitment to provide the necessary resources.

Above all the rejection of Woolf's 7th recommendation – to create a rule to end overcrowding – was to render nugatory Baker's claim that *Custody, Care and Justice* would 'chart the direction of the prison service for the rest of the century and beyond' (Hansard, HC 25.2.91). Joe Pilling, who had replaced Chris Train, as Director General regarded such a rule as 'an indispensable precondition of sustained and universal improvement in prison conditions.' Richard Tilt thought that 'the refusal of the Treasury to countenance limiting the prison population to CNA seriously undermined' the effectiveness of the service. One of us had asked David Faulkner at the time why the civil servants had not pressed harder for Woolf's proposed rule. On reflection he said that 'some people argued that given that the prison population was relatively stable, they did not think it was necessary'. Woolf had been careful not to ask for a limit to the overall size of the prison population – to which a stock refusal might be made on grounds that it would interfere with the independence of the judiciary – but simply 'that no establishment should hold more prisoners than is provided for in its certified normal level of occupation'. Baker told us that the Home Secretary must 'ensure that he gets sufficient money to maintain the prison estate and to expand it' where necessary although he also believed that 'far too many people were sent to prison'. He wanted to see greater awareness among judges about the costs of sending people to prison for different lengths of sentences and to that end toyed with the idea of introducing 'capita funding for prisoners' just as he had for students and pupils whilst at the Department of Education. He wondered whether judges might be given specific budgets within which to deliver appropriately parsimonious sentences. Although the idea of problem-solving courts, let alone judicial monitoring of sentences, had not really surfaced at that time, Baker's speculations about judicial control of local prison budgets may fit well with them – a matter to which we return in our conclusions. But it takes cross-party agreement and legislation to ensure that prisons are not used beyond their capacity and the opportunity was lost with the failure to deliver Woolf's proposed rule.

In fairness to Baker the budgets had probably already been set by the time the White Paper was published and the real bargaining would have had to come in the following round by which time he had moved on and at which time the prison population was stable. But the prison population did not remain stable for long. The building programme became – as they almost always do – less a matter of replacing old stock but more a desperate attempt to catch up. Baker had survived the fallout from the escape of two Category A prisoners from HMP Brixton arguing that 'the Home Secretary is responsible for policy in prison matters. The administration, development and running of the prisons are the responsibility of the Director General and of individual prison governors' (Hansard, HC 8.7.91).

Like Waddington before him, he also inherited Douglas Hurd's Criminal Justice Bill which he then saw through Parliament as the CJA 1991. A backbench amendment, however, allowed him to announce the contracting out of Blakenhurst for convicted prisoners without waiting for an evaluation of the 'experimental' letting of the Wolds to G4S for remand prisoners. Although the evaluation of the Wolds turned out to be positive this was undoubtedly an expansion of the commitment to privatisation. He hoped, as Hurd had done, that the Act with its unit fines and strictures about prison being only a last resort, would bring the prison population under control as well as lead to a stronger probation service.

On his watch there were more attempts to persuade private companies to offer employment to prisoners and ex-prisoners. He valued the reports of the Inspectorate and arranged for them to be published. He claimed to have good relationships with Judge Tumim, and he later enjoyed Ramsbotham's forthright approach to inspection but found their successors rather bland by contrast. He continued to pursue plans to move the headquarters of the prison service to the Midlands where accommodation had been found in Derby. He had hoped this would give the Director General and the prison service a clearer identity and greater independence, through greater physical distance, from the Home Office and the Home Secretary. He had commissioned the review of the organisa-tion of the prison service by Admiral Sir Raymond Lygo and he welcomed the report which supported his determination to develop the service as a Next Steps Agency in which responsibility for its operational performance would rest firmly with the Director General.

In the spring of 1992 'a General Election was on the way' and he had never been 'a member of the Prime Minister's inner circle. The Guard was changing' (Baker, 1993, pp 471–2). After 17 months in office, Baker resolved to return to the back benches and re-engage with the business world. The ensuing election marked a ramping up of law and order as an issue in which Labour was described both in the media and in the Commons as 'soft and flabby on crime.' His time in office had seen several major developments, often essentially continuations of recently evolving policy, in which he was 'ably served' by his Prisons Minister, the late Angela Rumbold. There is no doubt that Baker was genuinely aghast that the prison population which had stood at around 42,000 when he left office was double that on the day of our interview. He was replaced by Ken Clarke.

Ken Clarke (April 1992–May 1993)

Our interview with Ken Clarke took place at his office in Portcullis House on a hot mid-summer afternoon. It was an interview like no other – more a stream of consciousness which jumped between his time as Home Secretary and his later period as Minister of Justice and Lord Chancellor. Although this yielded much interesting material it did not always pertain to important events we wanted to explore that occurred a quarter of a century earlier. We were occasionally chas-tised for not asking questions but before we could do so the monologue had been resumed. This meant there were some quite startling omissions. There was, for example, no mention at all of his pursuit of the prison service as a Next Steps Agency or his appointment of Derek Lewis as the first Director General from the private sector. Even more surprising, when we checked his memoirs (Clarke, 2016) they were not mentioned there either. Indeed he told us 'I had all the same ideas about rehabilitation but I don't recall in the end that we did anything very much in particular about prisons'.

He had expected to be at the Home Office for the whole Parliament but in fact stayed there for only about 14 months. 'It was a huge department in those days,' he told us, 'but when I left … I was still getting my agenda sorted out'. He had intended to concentrate on reforming the Police Authorities, but on that he admitted 'I was pretty ineffective'. His main recollection of prisons at that time was about his determination to avoid the fate that had befallen David Waddington. In one incident when prisoners climbed onto the roof he was

> 'certainly not going to be told that this was nothing to do with the Secretary of State. I wasn't intending to take over personally but I did want to be aware of what was happening, make suggestions if I wanted to'.

As it happened there was no need because it started to pour with rain and the prisoners went back inside.

In fact Clarke had a mixed record on criminal justice policy but an excellent one in terms of his relations with his officials.

The CJA 1991 had been steered through Parliament by Kenneth Baker and came into force in October 1992. In its first few months, and possibly before that in anticipation of its passing, the effect was to reduce the use of custody whilst increasing the use of community sentences and fines. Just what had been intended. He dismissed his successors at the Home Office, in much the same terms used by Baker as 'a series of ministers playing to the gallery and trying to show they were tough law and order figures' with Michael Howard and David Blunkett among others in his sights. But as he wrote in his memoirs

> 'my reputation was not as liberal as most of my predecessors. I was in fact very liberal, but I had inherited some measures that went too far even for me .... on unit fines and on the relevance of previous convictions to the sentencing of criminals'.
>
> *(Clarke, 2016, p 292)*

He, therefore, reacted with remarkable speed when the popular press, aided and abetted by then Lord Chief Justice (LCJ) Taylor, ridiculed some examples of the operation of the unit fine system. Clarke had initially supported the scheme and he 'began to have discussions with officials about how to reform it' in ways suggested in evaluations by the Home Office Research Unit of some promising pilot studies. However, he 'despaired after a series of useless meetings with the leaders of the Magistrates Association ... a formidable collection of ladies' who were unwilling to change their ways and so he 'did as elegant a U-turn as I could manage ... and ... decided to abolish the system' (Clarke, 2016, p 293).

In addition to his remarks on unit fines, LCJ Taylor also chose to re-interpret what was meant by 'sentences being commensurate with the seriousness of the offence' as stated in the CJA 1991. The White Paper underpinning that Act had, on the basis of Home Office research, *explicitly* questioned the validity of notions of deterrence, and the Act *deliberately* made it more difficult to take previous convictions into account when determining the seriousness of the current offence. Lord Taylor ruled that the Act must mean 'commensurate with the punishment and deterrence which the seriousness of the offence requires' which it clearly did not. Clarke's announcement that he was abandoning unit fines completely in the CJA 1993 was made in May 1993 – just days before he departed for the Treasury – and the Act received the Royal Assent two months later. At the same time, it reversed section 29 of the CJA 1991 which limited the relevance of prior convictions in determining the gravity of the current offence, making it far easier for the courts to reach the conclusion that custody was justified. It was a remarkable *volte-face*. In two strokes Clarke had seriously undermined the CJA 1991 which he had previously 'dutifully defended for a few weeks' (Clarke, 2016, p 293). The 'principled sentencing' nurtured by Hurd and Faulkner was effectively reversed. Peter Raynor wondered whether Clarke 'had really done his homework'. These changes, he told us, meant that

> 'probation was left with the punitive rebranding, probation orders were now a punishment instead of an alternative to punishment, while all measures which would have made this a reasonable price to pay were summarily abolished. The rebranding of course, went on, including the abolition of consent to probation, but few politicians have ever been convinced that probation is punitive enough'.

Unlike his predecessor, Clarke was a lawyer by training and had practised briefly before entering parliament. Clarke had no background in business, but according to Phil Wheatley, 'he demonstrated a great belief in the power of the market to drive improvement and efficiency. He was agnostic about who the providers were but wanted sufficient of them, including from the public sector, to provide an effective market'. Following the recommendations of the Lygo Report, it fell to Clarke to establish the prison service as an Executive Agency in 1993 and he linked it to the White Paper *Custody Care and Justice* as a way of driving those aspirations forward. He appointed Derek Lewis as the first, and so far the only, Chief Executive from the private sector, and whom he trusted, in keeping with the arms-length principle of *Next Steps Agencies*, to get on with the job of prison reform without interference from the Minister. Lewis told us that Clarke was indeed the least hands-on, most supportive, and laid back of Home Secretaries. He expected the Chief Executive and the Prisons Board to make the final decisions on market testing and contracting out. However, Lewis's appointment was controversial and was made despite the claims of the well-regarded incumbent, Joe Pilling, who had earned the support and respect of prison staff as well as the Prisons Board. Clarke had apparently thought, albeit mistakenly, that Pilling would not take forward the idea of private prisons. This background to the appointment certainly meant that Lewis was greeted initially by a rather sullen Prisons Board. But the appointment signalled Clarke's faith in private sector solutions even though, as Lewis told us, his understanding of how the private sector actually worked was often seriously flawed. Lewis also confirmed Clarke's claim to us that he ran the department

> 'rather like a debating society where you thrash out with one another what you want to do before finally settling on a plan. You've got to have respect for the expertise of your officials and then you've got to decide and sign it off'.

Clarke had his own trusted adviser but he had no time for the new kind of special advisers (SpAds) – political appointees who are 'mainly obsessed with press relations.'

In fact he greatly accelerated the privatisation process. 'It was Douglas Hurd who announced his intention' he told us,

> 'but the Department wasn't really enthusiastic about it …. The Home Office was a good department but they could go very slowly. The prisons at that time varied greatly in quality – the best ones were alright but the worst were very bad. It needed up to date management and innovation and the best way to do that was through a variety of providers and competitive tenders'.

Like Baker before him, Clarke saw the threat of privatisation as a way of curbing once and for all the considerable power the POA retained even after *Fresh Start*. The initial contracting out of court escort services to Group 4 (later G4S after amalgamation with Securicor) occurred on his watch and some serious early problems were given extensive coverage in the Press. However, it did produce some immediate improvements in security because, as Phil Wheatley reminded us, the previous arrangements of getting prisoners to and from courts were sometimes reduced to 'using taxis and ordinary buses which had been hopelessly insecure'. The contracting out of court escorts also ended some of the perks which had become abused by the POA. When he announced to Parliament that he was inviting tenders for the operation of Doncaster Prison he looked forward to a time when the private sector would have 'a significant level of involvement' in the prison system (Hansard, HC 3.2.93). Moreover, this was not to be limited to new prisons: Strangeways, by now known simply as HMP Manchester, was among the first of the existing prisons to be market tested – although when the time came the public sector actually retained that contract against competition from private companies. Clarke introduced the contracting out of education services claiming they provided 'value for money' – although evidence to that effect was rarely offered. Within the public sector prisons 'new managerialism' prevailed. Like other Next Steps Agencies, the prison service had to have clear performance targets signed off by the Treasury before being given the necessary operational and financial freedoms which accompanied agency status. Clarke also initiated the creation of the post of Prisons Ombudsman – although the first, Sir Peter Woodhead, was not appointed until May 1994.

One of Clarke's Junior Ministers at the Home Office was Peter Lloyd, whom we were able to interview at his North London home. Peter Lloyd is most famous for having steered the Sunday Trading Law through Parliament, but he was twice closely involved in the Prisons brief – the first time, under Clarke 'because I was shoved there' and the second, under Howard, 'because I really made efforts to get back there … prisons is an area where with the right sustained policies things could be successful instead of being a problem'. Peter Lloyd was an old friend of Clarke's from Cambridge days and it was clear that he was highly regarded.

'I simply said to Peter that the prison service was his to get on with, but that if we were about to have a monumental row, he should tell me. Then we could sit down and work out together what to do. It took an enormous load off my desk'.

(Clarke, 2016 p 284)

Like other Junior Ministers who had the prison or probation brief Peter Lloyd remains interested in what has happened since and is still involved in the field now through his association with the charity the New Bridge Foundation. But he was also able to help us understand a number of issues then current and he was aghast at what had happened to prisons and probation under his successors. He was interested in our emerging ideas about how we might do better in future and we return to those matters in our conclusions.

Despite some reduction in the prison population and the completion of some 16 of the planned new prisons, the system was still overcrowded and reliant on the use of expensive police cells. On Clarke's watch, some of the key recommendations of the Reed Report were accepted late in 1992 requiring health authorities to include services for mentally disordered offenders in their plans, and there was a declaration that prison medical services should be brought closer to the NHS. Also the first sex offender treatment programmes were piloted in prisons. The plan to move headquarters to Derby, however, was dropped after £11.5 million had been spent on the proposal. Clarke was under pressure from Government belt-tightening and preferred to spend the money that would have been spent on building the new headquarters, to provide additional accommodation for prisoners. But according to some, Clarke was never much keen on the idea. The hopes of his predecessor – and Lygo – that removal to the Midlands would provide the distance from ministers implied in Agency status were lost.

Clarke's move to the Treasury in May 1993 after less than 14 months at the Home Office was occasioned by the belated removal of Norman Lamont after the travails of Black Wednesday. But by the time of Clarke's departure, the climate on law and order was changing. On 12 February 1993, the infant James Bulger was abducted and killed by two ten-year-old boys who were formally charged later that month. Understandably, this event shocked the nation and received huge press publicity and the politicians reacted. In that same month Tony Blair – who Clarke always thought of as a 'One Nation Conservative who admired Margaret Thatcher and had somehow wound up in the Labour Party because his wife was a left-wing political activist' (Clarke, 2016, p 292) – coined his mantra 'tough on crime and tough on the causes of crime'; and John Major delivered himself of the astonishing statement that 'society needs to condemn a little more and understand a little less'. Some of the political furore was directed at the CJA 1991 which was seen as too soft. Clarke defended the Act in Parliament: 'that legislation was taken through Parliament at the request of the courts and was supported by both sides of the House' he said, and since it had only come into effect five months earlier, we needed to see how well it was working 'before embarking

on any possible changes' (Hansard, HC 2.3.93). But the pressure was relentless and in that situation, Clarke told us, 'even the Judges do respond ... to the
newspapers ... a bit ... by putting sentences up.' Phil Wheatley recalled a speech
given by Lord Woolf himself to the Prison Conference that year outlining the
constraints the judiciary were under 'to up sentence lengths, without there being
any change in legislation' for fear that they would otherwise 'undermine respect
for the law'. The prison service 'became quickly overwhelmed by increasing
numbers.' Clarke's successor, Michael Howard, ushered in a sea change in the
direction of criminal justice policy.

Michael Howard (May 1993–May 1997)

We interviewed Michael Howard in a room at the House of Lords. When not
'playing to the gallery', as Ken Clarke had put it, Michael Howard is the quin-
tessentially perfect gentleman, personable and charming. We had decided to
steer clear of raking over old sores – like the notorious *Newsnight* interview with
Jeremy Paxman over whether or not he had instructed Derek Lewis to dismiss
John Marriott, the governor of HMP Parkhurst. Two months after we interviewed Howard we spoke to his Prisons Minister, Anne Widdecombe, by telephone. She was her usual no-nonsense self – telling things exactly as she saw
them. She had no qualms about everything being on the record saying, 'that's
no problem, the transcript will protect us both'. Her immediate predecessor,
Michael Forsyth, twice declined or failed to reply to our invitations to interview.

Our conversation with Michael Howard only became prickly when we
expressed our despair at the adversarial nature of British politics and he offered
a passionate defence on grounds that 'that's democracy for you.' When we asked
about ministerial churn, he agreed that 'it's a disadvantage of the system' but
that consensus on criminal justice was 'an unachievable ideal except in exceptional circumstances. Although people may agree on the objective they legiti-
mately differ on the way to achieve that objective'. When pressed, he said, rather
doubtfully, 'I suppose you could try and build up a real body of opinion – a real
consensus'.

The abduction and killing of James Bulger by two young children in February
1993 happened shortly before Michael Howard came into office and what followed represented a nadir for the British system of criminal justice, and neither
our Judges nor our Politicians nor our Press came out of it in a good light. In
England and Wales children of ten years are deemed to be criminally responsible – the lowest in Western Europe where the norm is 14 years. Governments
have repeatedly resisted attempts to raise that age. The young perpetrators, initially known only as A and B were tried in an *adult* court in the full glare of
publicity. And once convicted by the jury in November, the Judge – Mr Justice
Morland – insisted they be identified, on grounds that the 'public interest over-
rode the interest of the defendant'. Not only did this dog the later lives of these
children but the *parents* of the defendants were required to move and assume

new identities because of repeated death threats. Michael Howard wanted to intervene to extend the initial term of their sentence. Peter Lloyd, who had successfully got the prisons brief once more, told us that he advised against the intervention reckoning that 'it would be overturned by the European Court of Human Rights, but Michael was Home Secretary and so that was what happened'. In Lloyd's view, the outcry over Jamie Bulger's killing was 'the shadow that eclipsed much of the Woolf Agenda'.

Six years later the European Court of Human Rights did indeed find the case to be in breach of the right to a fair trial, and that there was no public interest in trying the case in an adult court or in identifying the defendants. Honest politicians should have pointed out that the case was extremely rare and not the beginning of an epidemic, and that hard cases make bad law. A quarter of a century earlier, in 1968, Mary Bell, the much-abused 11-year-old daughter of a prostitute, had also been found guilty in an adult court of the murder by strangulation of two young toddlers. She was similarly identified but then given a new identity and anonymity for a limited time when she was released, only to be tracked down and hounded by the Press. She later sought, and won, not only lifetime anonymity for herself but also her daughter and granddaughter. The parents of the victim – themselves, of course, also victims – should have been given maximum support. But there is no case for involving victims in sentencing or parole decisions. It took centuries for societies to replace the feud and the vendetta with disinterested systems of blind justice. The dust jacket of Morris and Hawkins' *The Honest Politician's Guide to Crime Control* has a picture of Justice lifting her blindfold from one eye. The last quarter-century has seen a systematic erosion of that civilised approach by arguments for placing victims at the heart of criminal justice. Apart from anything else, it introduces a new element of injustice. Some victims shout louder than others; some are listened to and others not. At the time of writing, the pleas of the father of Jack Merritt, who was murdered in the terrorist attack at Fishmongers' Hall in 2019 – that his son's work should be honoured by keeping open the educational route to rehabilitation and not to use his death for political advantage – were simply ignored by Boris Johnson.

Michael Howard was a QC who had practised for a short time at the Criminal Bar and briefly, as a Recorder, although mostly he had worked in the area of town planning. But when John Major called him to No 10 he was expecting to get the Treasury so it came as a surprise to be offered the Home Office. 'I was never expecting to be Home Secretary' he told us,

> 'and so I spent the first two or three months listening – in particular to the police. Their job was becoming impossible – it was hard enough to find the perpetrators; if they found them the chances are the CPS would say there's not enough evidence to prosecute; if there was enough evidence the chances were they'd be acquitted; and if by some miracle they were convicted they'd probably be sent away with sixpence from the poor box'.

Howard did not say whether he listened to the concerns and frustrations of those running the prisons and probation services. He was, however, briefed by his officials at the Home Office who presented him 'with a graph showing that crime had increased by about 5% a year on average over the last 50 years' and they told him that 'your job is to manage expectations in the face of this inevitable and inexorable rise in crime. Well that wasn't advice I was disposed to take.' Which was a pity because managing expectations about what a criminal justice system can do was very good advice indeed. Raising unrealistic expectations is a recipe for disaster. Much the same advice was given by Roy Jenkins to David Blunkett who similarly ignored it to all our costs.

In his raising expectations about what could be done about crime and what part prisons and probation could or should play in that process was less than honest with the public and it precipitated a competition between the two main political parties as to who could be the toughest on crime. In the course of his four-year term at the Home Office – one of the longest of any of our Ministers – he set in train a process of demoralisation in both prisons and probation which continued, though not without some respite in the early days of New Labour, to this day. He was convinced that probation was a soft option and set about undermining its social work ethos by withdrawing the funding for probation training in University courses approved by the Central Council for Education and Training in Social Work, and expressed concerns about the effectiveness of local Probation Committees. His announcement in September 1993 that it was the intention to have about 10% of the prison estate managed by the private sector gave numerical expression to what Clarke had described as *significant involvement*. But his rejection of the recommendation by HM Chief Inspector of Prisons, Stephen Tumim, in his report on the disturbance at HMP Wymott, that we should reduce and manage better the prison population, set a clearly different tone from his predecessor. This was made crystal clear in his 'Prison Works' speech to the Tory Party Conference on 6 October 1993 (ironically introduced, 'with typical gusto' as Martin Narey reminded us, by Jeffrey Archer). Howard also argued in Parliament that prison

> 'ensures we are protected from murderers, muggers and rapists – and it makes many who are tempted to commit crime think twice. This may mean more people go to prison. I do not shrink from that. We shall no longer judge the success of our system of justice by a fall in the prison population'.
>
> *(Hansard, HC 6.10.93)*

We are not aware of anyone who has offered such a criterion for the *success* of the system. But there are powerful reasons for thinking that a high prison population is expensive and largely ineffective and that overcrowding gets in the way of decent regimes and inhibits rehabilitative efforts. Yes, it has an incapacitation effect for the time they are incarcerated but prison almost certainly has little or no deterrent effect on offending as the research evidence showed at the time of the CJA 1991. But the net effect of the speech and legislation that followed was a dramatic increase in the prison population. Although by the end of 1993 all but one of the prisons in the building programme had been completed the prisons remained overcrowded.

Howard's speech – and his actions – had no less an effect upon the probation services which many feared were going to be dismantled. In the absence of any mention of 'alternatives to custody' what then was the point of probation? And with no obvious national spokesperson on behalf of probation, Graham Smith, HM Chief Inspector of Probation, sought to argue that probation could survive if it could demonstrate that it could bring about reductions in reoffending. In effect, Peter Raynor told us, 'he led the adoption of What Works?' Smith commissioned Andrew Underdown, the Assistant Chief Probation Officer for Manchester, to conduct a survey of projects where probation claimed success in bringing down reoffending. Raynor himself was one of the assessors for the evaluations, many of which were technically 'awful'. Smith decided not to publish the report whilst Howard was still in office but wait for more propitiate times in which to advance the case for 'evidence-based practice' which duly came under New Labour's Crime Reduction Programme.

Of the 27 points in Howard's Prison Works speech, 22 were embodied in the Criminal Justice and Public Order Bill designed to tilt the criminal justice system away from allegedly favouring the criminal and towards protecting the public. Among other things it introduced restrictions on bail, reversed the CJA 1991 requirement for pre-sentence reports in all triable either way offences, extended police powers for stop and search, changed the rules over the right to silence and introduced measures to control both travellers and rave parties. It was also the first statute to give a discount for guilty pleas. It was, in the words of one of our legal commentators, 'a right mess'. The bill became law the following year. As far as prisons were concerned it introduced powers for mandatory drug testing to deal with a growing problem of heroin use in prison. Howard's call for 'austere regimes', was not new – Kenneth Baker had used the same terminology – but in its latest iteration in the new climate, it began the unpicking of the Woolf agenda although Howard told us 'that was never my intention'. The prison service had long allowed prisoners a number of privileges which could be removed as part of a disciplinary process, although these were not consistently applied even across prisons of the same level of security. Howard argued that 'prisoners should not enjoy privileges as a matter of right', and Derek Lewis had been in favour of prisoners earning them. By the end of 1995 a new Incentive and Earned Privileges (IEP) scheme became fully operational. This was not necessarily incompatible with the Woolf agenda because Woolf had spoken for the need for incentives to guide a prisoner through a sentence plan as part of a contract or compact with prisoners which set out their 'legitimate expectations' (Cm 1456, para 12.129). But whether Howard intended it or not the change of tone in his call for austere regimes dramatically undermined that

agenda. Michael Howard defended his position by arguing that 'I didn't want them to slacken up on things like counting prisoners in or out of the gym, but I certainly did not mean that they should be any less humane in their everyday dealings with prisoners'.

Peter Lloyd offered us a kindlier interpretation of that period of Howard's time in office:

> 'I think he saw it as his duty to restore confidence in the criminal justice system, and didn't want me to get up and bleat about training prisoners for jobs that they could actually do outside. He thought it would confuse people, not because he couldn't care less'.

Lloyd regretted that there was never a real plan from the top as to how Woolf's agenda was to be delivered, or a timetable for delivery, or regular reviews of progress. As a result prisons remain he told us like 'a cheap hotel chain … expensive for the public but cheap in its facilities. They are remedial education establishments, nursing homes for people with mental afflictions, and now homes for geriatrics.' He came to recognise that his 'approach to prison and penal matters was not actually what the Home Secretary and, I think, the Prime Minister himself wanted at that time.' He was replaced by Michael Forsyth as Prisons Minister.

In 1995 a Green Paper on *Strengthening Punishment in the Community* reversed the spirit of the CJA 1991 which had looked towards diverting offenders from custody, and instead proposed the removal of the requirement for offenders to consent to community orders, to abolish the national training and social work qualification for probation officers, as well as to set new national standards and performance indicators to increase accountability. This would be a sea change for the nature of the relationship between offenders and their probation officers and seriously undermined the professional status of the latter. Unsurprisingly, there was widespread unease in the probation service and morale sank to a new low. A White Paper in June 1996 on *Protecting the Public* aimed 'to introduce automatic life sentences for serious violent and sex offenders, mandatory minimum prison sentences for persistent house burglars and drug dealers; and to introduce greater honesty into the sentencing process' (Hansard, HC 19.6 96) and formed the basis of the Crime (Sentences) Act 1997. The Act also replaced possible release from prison at the halfway point of sentence with the option to earn 20% off sentence for good behaviour, and required extended supervision for sex offenders.

Towards the end of 1993, there were repeated threats of strike action by the POA. Howard told us that 'everyone assumed that the prison officers were entitled to go on strike'. However, 'a clause in a bill enacted when Willie Whitelaw was Home Secretary … removed their right to strike. Everyone (in the Home Office) had pretended that it didn't exist'. Howard had a choice: 'between releasing prisoners or applying for an injunction on the basis of this law.' He told us that 'Derek Lewis said you can't possibly do that. You can't put thousands of prison officers in jail for contempt'. But Howard 'told number 10 what I was going to do, and John Major said are you really sure? And I said yes, I'm really sure … and we applied for the injunction and the injunction was of course, complied with'. Different accounts of these events were provided by other contributors to our research – but what is essential to know is that over the following years further legislation was passed to reinforce the ban on strikes, periodically relaxed in favour of voluntary agreements not to strike, and then reintroduced under New Labour when voluntary agreements broke down. Delivering writs to the private homes of POA representatives at the local level had nevertheless been an unseemly business.

Michael Howard's time in office is perhaps best remembered for his determination to avoid Waddington's fate by distancing himself from responsibility for events in the prison system. In September 1994 five 'exceptional risk' IRA prisoners attempted to escape from the Special Security Unit at HMP Whitemoor. They were armed and they shot and wounded a prison officer in the process. Howard immediately appointed Sir John Woodcock, a retired Chief Inspector of Constabulary and his police team to conduct an enquiry. At several points in his report (Cm 2741, paras 8.19, 9.4 and 9.27) Woodcock came close to saying that, had the security procedures which were already in place been fully implemented, the escape would have been prevented. Despite this, he went on to make a further 64 recommendations to improve security across the prison estate. Although very expensive, these were enthusiastically accepted by Howard. According to both Phil Wheatley and Richard Tilt, they were less expensive than they might have been, because the service reduced the number of prisons in which Category A prisoners were housed and much of the money would have been spent anyway replacing obsolete equipment. It is important to remember that whilst this attempted escape was undoubtedly a serious failure on the part of management at the prison because it could and should have been prevented, it was ultimately *unsuccessful* – the prisoners were all recaptured – by some brave prison officers who pursued the escapees and the last line of prison security – the police outside the perimeter.

A month after the Woodcock Report the prison service was again headline news. Serial killer, Fred West, committed suicide in HMP Birmingham and three prisoners, including two who were Category As, escaped from HMP Parkhurst and remained at large on the Isle of Wight for a week. Howard had already commissioned Quartermaster General Sir John Learmont to conduct a more general review of security and he was now also asked to report specifically on the Parkhurst escape. His report contained a surprising recommendation to build not one but two supermax prisons. In the second of these he wanted to house all of the most difficult to manage prisoners – a proposal which was contrary to all received wisdom and advice in relation to such prisoners since the Control Review Committee in 1984. But Howard was soon told by the then Chief Secretary to the Treasury, William Waldegrave, that there could be no further money for prisons after the costly implementation of the Woodcock recommendations. Anne Widdecombe told us:

'Michael wanted the Learmont Report for political reasons. He wanted to get rid of Derek Lewis – that was what Michael Forsyth had made clear to me when I took over from him. He used Learmont to get rid of Lewis (and so) he wasn't going to be that critical of the Learmont Report. But I was astounded at the slackness of it'.

'Slackness' was an expression she used several times in our interview. Despite her differences with Howard over the escapes and the sacking of Derek Lewis, who was soon vindicated in his claim for wrongful dismissal and received substantial damages, Widdecombe nevertheless felt that they had achieved a great deal. She pointed to the elimination of slopping out, reduced overcrowding, more hours in purposeful activity, reduced assaults and a huge reduction in the total number of escapes. 'So it was seriously well managed against a backdrop of a rising prison population – that's why I was so furious with Michael,' she told us. Not all of her claims can be justified. Martin Narey thought they were absurd given the number of Category A prisoners who escaped. Not surprisingly, Richard Tilt saw these developments, several of which happened on his watch as Director General, as a tribute to good prison service management which Anne Widdecombe did not always appreciate. In general, and in keeping with her political persuasion, she would have preferred someone with 'greater vision from the private sector' to have replaced Derek Lewis. She thought that Richard Tilt, as a prison service man, simply believed what he was told by his senior managers rather than checking with governors on the ground. Lewis, she thought, would just 'ring up the governors' and nip any problems in the bud. This was a view which received short shrift from Richard Tilt: 'that is just rubbish'.

Widdecombe spent much of her time trying to cope with the growing prison population. She had no truck with the idea of reducing the prison population and was adamant that the Prison Service had to cope with whoever the Courts so sentenced. 'You don't overcrowd, you don't say don't send people to prison, you find the extra places – it's your job.' Richard Tilt and his deputy, Tony Pearson, had persuaded Michael Howard that the ship which became HMP Weare could provide 'a reasonable and cheap option to avoid the use of expensive police cells' and after the election they had to persuade Jack Straw before it came into use late in 1997. Although intended as a temporary measure, HMP Weare remained in use throughout New Labour's first eight years of office. It invited mockery as a re-invention of the 'prison hulks'.

Douglas Hurd appointed Judge Stephen Tumim as HM Inspector of Prisons in 1987 and used his often shocking reports to encourage changes. Hurd's successors – Waddington and Baker – also accepted that such public criticism was useful, if not always comfortable, and Clarke extended Tumim's appointment soon after taking office. But in the new climate, Tumim's reports were seen as unwelcome and in 1995 Michael Howard refused to renew his appointment. Stephen Tumim died in 2003 but we were able to interview his successor David Ramsbotham in the House of Lords. His reports were equally trenchant and they quickly earned him the nickname of 'Rambo'. Ramsbotham told us that he was horrified when he heard about the handcuffing of women in labour – something which had greatly exercised Anne Widdecombe – and he had seen for himself 'the appalling conditions and treatment of women at HMP Holloway' (now closed). With a typical rhetorical flourish he asked, 'is this Mongolia in the year 900 or England in 1995?' He told the governor 'that I was going to send her a list of things that I expected to be done in the next six months' thereby inaugurating the six-month follow-up inspections. He claimed he had asked Richard Tilt 'who was the director of the women's estate?' only to discover that there wasn't one, only 'a civil servant in the policy department who issues paper instructions.' Howard created a 'special monitoring team' for his reports and Ramsbotham had to resist their attempts to challenge 'the facts'. He complained that one report had taken 'three years to get through the political process' before it was published. In his book, *Prisongate*, he declared that the recommendations of Baker's White Paper *Custody, Care and Justice* had 'never been implemented' (Ramsbotham, 2003, p 79). He was similarly disappointed that Lygo's recommendations, initially accepted, were subsequently undermined by the actions of Jack Straw and David Blunkett (p80).

Michael Howard and Ken Clarke had been law students together at Cambridge and knew each other very well but in office, they were very different characters and Derek Lewis told us that he thought Clarke would have handled the escapes in a very different way. His time in office came to an abrupt end with the general election in May 1997 which ushered in a New Labour Government. That same month, in a move designed to prevent Howard from becoming leader of the Conservative party, Ann Widdecombe had famously declared that 'there was something of the night about him.' The prison population had increased by some 16,000 during his term of office to around 61,000 driven by both a huge increase in the custody rate and by increases in the length of sentences. The probation service was changing beyond recognition – its professionalism undermined and its ways of working called into question.

Part two: The Directors of Prisons

The probation service at this time had no equivalent role to the Director General of the Prison Service. Chris Train, who had been Director General of the Prison Service at the time of the riots at Strangeways, died before our research began. But all former directors of service, both prisons and later probation, whom we interviewed retained a very active interest in what happened in their field long after they left office. They did not seek to interfere but put simply it had *got under their skin* and they still *cared*.

Joe Pilling

We met Joe Pilling in his London home where he told us about his continued association with prisons since leaving office through his work with the charities, the Koestler Trust and New Bridge. He was also an 'unpaid, non-executive member of the Sodexo management board', which at the time of our interview managed four prisons as well as being a private provider of probation services. He had been 'a career civil servant' and in his first stint at the Home Office Prison Department (HOPD) he was an 'Assistant Secretary … in charge of a very big division' regularly meeting with a lot of 'deputy governors'. Those meetings helped form his view 'that the relationship between prisons and headquarters, was far, far worse than you would expect it to be' and that 'we also had the trade unions that we deserved.' When we put to Pilling that the new 'Fresh Start' arrangement negotiated by Chris Train was intended to resolve industrial relations, his response quite simply was 'it hadn't'. Indeed negotiations with the union were to be a central feature of Pilling's time as Director General and he supported privatisation as a means to bring the POA to heel. His second stint in headquarters was as Director of Personnel and Finance, and it coincided with the Strangeways riot. He was expected to speak out on behalf of the Prison Service.

> 'I did one television interview on Strangeways although it was nothing to do with me. Ministers were trying to pretend it was nothing to do with them. My predecessor, Chris Train, of whom I was deeply fond … was the most hopeless performer on the media … he did not like to answer a question until he'd thought about it. This is not something that goes down very well on the Today programme'.

Pilling had been moved to the Northern Ireland Office at the time when Chris Train took early retirement, and

> 'somebody in the Home Office … said would I become the Director General? I took about 30 seconds to decide that I would do it, because it was the job above all others … that I most wanted to do. The Prison Service was far and away the most interesting and biggest thing that anybody was likely to ask me to run'.

As Director, he was soon faced with the Woolf Report. He had already reached the same conclusions as Woolf on relations between the field and headquarters and on the pressing need for highly visible leadership. When the White Paper, *Custody Care and Justice* (Cm 1647) was published he 'sat with Angela Rumbold and Kenneth Baker on a platform for the press conference.' They gave a show of unity in support of the new agenda which contrasted with the absence of David Waddington and Chris Train during the riot. When asked about this new agenda, Pilling focused on the introduction and pursuance of the 'idea of a Next Steps Agency', which Woolf didn't formally recommend but Pilling saw as a solution to his and Woolf's concerns about a distant headquarters. He had spoken to Woolf personally about the need for a more visible and audible leadership, and recalled being supported in his public appearances, both good and bad, by

Angela Rumbold and Ken Clarke: 'I think I dimly remember writing Clarke a note which said something like, you know, I'll get this wrong from time to time, and back came a response saying so do I'.

The idea of 'hiving off' areas of civil service work to separate agencies had been around for many years, as we discussed in Chapter 1, and it had its latest iteration in the Lygo Report (1991). Pilling told us the Prison Service might 'never have become a Next Steps agency if I hadn't pressed for it … the Permanent Secretary, Clive Whitmore was certainly against it.' When we asked whether Lygo's recommendation that the Director General should be recruited through open competition may have worked against Pilling's appointment, he said, rather ruefully, 'I gave it to him … he'd never heard of agencies I don't think'. Agency status for Pilling was about separating the Prison Service headquarters from the Home Office. He told us 'it's very difficult to think of another service as operational as the Prison Service within the Civil Service', and that 'prison officers didn't thank you for telling them that they were civil servants'. But, he told us, 'I could never really see …. a successful case for the Prison Service to be taken away from direct ministerial accountability to Parliament', more of a 'thinning out of accountability, making it slightly easier' all round.

> 'I felt completely confident that if I'd have remained in the job I would have continued to assure the Prison Service that I was one of them and on their side. But I would have also managed to convince the Permanent Secretary and the Home Secretary and Junior Ministers, that there was somebody in charge of the Prison Service who understood their problems …. That was the easy bit of the job from my point of view, I'd always done it'.

We asked him to reflect on the changes since his time in office. In his day he did not see the Treasury as a problem. 'I always thought that the best allies I had were in the Treasury'. But in those days nobody had 'the idea that you could run the same number of prisons much more cheaply with far fewer staff.' When he gave talks he used to say

> 'prison is very costly. We will do our best for prisoners, because we should … But please, nobody ever send somebody to us in order that we can help them. I thought the only reason for sending someone to prison was to protect the public, and as a deterrent, but not for rehabilitation'.

'It's infinitely worse now than it was when I knew it, partly because it involves probation, partly because the prison population's twice as big as it was when I was the Director General'. Whilst he certainly did not believe that 'every prisoner ought to be out' he did want Politicians, the Press and the Public to recognise that the 'nature of imprisonment is necessarily grim. And the idea that you have to keep ratcheting it up in length in order to make it really significant for people is just so barmy'. When asked about the director's post covering both prisons and probation, he reflected 'I never felt when I was running the Prison Service that what I really needed was a bigger job. It felt like quite a big job to me at the time'.

Relationships with Ministers have changed since his time as well. 'I didn't see them all that much. I might have met Ministers 10 or 12 times a year' so the move of Headquarters to Derby, which he had negotiated, would not have meant that we'd 'be on the train to London all the time.' Unfortunately, Ken Clarke, despite his hands off approach, scuppered the plan, because of his past experience 'in the Department of Health and Social Security' when 'it drove him mad having a load of important people in his life based in Leeds, and Parliament and he were based in London.'

Joe Pilling had predicted some difficulty in applying agency status to prisons,

> 'because what Agency said was that Ministers were interested in policy … and operations, were something that the management of the organisation should see to. But it was completely the opposite way round with Ministers and prisons … they are not interested in policy generally, but they are interested in operations. It's when things go badly wrong in prisons that Ministers, whether they like it or not, are in the middle of it, and that's why they tend to over react'.

He recalled the escape of two high-security prisoners from Brixton when the job of speaking to the media fell to him, and the first question asked was, 'do you think the Home Secretary should have dismissed the Governor or moved the Governor of Brixton?' The interview was

> 'completely disastrous. I could see the dangers of upsetting Kenneth Baker by my response, and I could see the dangers of upsetting prison governors by my response, but I couldn't quite see a way of answering the question without upsetting one or other of them … my mouth kept opening and nothing came out'.

The pre-agency division between ministerial responsibility for policy and service responsibility for operational matters was clear enough that he could speak to Ministers 'about what could and couldn't be done in prisons' in terms of policy, and in return for him to take a 'sharp and immediate personal responsibility' for any disasters.

Pilling was disarmingly honest about his famous 1992 Eve Saville Memorial lecture, *Back to Basics*, seen by most as a successful proclamation of what the Prison Service should be about. 'I did mean it, and it did express quite high values … I think it took people back a bit'. It earned him a lot of support within the service, among prison reform groups and the academic community.

> 'I blush to tell you that I knew it was going to, and that's why I did it … it was my responsibility to make it clear to prison staff how we needed to

treat prisoners ... be more liberal than the Government found completely comfortable ... my argument to Ministers was I've got a responsibility to keep the focus on treating people decently'.

He was less sure that the additional argument got across to those in charge of sentencing policy: that 'however flawless we were in not departing from the decency agenda, it was a terrible experience going to prison'.

Given his support for a Next Steps Agency, and for private prisons, if only to deal with the intransigent unions, and his evident support within the service it is rather surprising that Joe Pilling's candidacy for the top job as Head of the Agency was disregarded by Ken Clarke. He discovered later that he had 'succeeded in coming top of the list' for the job but Clarke had decided 'he wanted to try someone from the private sector ... the person who'd come third in the competition, Mr Lewis'.

Derek Lewis

We interviewed Derek Lewis at the Institute of Criminology in Cambridge and much of what we discussed had already been laid out in his book (Lewis, 1997) in which he declared 'The 1,014 days for which I was Director General of the Prison Service in England and Wales were the longest, toughest, most traumatic and yet most satisfying of my life' (p ix).

He told us that when he was head hunted his 'initial reaction was quite negative' but that he was persuaded to allow his name to go forward as one of three candidates. He 'was sold' the job on the prospect of implementing the recommendations of Woolf and the White Paper, with 'a clear agenda and sense of direction for the prison service.' His candidature was kept under wraps until he appeared at the press conference with Clarke after his selection because there were fears that Clarke's 'predilections for an outsider would cause a political furore'. Clarke asked only one question at the interview,

> 'whether I thought there was any limit to which the private sector could be employed to run prisons, then, kind of, lost interest. My answer was that provided the private sector performed, there was no limit, which was obviously the right answer'.

He told us that it was his lack of 'baggage' which meant that Pilling did not stand a chance. After the press conference he was escorted by the Permanent Secretary who 'pushed me in' and left him to introduce himself to an 'unwelcoming' Prisons Board grieving the loss of Pilling

The first major test for Lewis was the 'total disaster' of outsourcing to Group 4 the escort service to and from prisons, police stations and the courts. It was a done deal before his arrival, but, at first, with 'prisoners being delivered to public libraries ... it was just a nightmare and there was massive media attention'. But

Clarke told him, 'Just go and tell them that when you break new ground, things go wrong initially, then you fix them. I'll come and do it with you'. There was no 'we must have an enquiry'. However, problems relating to the prison custody and escort service did not go away and raised their head again a decade later. Unsurprisingly, Lewis described Clarke 'as an absolute delight to work with' but he told us that despite Clarke's fascination with the private sector he had little real understanding of it. Clarke wanted prison governors to be employed on 'fixed term contracts' to 'concentrate their minds', like they do in '*Marks & Spencer*'. Lewis had to explain that was not what *Marks and Spencer* did and that most of the private sector had staff on indefinite contracts. Clarke, expressed his surprise, saying, 'Oh, really?' Two weeks later Lewis 'heard him on the *Today* programme making exactly the same case.'

Lewis told us that 'Clarke was ideally suited to operate the theory of agency because he was delighted to leave things alone' and so the 'transition to agency status was a fairly painless process.' But his reversal of parts of the CJA 1991 in the CJA 1993 which he admitted meant 'increasing the prison population by an estimated 5,000' caused major problems for the Prison Service. When Lewis raised the problems with Clarke 'he said that there wasn't time to discuss them' ramming home 'how little control the Prison Service had over its own destiny' (Lewis, 1997, p 95). When Clarke became Chancellor of the Exchequer, he compounded the problems by refusing to fund the extra accommodation, leaving Lewis to find the money and forcing him 'to cancel long planned capital spending to improve security, conditions and regimes' (p 112). This included improvements to the security at Parkhurst prison, the lack of which, along with serious failures of management to ensure that staff followed basic procedures, featured in the high profile escapes that led to Lewis' demise.

Although Lewis described Howard as an 'inherently polite and courteous individual' there was little evidence that he listened to the views of the prison service in ways that he claimed to have done with the police. Lewis told us that Howard's public support for the White Paper agenda was never evident in private discussions where he showed a clear 'desire to shift the emphasis away from rehabilitation towards punishment and security … advocating greater austerity.' Lewis took the 'Prison Works' speech to be part of Howard's drive to make 'his reputation in the Home Office on his way to No.10'. Howard paid close attention to the 'media world … what happened to be in the press cuttings that day was actually what set the agenda for him'. The frequency of contact remained fortnightly, but 'the concept of having an autonomous agency' he told us 'was just, alien to him when it came to things that he thought affected his political reputation.' Howard made it clear that 'agency status' could not 'insulate' the service 'from the political world'.

An early example of interference was over Woolf's recommendation for, and the White Paper's commitment to, 'a code of standards'. Lewis told us that Howard saw this as 'a charter of rights for prisoners, which to him was a very alien concept' and so he 'delayed and delayed'. During those delays Lewis 'got a call from David Cameron, then Howard's special adviser', who told him that 'the Home Secretary had apparently given his wife a copy of this draft code of standards and she's made a lot of comments on it, which he would like me to review with you, and asks that you adopt or pursue them wherever possible'.

This episode was described in his book (p 117) but was hotly denied following publication. The amended code of standards, with 'a greater feel of austerity' took a further five months to agree and the general point remains, Howard was 'hands on', not 'arms-length' and his stance 'infected' relations between the Home Secretary and the Prison Service. Lewis was able to maintain much better relations with successive Junior Ministers, Peter Lloyd, Michael Forsyth and especially Anne Widdecombe who recognised 'that there were no simple solutions in prisons' (p 128).

One rare subject on which Lewis and Howard were agreed was the need to deal with an intransigent Prison Officers' Association, although their respective accounts as to who deserved the credit differed. Lewis was advised that the POA was not a 'proper' trade union because, by virtue of the nature of the job, they had the 'powers of a constable' similar to the police. This meant that they were not immune from legal action by their employers in the event of industrial action. This had apparently been a well-kept secret within the Home Office for many years and no one had been prepared to put it to the test. The expansion of privatisation had led to the POA 'preparing for war' (p 135) and Lewis decided this was the 'legal weapon' (p 136) needed to break the stalemate. According to Lewis, Howard took some persuading, but was in the end supportive in Cabinet negotiations and the first legal action seeking an injunction against the POA's threatened strike, was sought and won. In any event legislation followed in the Criminal Justice and Public Order Act 1994 to confirm the Government's position in statute. 'The war was all but won' wrote Lewis. 'Prison Service management and ministers had given governors back their authority' (p 139).

Despite some success in addressing industrial relations, establishing some standards in accordance with Woolf and the White Paper, as well as meeting seven of the eight performance targets in 1993 and all eight the following year (although they fell back to five out of nine in 1995), Lewis is most remembered for his infamous sacking by Michael Howard. The deed was officially done, as is the way in these matters, by the Permanent Secretary, Richard Wilson. Lewis freely admitted that the escape of six 'exceptional risk' IRA prisoners, from the Special Security Unit at HMP Whitemoor in September 1994 was 'wholly indefensible' even though it was ultimately unsuccessful. Whereas he thought Clarke might have 'taken the line … they didn't get away … there are lessons we can learn from this, and we will learn them but … I'm not going to be diverted into big enquiries'. Howard took a very different view and appointed Woodcock to conduct an inquiry, which was described by Lewis as like a 'criminal investigation' (p 156) but without the protection of the law, and the final report as 'sensationalised'. Some of the practices in HMP Whitemoor had actually been signed off by Angela Rumbold because of the 'sensitivity of the Irish position' and had become 'established practice'. 'Howard was keen to accept all sixty-four recommendations ... before anyone had a chance to assess whether they were affordable' (p 159). The Treasury, caught unawares, agreed to fund it. 'More than the security breach' he told us, 'what was personally embarrassing to Michael Howard' was the 'manipulation and intimidation of prison officers, and the initiation of practices that really could not be justified'.

Four months later the escape of three prisoners from HMP Parkhurst high-security prison, who remained at large on the Isle of Wight for a week, 'revealed the extent to which ... the Woolf agenda ... had been exploited by some of the smartest prisoners in the system'. In Parkhurst, Lewis told us, 'there had become a tolerance of practices that if you took them out and examined them in the light of day' could not be justified – although he admitted he had 'not personally picked up on them'. Unlike HMP Whitemoor, where the governor was relatively new to the post, the poor practices at Parkhurst 'had grown up under the governor's regime'. Lewis took the view that the governor should and would be investigated, but until a final decision was made he was entitled to continued employment. Howard, however, 'blew his top and said, that's not acceptable and that he must be suspended'. An uneasy truce was reached but the controversy 'that the Home Secretary had interfered and then lied' (p 171) about that interference continued into the next Parliament, damaging his reputation and blocking his way to the job of leader of the opposition – albeit only for a few years. Despite Howard's evident involvement in operations, he now made a clear distinction between his responsibility for policy and Lewis' for operations.

The Learmont enquiry followed. 'The thoroughness and openness of the Woolf Inquiry contrasted sharply with the superficiality and covertness of Learmont' (p 176). An in-depth study of the relationship between Ministers and the service was recommended 'with a view to giving the Prison Service the greater operational independence that agency status was meant to confer' but this never happened. When the report was published a covering letter apparently made it clear that the Home Secretary was not to be implicated, and the buck stopped with Lewis. Howard immediately initiated the process to sack Lewis, despite an earlier statement of support, and the continued support from Junior Ministers and the Prisons Board. Derek Lewis told us that Clarke would have been content with internal investigations by the Director of Security perhaps assisted by HM Chief Inspector of Prisons, and much more likely to stand by his Chief Executive. Others thought it unlikely that any Director General could survive such a multiplicity of escapes by Category A prisoners.

Lewis went out fighting and won his claim for unfair dismissal. He was replaced by Richard Tilt.

Richard Tilt

We interviewed Richard Tilt at his Northamptonshire home over tea and biscuits. It provided an opportunity for reminiscences because he had been governor of HMP Gartree when one of us had conducted research there in the 1980s. We reminded him that he had initiated the Master's Programme in Cambridge which was then intended just for prison service managers. He had left Gartree just two months before a hijacked helicopter landed in the exercise yard and spirited away prisoners Kendal, serving eight years, and Draper, a lifer. Kendall was recaptured ten days later but Draper was on the run for just over a year. Bob Duncan, who had succeeded Tilt as governor, was so new that he could scarcely be held responsible and Tilt was protected because he had sent several memoranda to HQ pointing to the vulnerability of the exercise area and asking for the installation of anti-helicopter wires. With a grin Tilt told us, 'you will not be surprised to learn that the wires were installed a few weeks after the escape'.

Tilt took the helm aware that he was not Howard's preferred choice to replace Derek Lewis but knowing 'the service was in such a mess' and feeling he had a 'duty to do it'. 'I was acting Director General for about a year. Michael Howard was busy trying to find someone else to do the job – which I knew about because people kept telling me. But he didn't get any takers'. Tilt thus became the first Director General promoted from within the service and it was very warmly welcomed by his colleagues. His term of office bridged the end of the Tory Government and the beginning of New Labour. What Tilt took from the Woodcock and Learmont Reports was that 'prison service policies were fine. The problem was they weren't being implemented. And there was no way of checking whether people were implementing them or not'. Accordingly, he quickly introduced a 'management system of auditing standards' whereby teams were sent around the prisons to check that policies were being implemented as intended. He thought that the new 'standards audit system did pull the service together'. However, Tilt said that Learmont showed 'no kind of understanding at all' about prisons, and in time-honoured fashion, Tilt set up a working party (to which one of us acted as adviser) to look into the feasibility of the recommendation to build two supermax prisons. He recalled a successful 'period of attrition … a lot of meetings with Michael Howard', delaying the final decision into the next Parliament. In fact Howard had been told by Waldegrave that there was no money for it, but Tilt was able to argue that after the implementation of Woodcock's security measures there was no need for it.

Tilt told us he would be very happy with a version of the Prison Service Agency which kept 'policy and operations largely together', with the targets and objectives agreed in the framework document coming from the Treasury. The original framework did bring two or three hundred people from the Home Office, including all the prison policy people, into the Agency. But 'Howard just couldn't cope with somebody doing something he didn't agree with', and so he would 'wade in with both feet … never mind the bloody Next Steps Agency'. Howard did not recognise the dual point of agency, to protect Ministers from the kind of 'tiny, individual injustice' that becomes a 'huge political issue over-night' on the one hand, whilst freeing up services to get on with the job, on the other. Tilt recalled that 'Michael Howard intervened a lot'. On one occasion a young offender had started a roof-top protest, and 'in the middle of the night, the Home Secretary rang the operations room and told them to hose him off'. Tilt was quickly contacted and the action was forestalled. The next morning he pointed out to Howard that not only was it 'the wrong thing to do' but also 'if it goes wrong, you're finished'. Howard conceded the point. Another incursion into operational matters was over IEP but over this it was Tilt who graciously conceded. Tilt and his senior management team had

> 'argued strenuously against the IEP on grounds that we did not think we could operate it fairly but it soon became apparent that it was working well and was liked by both staff and prisoners ... it was hugely successful'.

In essence, under the scheme, all new receptions are assigned 'entry' level sta-tus, but can be promoted to 'standard' level if they fulfil all the requirements of induction, and apply for 'enhanced' status after a further three months of good behaviour. A basic level can be imposed as a punishment. Tilt was in favour of introducing TVs in cells and payphones for prisoner use, but both were anathema to Howard as counter to his idea of 'decent but austere' regimes. However, in time, he told us 'I was able to persuade Jack Straw of the likely benefits of both'.

Richard Tilt thought that Junior Ministers 'didn't have any power, or effect'. It has to be said that Anne Widdecombe thought that things got 'slacker' under Tilt's stewardship than they had been under Lewis. She, like Ramsbotham, had become concerned at reports that woman prisoners were being handcuffed to beds in hospital maternity wards. Tilt explained that in the case which had caused all the headlines

> 'officers correctly followed procedures and removed her restraints as soon as the woman went into labour. But her labour stopped and when this was confirmed by the midwifery staff they reapplied the restraints – which was not the common sense thing to do'.

He went on,

> 'I was horrified by the whole business. My memory of Anne's view was that she was perfectly OK with what happened but didn't like the publicity. She asked me to sort it out which I did by meeting, and agreeing a protocol with, the Royal College of Midwives which has stood the test of time'.

Tilt also found himself at odds with Howard over the calculation of the number of days spent in custody on remand which could be deducted from the sentence. This was recognised as problematic because there were cross-cutting statutory instruments affecting how things should be calculated. There were 'challenges in the pipeline'. An instruction was given to interpret the Rules differently. Tilt accepted that he was partly to blame because he 'didn't tell the Home Secretary' because 'it didn't seem a big issue' having been told it only affected about 50 prisoners. It turned out that 600 prisoners were released somewhat earlier than expected and Howard became 'incandescent about it.' Disaster did not follow in the form of serious further offending and after a High Court ruling, the legislation was changed – but it did produce unwelcome headlines. However, it was not a problem that went away – Section 240 of the CJA 2003 required the judiciary to do the calculations and they devised a formula which allowed the number of days to be administratively calculated.

Tilt was an early advocate of bringing prisons and probation together, 'trying to create one service on the basis that an offender is best dealt with by one organisation from the point at which they come in.' He had been influenced by a visit to Canada where they had merged the two services and he 'was impressed by the much greater breadth of working for staff enhancing the role of the prison officer.' It also offered 'the logical connection between work that needed doing with an offender during sentence and to be continued after release.' But the Canadians told him that it had taken 25 years before they could see it bearing fruit – a time frame unlike anything tried in the UK. Tilt was angry about Howard's downgrading of probation training which he said was 'really dreadful'. He remembered Howard asking everyone 'why social work was a core element in probation training?' Dissatisfied with answers that did not fit his prejudices he ordered 'its removal from the syllabus'. But looking at what was to happen later he was even more angry about Grayling's so-called 'reforms' which he said 'just seem like madness to me.'

Richard Tilt was probably the only one of our prison directors who left the service without anger or regret at a time of his own choosing – though he too continues a keen interest in what has happened since.

References

Baker, K. (1993) *The Turbulent Years: My Life in Politics*, London: Faber and Faber.

Clarke, K. (2016) *Kind of Blue: a Political Memoir*, London: Macmillan.

Lewis, D. (1997) *Hidden Agendas: Politics, Law and Disorder*, London: Hamish Hamilton.

Lygo Report (1991) *Management of the Prison Service*, London: Home Office.

Ramsbotham, D. (2003) *Prisongate: The Shocking State of Britain's Prisons and the Need for Visionary Change*, London: The Free Press.

Woolf Report (1991) *Prison Disturbances April 1990*, Report of and Inquiry by the Rt. Hon. Lord Chief Justice (Parts I and II) and His Honour Judge Stephen Tumim (Part II) Cm.1456, London: HMSO.

3

THE NEW LABOUR YEARS 1997–2010

Introduction

In opposition, New Labour sought to ensure that they would never be outflanked by the right on law and order. The strategy helped Tony Blair to win three successive elections in 1997, 2001 and 2005. In government, his was the dominant voice on these issues and, according to Ken Clarke, he 'only appointed Home Secretaries who applied policies in line with editorials in the tabloid newspapers'. Blair had cultivated a relationship with Rupert Murdoch and his acolytes which helped secure the switch of support to New Labour from the Conservatives. According to one of our respondents, it was rather like 'always managing towards the Führer. He never seemed to make decisions, but everybody knew what he wanted.' In furtherance of Blair's 'tough on crime – tough on the causes of crime' mantra – to which all of his Home Secretaries and later Justice Secretaries signed up – New Labour wanted to close 'the justice gap' and 'rebalance the criminal justice system' through a bifurcated approach. At the top end were long, mandatory and often indeterminate sentences for the most serious offenders and at the bottom end, Anti-Social Behaviour Orders (ASBOs) and other measures to deal expeditiously with more minor incivilities. The prison population grew from 61,000 in 1997 to 85,000 in 2010. The probation service was encouraged to enforce order requirements more consistently through regularly updated National Standards and the total annual probation case load, comprising court orders and pre- and post-release supervision, rose from around 170,000 to about 240,000 over the same period.

It has to be said that New Labour, particularly in its first term, managed to generate an air of optimism that the government could 'do good' and was prepared to invest to achieve that end. It was generous in supporting programmes to reduce individual criminality, through its Crime Reduction Programme, for

DOI: 10.4324/9781003201748-4

example, and that other programmes, including 'Sure Start', strengthened local communities by providing assistance in childcare, early education, health and support for families. In his memoirs, Blair noted that Ministers in incoming governments 'spend several years relearning what the last incumbent could have told you from experience' (Blair, 2011, pp 643–4). However, as far as criminal justice was concerned, New Labour, quickly adopted some Tory policies they had opposed in opposition. New Labour was prolific in introducing legislative changes some of which had disastrous consequences. Lord Chief Justice (LCJ) Igor Judge complained that 2003 saw six major statutes passed on criminal justice matters, 'the great Daddy of them all being (David Blunkett's) Criminal Justice Act, which had 1,169 paragraphs' (BBC News Channel, 15.7.09). Under Blair's regime, the traditional role of the civil service was moved away from 'giving policy advice' and more towards the 'management of services', whilst imported outsiders advised on policy. There were also major administrative changes too. To cover all these here would be impossible. Instead we focus on what seem to us to be the major events. We indicate some of them and the main *dramatis personae* in Table 3.1.

Part one: The politicians

Jack Straw (May 1997–June 2001)

We interviewed Jack Straw at his home on 6 November 2018. He had just recovered from pneumonia, but sped us through the interview with a brisk 'Right, next question?'. In marked contrast to some of his Conservative predecessors, Straw, whose second wife was a career civil servant, wrote in his memoirs that he 'never had the slightest doubt about the loyalty' of his civil servants (Straw, 2012, p 206). We had already interviewed Joyce Quin, whose job title at Straw's insistence was Prisons *and* Probation Minister, and who like others before and since found the job absorbing. She regretted that she had only a year in the job. She had no handover package from her predecessor, Anne Widdecombe, whom she nevertheless respected for trying to 'ensure good prison regimes' – nor did she talk in detail to any of her successors. With no prior experience of the field she found herself on a 'steep learning curve.' She did not even have a prison in her constituency though she had regularly seen some 'campaigning probation officers' at her surgery. She believed that Ministers needed at least two years in the job both to master the subject and build up relationships.

Straw did not need a handover arrangement. After three years as Shadow Home Secretary, he had a 'very clear agenda,' signed off by Blair, and was ready to 'hit the ground running'. His first priority was to see the Crime and Disorder Bill successfully through Parliament. Although this became one of the principal legacies of his term in office, through the creation of the Youth Justice Board and the means for establishing local Youth Offending Teams (YOTs) under the Crime and Disorder Act 1998, we have mostly had to confine our attention, on

TABLE 3.1 New Labour Ministers, Directors of Service(s), Key Legislation, Department and Service Reorganisation 1997–2010

Year/ month (general election in bold)	Home Secretary/ Justice Secretary & Lord Chancellor	Key legislation for prisons & probation	Prisons & Probation Minister (combined at the start of this period)	CEO of Her Majesty's Prison Service (HMPS) agency	Director of the National Probation Service (NPS)	Commissioner of Corrections/ CEO of National Offender Management Service (NOMS)/ DG of NOMS agency	Department & Service Reorganisation
1997 May	Jack Straw	**Crime & Disorder Act 1998 & Criminal Justice & Court Services Act 2000 (& Sexual Offences Act 1997)** establish NPS & rebrand it as a law enforcement agency with licensing & recall remit.	Joyce Quin	Richard Tilt continued	N/A	N/A	N/A
1998 Jul			Lord Williams of Mostyn (D)				
1998 Dec				Martin Narey			
1999 Aug			Paul Boetang				
2001 Apr		Brings into force **Crime (Sentences) Act 1997** automatic & mandatory sentences.					
2001 Jun	David Blunkett		Beverley Hughes		Eithne Wallis		1st **NPS** fully funded centrally & 1st Director of NPS; 54 committees reduced to 42 boards coterminous with Police Authorities.
2002 May							
2003 Mar		**Criminal Justice Act (CJA) 2003** followed 4 high profile child murders & ECHR judgment to remove the Home Secretary's right to set murder tariffs; new 5 purposes of sentencing framework reverses 'deserts' sentencing and expansion of public protection sentencing; to increase use of community sentences; new indeterminate Imprisonment for Public Protection (IPP) sentences; new schedule 21 specifies mandatory minimum 'starting points' for life sentences; new sentencing guidelines council (SGC) to improve sentencing consistency.	Hilary Benn			Martin Narey	
2003 May			Paul Goggins (D)	Phil Wheatley			1st **NOMS** Commissioner of Corrections made a Permanent Secretary to commission & manage offender services across prison & probation, & inform sentencing; HMPS agency and NPS retained separate directors.
2004 Jan							
2004?							
2004 Dec	Charles Clarke				Steve Murphy		
2005 Apr					Roger Hill		
2005 May			Fiona McTaggart & Baroness Scotland				
2005 Oct						Helen Edwards	2nd **NOMS** Commissioner of Corrections resigns & Permanent Secretary status revoked following loss of **Management and Sentencing of Offenders Bill** (& remit of SGC to manage correctional service capacity).
2006 May	John Reid		Gerry Sutcliffe				
2007 May	Lord Falconer		David Hanson				New **Ministry of Justice** (MoJ) moves prisons & probation out of Home Office, & combines with Dept of Constitutional Affairs (that replaced the Lord Chancellor's Department in 2003). The Lord Chancellor & new Justice Secretary positions combined.
2007 Jun	Jack Straw	**Offender Management Act (OMA) 2007** after 4 years of debate & 2 Bills permits the privatization of all probation services. Probation Boards to move to Trust status, with whom the Minister *may* contract services. Blunkett's prison cap lost in Clarke's second iteration of Bill.		N/A		Phil Wheatley	
2008 Apr							1st **NOMS** agency joins commissioning & delivery of prison & probation services regionally & centrally; HMPS loses agency status & separate director.
2009 Mar					N/A		Separate director of probation removed.
2009 Jun		**Coroners and Justice Act 2009** Sentencing Council replaces SGC to improve consistency & inform on resource needs but *not* manage service capacity.	Maria Eagle				2004–2010: 42 probation boards move to 35 trusts.

space grounds, to matters affecting adults. More controversially the Act introduced the Anti-social Behaviour Order (ASBO), through which New Labour sought to show that they understood and cared about the concerns of ordinary people. ASBOs were imposed under civil law but once breached the offender became liable to criminal sanctions thus contributing both to net-widening and the burdens on the prison and probation services. It was also the harbinger of what was to come in a stream of out-of-court penalties. ASBOs, as such, were repealed in 2014. Straw was responsible for introducing the Human Rights Act 1998 and the Freedom of Information Act 2000 although we had insufficient time to discuss them in our interview. As he put it in his memoirs, 'one damned by the popular press, the other by ministers and officials alike – and I was to blame for both' (2012, p 269). These had been long-standing elements of the Labour Party's agenda and had become firm commitments in a speech by Blair in honour of his predecessor John Smith.

After the abrasive intrusions of Michael Howard's *Prison Works*, Straw was determined to 'restore good relations with the prison service and with other officials' believing he would 'achieve more' if they thought he 'was on their side'. He signalled the change of approach in a speech, carefully crafted by his officials to whom we spoke, under the artful title *Making Prisons Work*. Joyce Quin told us there was a huge sigh of relief in the prison service when Michael Howard departed and she was able to reassure managers that there would be no more 'day-to-day interference by ministers.' Her arrangement with Richard Tilt was one of a partnership in which they shared objectives and reviewed progress and problems at regular weekly meetings. Quin described Straw's approach as 'very collegial' and everyone had a chance 'to have their say'. She also developed good relationships with several Chief Probation Officers as well as the Chief Inspectors of Prisons (David Ramsbotham) and Probation (Graham Smith) but she 'worried' that Rambo's reports were sometimes so 'hard hitting' that they would leave prison staff 'downhearted,' that their hard work was not sufficiently appreciated.

There is little doubt that in the early days of New Labour, relations between the prisons and probation services and Ministers were constructive and cordial. New Labour bought into the idea of 'What Works' as part of its commitment to evidence-based policies for which Graham Smith had been a staunch advocate. This excited prison and probation staff because there was money for programmes for offending behaviour and education, and it excited the academic community because they would provide the evidence through evaluative research. A good deal of money was spent on the development of treatment programmes especially for drugs and sex offenders. Straw told us that he thought 'prisons were bloody awful places', and that he believed that people were 'sent to prison as punishment, not for punishment'. He therefore supported regime improvements in line with the decency agenda. Reversing Howard's policy not to allow televisions in cells, was both affordable and fitted well with Incentives and Earned Privileges (IEP) arrangements, and went some way towards mitigating the effects of 23 hours lock-down. But he insisted to us that one could not deal with the overcrowding by capping the prison population in a way 'that trumps other considerations.' Straw extended Release on Temporary Licence (ROTL) as a means of getting offenders back to work from young offenders, then to women and finally to adult males. Straw and Quin told us that they believed that the language of toughness allowed them scope for 'doing good by stealth.'

Straw regarded Howard's insistence that the Chief Executive report directly to parliament, as no more than an attempt to evade ministerial responsibility. For Straw, the distinction between accountability for policy and responsibility for operations was 'intellectually threadbare ... because the only test of a policy is how it operates'. He therefore returned to the practice whereby the Minister replied to questions in the House, thus eroding the extent to which the Chief Executive could have a public voice. But in regular meetings with Richard Tilt, he tried to agree ways forward on matters such as raising standards, and reducing the turnover of prison governors which had been a long-standing problem. In opposition he had proclaimed that 'the provision of private prisons was quite immoral', something which in our interview he ruefully regretted, because once in government he faced the problem of 'what the devil do you do about them' given a rising prison population and overcrowding in prisons. He quickly came to see both that market testing was a way of limiting the power of the militant POA and that Gordon Brown would only approve new prisons if they were done by the private sector under the Private Finance Initiative. He told us, however, that market testing was a 'two-way street' and that at the end of a private contract, the public sector could compete to run what had been a privately run establishment.

On other matters, however, Straw told us that before Michael Howard 'Labour had been very critical of the really complacent attitude the Conservatives had over rising crime', so they could hardly do other than accept much of what Howard had enacted 'and most of those measures stayed on the statute book'. That was broadly true, although in fact he refused to implement the sections of the Crime (Sentences) Act 1997 which demanded that 'honesty in sentencing' required some prisoners to serve their full sentence without the possibility of parole. His own idea of honesty in sentencing simply required judges 'to explain what the sentence means in practice ... time to be spent in prison, the period of supervision after release and the period during which the offender might be recalled to prison'. Although he was initially reluctant to bring in provisions for automatic sentences for violent and sexual offenders, and mandatory minimum sentences for third-time burglars and drug offenders, it was unclear why he did not resist opposition demands to do so in 1999 given the size of the Labour majority.

Straw introduced important changes to probation. He thought that Howard's 'decision to end professional training for probation officers was crazy' and he introduced a new Diploma in Probation albeit one which was no longer linked to social work and constituted a lower entry qualification to what was becoming a less professional service. Like Howard, however, he was concerned that probation was falling 'into disrepute' because during his two years at the Criminal Bar, offenders were saying they had 'got off' when sentenced to probation. The removal of the requirement for offenders to consent to probation – something which had been proposed by Howard in 1995 (Cm 2780) – greatly changed the relationship between offenders and their probation officers. Straw did not 'see rehabilitation as being inconsistent with law enforcement' and was 'unrepentant' about the use of sanctions for those who did not comply, seeing 'no case for having a probation service at all if it wasn't going to be effective.' He wanted to bring the probation service closer to the prison service. In his last year at the Home Office, the Criminal Justice and Court Services Act 2000 introduced far-reaching, if short-lived, changes: it established for the first time a National Probation Service (NPS) with Eithne Wallis as the first Director of Probation and reduced the 54 Probation Committees to 42 Probation Boards which were coterminous with police boundaries. The police and probation services were required to manage the risk of violent and sexual offenders through new Multi-Agency Public Protection Arrangements (MAPPA). This marked a significant shift in probation work, according to Sonia Flynn, at the time of writing the Chief Officer of Probation whom we interviewed at her office in Petty France. She told us that 'it changed our purpose from advise, assist and befriend to surveillance and protection'. The Act removed the involvement of the Home Secretary in the sentencing of young people for grave crimes, in light of decisions by the House of Lords (1997) and the European Court of Human Rights (1999) in respect of Venables and Thompson who had killed Jamie Bulger.

Around this time also came the introduction of electronically monitored Home Detention Curfews (HDCs) – a modestly useful mechanism for combining some relief on population pressures with opportunities for rehabilitative activity. Drug Testing and Treatment Orders (DTTOs), perhaps following the example of the much visited Red Hook court in New York, were introduced and gave discretion to sentencers to set treatments for drug offenders in the community, and then to monitor their progress. The first cautious steps towards what were to become Sentencing Guidelines were made through the creation of the Sentencing Advisory Panel to the Court of Appeal and the Powers of Criminal Courts (Sentencing) Act 2000, introduced by the Law Commission, was intended to codify sentencing for a whole generation (though much of it was soon to be amended by the CJA 2003).

In December 1999, the Lord Chancellor, Lord Irvine, had commissioned a review of the Courts by Sir Robin Auld (2001) and in May 2000, Straw had called for a review of the sentencing framework by former Home Office Civil Servant John Halliday (2001). Straw then published a White Paper *Criminal Justice: The Way Ahead* with, ostensibly, the laudable aim of codifying the criminal law to establish a more permanent system avoiding the churn of criminal justice bills. But the White Paper used inappropriate official statistics of police recorded crime and the numbers of convictions that conveniently showed a ratio between them which was *high* enough to suggest that the criminal justice system was ineffective but also *low* enough to suggest that radical tough reforms could get on top of the problem and provide 'a cure for crime'. Had the White Paper used data from the British Crime Surveys, these would have shown a ratio that was *so high* that there was no reasonable expectation that the criminal justice system, however tough, could have much impact upon the level of crime.

On several occasions, Straw had found himself at odds with No 10 – he was the least right wing of the New Labour Home Secretaries – even though he complained that the terms 'after-care' and 'through-care' sounded too much like part of caring services, and insisted that 'resettlement' should be used instead. But during those last months before the 2001 General Election, his time at the Home Office became very difficult. On the one hand, he wrote in his memoirs: 'David Blunkett coveted my job and ran a brazen and very public campaign for it with help from papers like the Sun.' On the other hand, John Birt, the former Director General of the BBC, had

> 'somehow inveigled himself into Downing Street ... and got others there to believe that he would ... find the holy grail of crime reduction policies. Unleashed by Number 10 he began to interfere, for no good reason ... and with even less understanding'.
>
> *(Straw, 2012, p 320)*

Within six months of the election in 1997 the prison population had risen by 3,000 mostly as a result of earlier changes to sentencing policy. Thereafter, the population remained relatively stable but there were significant increases in recall rates as a result of the increased emphasis on the law enforcement role for probation officers. Whilst Reports of the Chief Inspector of Probation had many positive things to say, those from the Chief Inspector of Prisons expressed concerns that the prisons were falling back to the conditions of the pre-Woolf era. After the election Blunkett did indeed replace Jack Straw at the Home Office.

David Blunkett (June 2001–December 2004)

We interviewed David Blunkett on 6 September 2018 in his room at the House of Lords, and we got refreshingly direct and candid answers to all our questions. We also interviewed Junior Ministers Beverley Hughes by telephone and Hilary Benn in a rather public room in Portcullis House.

David Blunkett told us that Roy Jenkins had said to him 'don't believe you can have any influence over the level of crime ... and I just didn't agree with that at all'. He went on to make much the same kind of mistakes as Michael Howard had done. Both clearly claimed that they were doing what the public wanted and both thought that they could deal with the crime problem through tougher sentencing, although Blunkett and New Labour generally also hoped that a renewed emphasis on rehabilitation would reduce reoffending. It was clear that the Prime Minister felt much more comfortable with his new appointee at the Home Office. 'For the first time, I felt with Charles (Clarke), Alan Milburn and David Blunkett I had people alongside me fully in tune with what I wanted to do and why' (Blair, 2011, p 487). Gordon Brown, according to Blair, 'argued that immigration and law and order issues were only of great salience because we insisted on talking about them. David was accused of inciting the issues rather than responding to them' (p 494). But as far as Blair was concerned, 'David Blunkett was motoring on the law and order agenda and to great effect' (p 492).

Blunkett had to contend with some high profile events on his watch which raised the temperature. He said he had 'no option' but to accept the release on parole of the two young men who, as children, had killed the infant Jamie Bulger. The murders of four young girls in July 2000, and March and August 2002, added to the pressure as did the later murder of John Monckton in November 2004. Ministers felt exposed to public criticism, especially if offenders committed serious further offences whilst under supervision. But there was no real attempt to explain the rarity of such events, or the impossibility of eliminating risk, or even to point out that crime rates were actually falling. So concerned were New Labour to cement their law and order credentials that they were reluctant to boast about the success of some of their community initiatives or the diversion of large numbers of young persons from the criminal justice system into Intensive Support and Surveillance Programmes (ISSPs). Blunkett told us that he was proud of those achievements. But to observers at the time it seemed as if an opportunistic Blunkett was over-reacting like Michael Howard on steroids.

The number of prison places had been increased substantially but there was continuing concern about overcrowding in prisons, and the poor condition of much of the prison estate. The prison ship, HMS Weare, was still in use. Blunkett had wanted to borrow money in advance to enable new accommodation to come on stream, but Gordon Brown refused to allow loan funds. Bringing about major improvements required 'the Treasury's help to do it, but there are no votes in prisons' said Blunkett. Instead, an emergency programme using temporary buildings and infill continued and long-planned refurbishments were deferred. Yet, as Benn pointed out, there was 'money allied to reform' through the development and evaluation of programmes which might help towards rehabilitation. Compared to building new prisons these were comparatively cheap, short term and potentially easy to terminate. Although they were greatly welcomed within the prison service, such programmes are difficult to organise and sustain in a system so overburdened that it was difficult to find places for prisoners to sleep.

In November 2002 the prison population stood at 72,600 and some 500 prisoners were regularly held in expensive police cells. After Lord Woolf made a speech urging that custody be reserved for the most serious offenders, Blunkett, the Lord Chancellor, Derry Irvine and the Attorney General, Peter Goldsmith issued a joint statement urging judges and magistrates to think carefully about whether custody is the most effective sentence available (*The Times*, 4.11.02). According to Blunkett, this presaged a very modest agreement that the proposed Sentencing Guidelines Council, to be set up under the CJA 2003 with the aim of bringing about greater consistency in sentencing among judges, might enable the prison population – which was otherwise projected to rise to 93,000 – to be stabilised at 80,000 by tweaking the guidelines. It began to look as though the Executive and the Judiciary might be speaking with one voice – but it was not to last. Blunkett told us this was scuppered by an interview which Derry Irvine gave to James Naughtie on the *Today* programme in January 2003. Without prior consultation either with Blair or Blunkett, so his story goes,

> 'Derry talked about three strikes and you're *in* and … so we were actually sending an alternative message to magistrates and district judges …. to get tougher … when we wanted more community sentencing, more restorative justice, more tagging and more early release with proper supervision'.

There is no mention of this incident in Blunkett's memoirs but the record in Hansard after Irvine's interview actually shows that the Government was under attack for Irvine's advocacy of prisons as a place of last resort.

After receiving the Halliday Report – which Blunkett called a 'boring deadly document' – in July 2001, and the old Auld Review three months later, Blunkett published a White Paper *Justice for All* in 2002 which built in part on Straw's *The Way Ahead* and led to the Criminal Justice Bill eventually enacted as the CJA 2003. Halliday argued that there had been an erosion of the 'just deserts' principle enshrined in the CJA 1991 which maintained that sentences should be no longer than could be justified by the current offence. He also argued, rather optimistically in the views of some of our sources, that it was necessary to put into practice what was known of 'what works' and develop the probation service, the better to reduce reoffending. Halliday thought the re-establishment of a principled sentencing framework would increase public confidence. Blunkett's CJA 2003 claimed to put forward just such a framework which, however, 'put public protection at its heart.'

But the promise of a clear statement of the purposes of sentencing was not fulfilled. Rather the Act listed five, potentially conflicting purposes but with no indication of priorities:

i. Punishment of offenders
ii. Reduction of crime (including through deterrence which the CJA 1991 had specifically ruled out)

iii. Reform and rehabilitation of offenders
iv. Protecting the public
v. Making reparations to victims by offenders

Controversially, the CJA 2003 introduced indeterminate sentences of Imprisonment for Public Protection (IPP) which were to be imposed, ostensibly on grounds of serious future risk regardless of the seriousness of the current offence, and with release dependent upon the demonstration that the risk had been substantially reduced. In practice, the successful completion of appropriate programmes intended to reduce those risks became the accepted criterion for such a demonstration. David Blunkett seems genuinely to have believed that IPPs were 'progressive' but it was naïve not to recognise that the assessment of future risk would be subject to widely differing interpretations, or to believe that there were programmes, the completion of which could reliably indicate the reduction of risk, or that such programmes as there were would be easily accessible to IPP prisoners. But he clearly persuaded himself that this was what the public wanted. He disregarded his civil servants because they were 'floating above things' and it 'was never clear whether you're talking to people who have a clue.' Had he listened more to his officials' wiser counsels might have prevailed. He later apologised for some of the anomalies and injustices that IPP produced and told us 'I think that IPP is a blot on my copybook because I should have foreseen the dangers'. But he attributed most of the blame to the way judges chose to interpret and implement the legislation –

> 'why they would say this would have been a very low tariff, like two years, but we're sentencing you to an IPP ... when the whole purpose was to detain people that weren't safe to be let out on a tariff?'

He told us that 'I still stand by the Criminal Justice Act other than the implementation of IPP'. Hilary Benn, also defended it both as 'an accountable politician' and because he thought 'the objective was a reasonable one, but', he told us, 'it's not uncommon in legislation' that it can be used 'in a way that wasn't intended.' It takes time and careful drafting to frame legislation to meet the precise intentions behind the expressed desires of politicians – but Blunkett was in a hurry. When the opposition argued in favour of leaving sentencing matters with the newly planned Sentencing Guidelines Council, Blunkett responded 'there's insufficient time' (Hansard, HC 20.5.03). One of our respondents told us that Blunkett ran the Home Office with 'an iron fist,' and that IPP's were an overreaction and 'a big mistake.'

Unsurprisingly, none of the former Lord Chief Justices we spoke to could find anything to say in favour of the IPP sentence, but they were even more concerned about the consequences of Schedule 21 of Blunkett's Act which is perhaps an even bigger blot on his copybook. This set new minimum terms to be served for life sentences in different types of murder. Blunkett had been incensed – or as Hilary Benn put it 'quite cross' – after the House of Lords had, at long last, overturned the Home Secretary's power to set tariffs for lifers ruling that this was a judicial and not a political function. Benn told us that he had been 'the last minister to set tariffs for murder cases' and that his first red box required seven such decisions. He was relieved when he no longer had those decisions to make. Some six months before, the CJA 2003 received the Royal assent, Harry Woolf, the Lord Chief Justice, who was to become the Chair of the Sentencing Guidelines Council, had proposed a change in the presumptive starting points for life sentences from 14 years to 16 years for the more serious cases and 12 years for the less serious, and said there was a strong case for the abolition of mandatory life sentences (*The Guardian*, 8.5.03). Blunkett, however, was determined to tie the hands of judges by enshrining his views on seriousness in law. He regarded paedophiles as 'the scum of the earth' (Hansard, HC 4.12.02) and Section 21 extended the applicability of whole life sentences to include terrorists, those guilty of multiple killings and serious child sex offenders. It set a new starting point of 30 years rather than 20 years for contract killers and those who killed police officers, and 15 years for the least serious cases. In 1962, when one of us was a student at the Institute of Criminology, the average term *actually served* by life sentence prisoners had been nine years. We discuss the views of the Judges on these matters in Chapter 6.

Although Blunkett wanted to be very tough with those guilty of the most serious offences, he endorsed Halliday's recommendation of a return to the twin track approach and wished to find alternatives to custody for the many for whom he agreed custody was not necessary. But it was always the tough end of the spectrum which took precedence, whilst the second track became tougher as well. For New Labour public confidence in tougher non-custodial sentences and a determination that they should be seen to be enforced, had become the *sine qua non* for any cutting back on custodial sentences. New sentences were proposed: *custody minus* – a suspended sentence, favoured by the judiciary; *custody plus* which would require prisoners to serve the whole of their remission period under supervision by the probation service – a sentence deemed so costly it was not brought into effect and more interestingly, *intermittent custody* at weekends for those who had jobs, or during the week, for those who had family commitments but no jobs. Despite two completed pilot studies, one for men and one for women, which were said to have worked well, intermittent custody never took off and was abandoned in 2007 (HO Findings 208).

These were times when things happened very quickly with Downing Street taking a lead in most things. Not only was John Birt expected to deliver the 'holy grail of crime reduction' – a phrase also used by Hilary Benn in our interview – but in March 2003, Lord Patrick Carter was commissioned by a powerful triumvirate, of the Prime Minister, the Home Secretary and the Chief Secretary to the Treasury, to review the correctional services. In December, Carter (2003) delivered his report *Managing Offenders – Reducing Crime* which tapped into two New Labour themes – the need to control the growth of the prison population and the linking up of the separate services of prisons and probation.

New Labour had become obsessed by the need, as they saw it, to join up the various parts of the criminal justice system and in 2003, Blunkett had established a new Correctional Services Board under the chairmanship of Martin Narey, until then Director of Prisons but who now, if briefly, enjoyed the title of Commissioner of Corrections as well as the status of Permanent Secretary. Phil Wheatley took over as Director of Prisons and became a member of the new Board, together with Eithne Wallis, Director of Probation and Norman Warner, the Chair of the Youth Justice Board. Later that year, the first joint report on the resettlement of offenders was published by the Inspectors of Prisons and Probation under the title *Through the Gate*. But it was Pat Carter's report, delivered in December 2003 which set the agenda for change. It is not clear why Carter, was chosen to conduct such a review singlehandedly. He was a close friend, and best man at the weddings, of Jack Straw but he was also a friend of Norman Warner on whose recommendation he had become a non-executive member of the Prisons Board. Although Carter acknowledged inputs from the Home Office Strategy Unit, the Department for Constitutional Affairs, and the Treasury as well as the prison and probation services it was, as he put it to us when we interviewed him in the House of Lords, essentially the work of 'an amateur'. He told us that he had earlier received much sound advice from Richard Tilt, and his deputy Tony Pearson and had walked an 'awful lot of landings' and visited a great many prisons both here and abroad. He had earlier, in January 2001, been asked to conduct an internal review of how 3% efficiency savings required by the Treasury could be achieved in the prisons budget.

His report recommended that sentencing policy should take better account of the resources available through the advice of the Sentencing Guidelines Council. Although the CJA 2003, in Section 172, simply required sentencers to pay attention to the advice of the Council, there was now an attempt to include more specific advice in the draft Management of Offenders and Sentencing Bill. This would require sentencing to take account of the cost of different sentences and their effectiveness in preventing reoffending, and the resources that are, or are likely to be, available. Blunkett told the House of Commons that he had agreed this with the Lord Chief Justice and the Lord Chancellor (Hansard, HC 4.1.04). The other main recommendation was that the prisons and probation services be brought together under a new body, the National Offender Management Service (NOMS), with the extremely ambitious aspiration of 'end-to-end' management of offenders – from the beginning of their sentence of imprisonment to the end of their supervision in the community. In January 2004, Blunkett appointed Martin Narey as the Chief Executive of NOMS. Ten Regional Offender Managers (ROMs) were appointed to commission both prison and probation services for each region. Of these appointments, six were from probation and three from prison backgrounds, and one was an external candidate with commissioning experience at British Telecom. They were, in turn, accountable to the National Offender Manager, and effectively Narey's deputy, Christine Knott, who had previously been a Chief Officer of Probation. The regions coincided with existing prison areas rather than the recently re-organised 42 Probation Boards. In this first iteration of NOMS, it sat alongside the Prison Service Executive Agency and the primary role of NOMS was to commission and contract for all prison and probation places and services, and case management.

NOMS formally came into being in June 2004, and in October a pathfinder pilot of how NOMS would actually work was being tested in the north-west region. NOMS was not greatly welcomed by either service each having its own history, professional culture and managerial arrangements which were adapted to, and appropriate for, their very different tasks. Probation officers had previously been seconded to work in prisons. They had replaced old style welfare officers to provide a point of contact with prisoners and their families during their imprisonment, as well as a link to the probation service in the community to which the prisoner would be released, but now they gave way to offender supervisors in prisons. It was never really clear just how bringing the two services together in this way was supposed to work in practice although at the heart of offender management was to be a common IT system, called C–NOMIS, that was to be accessible across prisons and probation as a management tool tracking offenders through their time in custody and subsequent supervision. Unfortunately, it became one of the more celebrated *Blunders of our Governments* described by Antony King and Ivor Crewe (2014, p 191), the lifetime cost of which to 2020 was approved at £234 million but two years later had almost tripled to £690 million. When we interviewed him some 15 years after the introduction of NOMS, Carter acknowledged that

> 'we didn't capture the technology or that culturally the difference between the probation service and the prison service was too great. If you looked at Eithne Wallis's management style and Martin Narey's and Phil Wheatley's … they were very different'.

Like most shot-gun weddings, NOMS did not prosper. Sonia Flynn, made it clear there were costs as well as benefits. Like most others we spoke to, she felt that probation was 'the poor relation'. On the one hand, it meant we were better able to share 'best practice around integrated offender management'. But on the other hand, 'the way end-to-end offender management was set up actually signalled the departure of probation officers from prisons.' And instead, 'the probation officer responsible for that prisoner was in the community, and you had an offender supervisor in the prison.' The ability to collaborate 'at that micro level just wasn't there anymore'.

Though Blunkett was committed to the success of NOMS, he left office 'part way through the passage of the Bill.' He told us that

> 'the prison service didn't want it …. the probation service liked the idea but they weren't keen on engaging. So why didn't it work? Probably not enough resources, probably because the political commitment diminished. Martin Narey was very able but …. was defending his corner – he'd been the head of the prison service and wasn't too keen on NOMS'.

When we probed about why there wasn't greater continuity when a new Minister takes over the portfolio, he sighed and said:

> 'That's a fantastically wonderful question about how things work. Ministers don't have a proper induction and they rarely speak to the person who has just done the job. The person who moves on has either just been sacked and is grumpy or has just been promoted and no longer cares. What we need is a proper portfolio with induction and handover every time someone changes – even when it is a change of government. The new person will have their own priorities but hopefully they will pick up the best of what has been going on'.

Despite those reflections when Hilary Benn was offered the post in International Development but was reluctant to accept it because he had by then developed a keen interest in the prisons brief, Blunkett told him not to be silly and to think of his career. And Benn himself asked the question 'who makes their name as Prison Minister?' and answered it 'you've really got to care.'

In the last 18 months of David Blunkett's time at the Home Office, plans had been emerging for constitutional changes. These centred on the anomalous role of the Lord Chancellor which straddled the three pillars of state: Parliament – as Speaker of the House of Lords; the Executive – as a Privy Councillor and Cabinet Minister with responsibility for the administration of the courts, including legal aid and some judicial appointments; and as Head of the Judiciary – who could sit on cases as a Law Lord. It had worked well enough in a British kind of way, based on mutual understandings and neither successive Lord Chancellors nor Lord Chief Justices were disposed to change it. However, the evident breach of the doctrine of Separation of Powers did not sit well in the light of the European Convention on Human Rights, which had been incorporated into domestic law by Jack Straw in the Human Rights Act (1988). Initially, it had simply been intended to abolish the role of Lord Chancellor. But it turned out to be not at all simple. There had been no Green or White Papers setting out proposals, and no consultations with the Lord Chancellor or the Lord Chief Justice, and hardly any serious thought given to the problems. It had, astonishingly, not even been realised that abolition would require primary legislation, until that was pointed out to them by Lord Irvine as soon as he got wind of the proposals. When he remonstrated with Blair, his former pupil in Chambers, he was told that there could not have been consultations because of fear of leaks. Lord Irvine resigned and six years later, on 26 October 2009, submitted a paper to the Select Committee on the Constitution, in an attempt to set the record straight. Irvine revealed that there had been two acrimonious meetings with Tony Blair in which he had suggested alternative ways forward, and when these were rejected he handed back his Great Seal of office to the Queen on 12 June 2003. As an interim measure, Charlie Falconer, who had served in the Home Office as a Junior Minister responsible for criminal justice, sentencing and law reform, became Lord Chancellor but in the newly created Department for Constitutional Affairs. Then in February 2004, the Constitutional Reform Bill was introduced in the House of Lords with the intention to implement Blair's plan.

Blunkett, like Jack Straw before him and Michael Gove after him, had been much impressed by the problem-solving court at Red Hook in New York. Blunkett, Harry Woolf and Derry Irvine had all visited it at different times and they were all very keen on introducing something similar in this country. Blunkett told us that 'when we came back we established the North Liverpool Court which worked for a time'. What particularly appealed to him was

> 'the idea of getting both the defence and the prosecution to get brownie points for doing the right thing .... having heard the case and considered the evidence ... this person needs psychiatric and social work help .... instead of the prosecution getting accolades for getting the person sent down'.

It was certainly a different way of doing justice. The North Liverpool Community Justice Centre, as it was officially called, was closed by the MoJ under Chris Grayling in 2014. There were a number of similar developments, mostly unsung, but there seem to have been few serious independent academic evaluations.

Hilary Benn told us that for Senior Ministers, dedicated to 'the holy grail of reducing offending', Martin Narey's focus on overcoming the 'indignity of prison conditions' was simply not enough. They had to be able to say that the people 'coming out of prison are less likely to burgle you.' Beverley Hughes, in our telephone interview, confirmed that she had 'regular meetings' with Narey, whom she suspected wasn't used to such 'close ministerial oversight.' Both Benn and Hughes developed a good understanding of the complexity of running prisons and Benn told us that, in the end, 'the overriding requirement is that the system operates and doesn't come to a grinding halt'. If one wanted to change things then you had to either have support from the top or else be very determined and prepared to take the consequences. As Blunkett himself reflected 'we're still ... not clear where the political and the administrative part company

… who's responsible for what … politicians believe they have operational control … but they don't.'

During Blunkett's time in office, the average daily population increased by over 9,000 prisoners. He was succeeded by Charles Clarke.

Charles Clarke (December 2004–May 2006)

We interviewed Charles Clarke on 31 August 2018 in the café at St Mary's Church in Cambridge, further testing our transcription service with the challenge of a background of rattling crockery and cutlery. Unlike Blunkett, Charles Clarke had not coveted the Home Office brief. He had served as a Junior Minister in the Home Office in 1999, but when Blair invited him to take up the job he initially refused. 'Then Tony said "are you really going to turn down one of the three great offices of state? …. and I decided that I wouldn't … couldn't'. He thought that prior experience of a particular field was not necessary for a new Minister, and might actually bring an unhelpful narrowness of approach when a wider view was needed. But his suggestion that it took him about a year 'to feel on top of the subjects I was dealing with in a big public ministry' only reinforced the need for a reduction in ministerial churn.

His first tasks were to oversee the bringing into force of the provisions for IPP – which he regarded as necessary to 'convince people that we were protecting them' and which would give them space 'for this other stuff' they wanted to do. This 'other stuff' also stemmed from the CJA 2003 and included new community sentences, new release and recall procedures, and so-called *custody minus* (but not *custody plus* because of funding issues) and *intermittent custody* (for which he extended the pilot studies). But, in response to the report by HM Chief Inspector of Probation on the murder of John Monckton by a prisoner on licence, it also included the extension of the licence period from the three quarters point to the full term. This was actually backdated, amending the CJA 1991 and effectively increased the length of the sentence intended by the courts. He was greatly 'exercised' by the decisions the Parole Board had to make and 'how to get them right'. He told us that he believed that 'if you commit serious offences you lose significant rights.' However, he recognised that it was 'massively difficult to make an assessment of people's potential actions.' Prison and probation staff were told not to place too much emphasis on good behaviour in prison as an indication of the reduction of risk. There *are* statistical methods for assessing the level of risk of future offences for particular *categories* of offender but no reliable methods for assessing individual risks within those categories. Behaviour in prison will not be an infallible guide, but will likely be as good or better than other indicators. The point remains that trying to build risk into criminal justice is fraught with the dangers of injustice.

Meanwhile, the Constitutional Reform Bill was proceeding on a tortuous path between the Lords and the Commons. Instead of abolishing the office of Lord Chancellor a series of amendments led to its retention, albeit in a radically amended form. Among the far-reaching changes which were eventually incorporated into the Constitutional Reform Act 2005 were the following: the Lord Chancellor's role as Speaker of the House of Lords was given over to an elected Speaker, the Law Lords were replaced by a new Supreme Court, judicial appointments became the responsibility of an independent Judicial Appointments Commission, and the Lord Chief Justice replaced the Lord Chancellor as Head of the Judiciary. The new arrangements were met with little favour from the Judiciary as we note in Chapter 6. Lord Falconer, who had previously supported abolition, now found himself in that role, and had to reassure the judges that he would faithfully uphold their independence. It says much for his abilities that he was largely able to do so and some regarded him as the last of the old-style Lord Chancellors.

Clarke also had to pick up Blunkett's introduction of NOMS. The proposals for a new commissioning model for prisons and probation, splitting 'offender management' from 'intervention' services, and raising issues about privatisation, regionalisation and centralisation, were all so controversial that they had been debated, amended and then changed again for the best part of two years. Even so, there were accusations of excessive haste to introduce poorly thought-out proposals, extravagant costs and lack of transparency. Of particular concern was the removal of powers from Probation Boards and placing them with NOMS, and ultimately the Secretary of State, and the introduction of providers from outside the NPS. Although Blunkett had blamed the failure of NOMS on the lack of sustained interest of his successors, Clarke told us that he was 'totally committed to NOMS.' In March 2005, the Junior Minister, the late Paul Goggins, announced a competition for the running of three new prisons on the Isle of Sheppey, further assistance for Probation Boards to develop offender management in their areas, as well as a range of other matters including connecting up IT systems (which was already well behind schedule), and in developing some 28 performance targets against which the work of NOMS might be assessed.

Clarke announced the closure of HMP Weare in March 2005 and, following a brief re-opening, it was eventually sold after being condemned by the Chief Inspector of Prisons, Anne Owers. Clarke believed that Gordon Brown had orchestrated public criticism of him over the matter and it was widely thought that Clarke considered himself to be the right candidate to replace Blair as Prime Minister when the time came. There is no doubt that Blair saw him as a kindred spirit. Towards the end of his first year, Clarke gave a major speech to the Prison Reform Trust (PRT) in which he set out his considered views on *Where Next for Penal Policy*. He told us that his 'predecessors David Blunkett and Jack Straw could not and would not have given a lecture like that.' It set out both a populist, Blairite stance combined with far-reaching redemptive plans to achieve the holy grail of rehabilitation and may have represented what he saw as his pathway to No 10. He thought 'the British people' wanted three things: 'first … to feel secure … ; second … that the offender will be caught, justice will be done …; and third … that when offenders leave the criminal justice system they will …

become constructive contributors to society.' In elaboration of the second of these, he emphasised that the government would 'continue to be tough on crime and criminals' (a telling extension to the usual mantra) and he pointed approvingly to the introduction of IPP sentences as evidence of that. Whether or not these were the *people's* priorities, they certainly were for the Government. In order to achieve the third, he contended, it would require 'all parts of our society working together.' He pointed to the operation of the YOTs and the principles of the Sure Start programme in education as contributing to the continuing fall in crime, and he focussed the rest of his talk on how best to reduce reoffending.

He spoke of the £300 million a year investment made in developing rehabilitative regimes and providing thousands of prisoners with education, skills and drug treatment programmes, as well as improving primary healthcare in prisons to NHS standards.

There was no doubt that in the first two terms of New Labour, money for the development of programmes was much more easily available – and this was indeed often remarked upon by the people we interviewed from the prison and probation services. These were considerable achievements. But Clarke also wanted real *community prisons* to bridge the gap between custody and community, as had been proposed by Woolf, and he dismissed the operational case, argued by officials, that it was near impossible to create such prisons when the system was running at, or beyond, capacity as an unacceptable 'excuse'. He looked forward to a contract whereby offenders would commit to 'going straight' and the agencies commit to providing programmes and interventions to help them – again congruent with the Woolf agenda. He envisaged individualised support packages for each offender including health, education, employment, social and family links and housing – all in his view sorely needed by what he rightly described as 'the least educated and least healthy people in the country.' He wasn't the first to see himself as turning prisons away from being 'universities of crime' to becoming institutions ensuring that offenders become 'working and productive members of society upon release.'

But Clarke was adamantly opposed to introducing any kind of cap on the prison population in part because he, mistakenly, believed that the Judiciary would be universally opposed. In his lecture Clarke said that he had already discovered 'it is always dangerous for a politician to tread on the toes of the Judiciary' – a reference, presumably to judges overturning his attempts to deport terror suspects which were held to breach the Human Rights Act – and he remained wary about these relationships. He nevertheless went on to advise the courts to make good use of indeterminate sentences, to maintain their authority by rigorously enforcing penalties, to make flexible and positive use of tougher community sentences as well as fines, and to take proper account of the guidelines issued by the Sentencing Guidelines Council. In our interview, he spoke of Lord Bingham's assertion that the LCJ and the Secretary of State should not have formal meetings but he thought it permissible to meet informally as he clearly did with both Lord Philips and Lord Judge.

In February 2006, Charles Clarke released his *Five Year Strategy for Reducing Reoffending and Protecting the Public* and a month later he published a consultation paper on *Restructuring Probation to Reduce Reoffending*, although this was derided by some, as consultation after the fact. Such a programme would be extraordinarily ambitious, expensive and inordinately complex to deliver. In our interview, he looked back and asked himself 'whether it was practical … maybe utopian?' but he felt, like some others among both politicians and practitioners, 'you've got to try'. Clarke had expected to be at the Home Office for a full five-year term by the end of which he had hoped to have made significant progress in his long-term plans for a step-by-step reorganisation of both prisons and probation. He recognised that many difficulties would have to be overcome but even his own estimate that it would take 'five years – at the minimum' would involve a continuity of planning by successive Home Secretaries of a kind not previously seen – at least for several decades.

It was not long, however, before disillusion set in. Clarke told us that he did not have 'a high regard for John Gieve who was the Permanent Secretary' and was much happier when Gieve was replaced by David Normington who had been Clarke's Permanent Secretary at Education. However, he 'also had serious issues' with people at what he called 'Deputy Secretary levels.' He did not get on with Martin Narey, who was actually one of three Permanent Secretaries at that time, and he told us that 'I certainly found him an exceptionally difficult and frustrating man to work with.' Clarke had been careful to get the support of Tony Blair – who had actually chaired the early planning meetings for NOMS – but he 'felt it was a struggle …. to get key officials, including Martin Narey, to try and carry that approach through'. This was a view vigorously rejected by Narey as 'pure nonsense'. He told us that although Clarke preached a philosophy of wanting his civil servants to speak truth to power in practice this was something he found difficult to tolerate. Clarke also found the late Harry Fletcher, former General Secretary of the National Association of Probation Officers (NAPO) as extremely negative, 'trying to resist NOMS at every turn.' Like Blunkett before him, Clarke saw Narey as someone protecting his prison fiefdom who did not welcome the intrusion of the probation service into his domain. But Narey's position was that without a mechanism for controlling the size of the prison population – the cap agreed by Blunkett, Woolf and Falconer and for which he believed he had secured Blair's support after Blunkett had departed – the prison service would be so busy moving prisoners around it would be completely unable to plan for or deliver the changes that Clarke wanted to see.

Martin Narey had come to believe that whilst rehabilitation was a desirable ambition it was extremely difficult to achieve on any large scale in any scenario he was likely to experience. He was much more concerned that prisoners should be treated with humanity and dignity which was difficult enough, and once it became clear that Clarke had effectively ripped up the agreement for a cap on the population by withdrawing the draft of the Management of Offenders and Sentencing Bill, Narey resigned. In an unfortunate interview on *Newsnight*, Clarke indicated he was pleased that Narey had gone and managed to convey the impression that he had been sacked. Narey demanded and got a written apology from Clarke and a similar apology was broadcast before a subsequent edition of *Newsnight*. In retrospect, Clarke reflected

> 'there are serious important questions about how possible it was to bring together the highly centralised prison system and the highly decentralised probation service. Was it a silly idea to bring them together and were the difficulties that arose inevitable? Good questions but I wouldn't say the official advice in that area was particularly good'.

They had certainly been good questions at the time of the Carter Report but they received little serious attention. Indeed, Clarke ultimately attributed the failure of NOMS, not so much to personalities as to insufficient attention having been given to the practical difficulties of joining up such radically different services: 'It was done from a principled point of view rather than a practical point of view'. Martin Narey was succeeded by Helen Edwards as Chief Executive of NOMS.

Clarke did not get to serve the full term he had hoped for but it was perhaps naïve of him to 'believe if I'd had the chance to carry this through I could have made an impact in these areas.' It is also important to note that, like others before and since, he looked for ways to reduce the numbers of women, drug offenders and people with mental health problems in prison. He brought the problems of the women's estate more sharply into focus, and commissioned the report on women in prison by Jean Corston following several deaths in custody at HMP Styal. Initiatives begun under Blunkett were continued, including a pilot of the one-stop community centres, later to form a major part of Corston's report. However, during the questions after his PRT talk he was asked whether he realised that some 10,000 of those in custody were in fact foreign prisoners who were possibly eligible for deportation. Extraordinary as it might seem, he had *not* known that. But once it had been drawn to his attention he highlighted the need to do more about speeding up the deportation process which was immediately taken up by the Press. It was the controversy over these prisoners which was to dog him thereafter and eventually to cause his downfall amidst huge adverse publicity. After less than 18 months in office he resigned and returned to the back benches, despite Blair's attempt to persuade him at first to stay on and then to give him the Defence portfolio. He had been on the point of announcing the establishment of drug court pilots to run for 18 months at Leeds and West London Magistrate's Courts. He was replaced by John Reid.

John Reid (May 2006–May 2007)

We interviewed John Reid on 11 July 2019 over cups of coffee in the House of Lords. He was the only one of our interviewees who declined to be recorded – we presumed because of past hounding by journalists, especially Rebekah

Brooks. Everything was to be regarded as a background briefing unless it was already in the public record. So after hurriedly finding pen and paper, one of us asked the questions whilst the other took notes.

Reid identified himself as a Blairite and had little time for Gordon Brown. He clearly relished his role as Tony Blair's 'Mr Fixit' – being sent in to clear things up whenever and wherever they had gone wrong. As a result, he occupied nine ministerial posts between May 1997 and June 2007 – which he regarded as far too many. His 13 months at the Home Office was exactly average for his ministerial career. He should therefore know all about the politics of churn. But whilst he regarded ministerial churn as a problem for departmental governance he also saw it as inevitable in a system emphasising parliamentary accountability – when Harold Macmillan was asked what was the most troubling problem for his government, he was widely reported to have replied 'events, dear boy, events'. Unlike many Ministers, however, Reid was able to leave the Home Office by choice, having said he would quit when Brown became PM and he was good to his word.

His period at the Home Office was profoundly consequential. He came in determined to sort things out and in short order made precipitate and controversial decisions to transfer prisons and probation to a new Ministry of Justice. The Home Office was still a sprawling department covering immigration, terrorism, criminal justice, police, prisons, probation and fire services, although licensing, alcohol, gaming and betting and film and video censorship had been transferred to Culture, Media and Sport in 2001. Immigration, terrorism and the matter of foreign prisoners, which had brought down Charles Clarke, were still issues of enormous continuing concern and had grown since the attack on the World Trade Centre and the wars in Iraq and Afghanistan. Immediately on his appointment, Reid had reportedly asked each head of department to 'bring out the bodies' promising his support in return for an honest appraisal of the problems and potential solutions.

Almost immediately on taking office he had to respond to reports on Serious Further Offences (SFOs) – murders committed by offenders whilst on licence, on probation or whilst in prison and he commissioned reviews of the management of child sex offenders and of anti-corruption policies in prisons. In June 2006, there were also heated exchanges between David Cameron and Tony Blair over who was to blame for 53 life sentence prisoners being released after serving less than five years, even though the average time served by 'lifers' had dramatically increased to over 14 years with many, of course, serving very much longer than that. Reid promised to tighten things up. Particular attention was paid to the case of Craig Sweeney, much of it ill-informed. Sweeney, a paedophile who had just completed a sentence for an earlier offence against a child, was sentenced to life imprisonment for abducting and sexually assaulting the daughter of a woman whom he had befriended. The sentencing judge, following precedent and the guidelines, indicated what length of determinate sentence he would have imposed had he not been minded to pass a life sentence – namely 18 years.

In accordance with the rules this would be reduced to 12 years in recognition of an early plea of guilty. This meant that the earliest point at which release on parole could have been considered would be after six years. There was, of course no requirement that he *should* be paroled after six years, or indeed *ever* – for life sentences are indeterminate – but that was not how it was reported in much of the Press. Reid called on Lord Goldsmith, the Attorney General, to appeal the sentence but he refused on grounds that it would give the impression of political pressure on independent judicial figures. But the case was expected to accelerate a review of the rules permitting judges to give a discount for early guilty pleas as well as changes to parole. Reid was attacked in Parliament and in the Press for seeking to blame 'the judges, the civil servants, and the public' (*The Guardian*, 14.6.06) for the problems in the criminal justice system.

The 2006 Report on *Rebalancing the Criminal Justice System* was premised on the populist perception that clever defence lawyers were misusing the Human Rights Act for the benefit of their clients and so putting the public at risk. The *Child Sex Offender Review* (2007) made provisions for the pilot of what was often called Sarah's Law in four police areas. Sarah Payne had been abducted and murdered by Roy Whiting, a convicted paedophile in July 2000. Sarah's mother, Sara Payne, played a key role in the establishment of the Review after a long and highly publicised campaign to give concerned parents the right to seek disclosure of whether adults with unsupervised access to their children had previous convictions for sexual abuse of children. The scheme was subsequently rolled out to all police areas. Reid was keen to point out during the parliamentary debate on the *Review* (Hansard, HC 18.7.06) that the 'metropolitan elite … confuse populism with listening to the views of ordinary people'. It marked another step, along the route of placing victims at the heart of criminal justice – a path which subsequent governments felt bound to follow. At the time of writing, a somewhat similar campaign is being mounted to increase the sentences on three youths convicted of the manslaughter of a police constable and the case has been referred to the Attorney General. Significantly, when we interviewed LCJ Phillips, he told us that he was 'strongly in favour of the discount for guilty pleas' which he regarded as 'essential' and that involving victims in the justice process was 'not a good idea'.

In the Summer of 2006, the prisons were full to overflowing and the prison service had to set up a 24-hour team working in shifts to find places for prisoners who were sentenced that day. To accommodate the growing number of adult men sentenced to custody two women's prisons were re-assigned to the men's estate, there was a more intensive use of open prisons, and the search was on for army barracks and former secure hospital sites for possible prison use. Like Clarke, Reid was opposed to early release as a partial solution which had in any case been vetoed by Blair. In July 2006, he was able to announce that the Treasury had agreed to fund 8,000 new prison places as part of the commitment 'to rebalance the criminal justice system in favour of the law abiding majority … to keep dangerous prisoners in for longer (for which) more prison places is the sine qua non'. But he stressed 'there is a legitimacy to alternatives other than prison' for less dangerous offenders and he expressed his support for the problem-solving courts in Liverpool and Manchester (Hansard, HC 18.7.06).

The Sentencing Guidelines which were supposed to balance the increase in the length of sentences at the deep end, by more community sentences instead of custody at the shallow end, were not working. Had they worked as intended they had been expected to bring about a reduction of 15% in the numbers of short sentences because, as Reid put it, 'people did not want to pay £40,000 in bed and breakfast' (*The Guardian*, 29.1.07). Like Blunkett and Clarke, he blamed the Judiciary for their over-use of IPPs although he made no apologies about the principle behind those sentences. He also blamed the Judiciary for their under-use of community sentences. Lord Phillips told us that it was not the fault of the judges whose lack of confidence in community sentence was not because they were too soft but because they doubted whether 'the facilities are going to be provided'. He famously spent a day, incognito, doing a day of community pay-back, and although this was dismissed in some quarters as a publicity stunt he was able to speak from experience.

As Chair of the Criminal Justice Board, Reid had been encouraged by the Lord Chief Justice to write about the issue of community sentences and to put it on the website of the Sentencing Guidelines Council, which, towards the end of January 2007, he duly did. It caused an immediate uproar with one judge complaining that he was 'seeking to hamstring the court's ability to issue appropriate sentences' and another that as a result he had to sentence a 'sex offender to a suspended jail term because he had to take account of Government advice' (*The Guardian*, 26.1.07). Not for the first time, there were calls for his resignation although LCJ Phillips came to his support telling us that he made it clear that Reid had 'not sought to instruct judges to stop imposing sentences of imprisonment'. A defiant Reid indicated that he would not be quitting, that his mission to sort out the problems at the Home Office would take time and that the public did not want a change of Home Secretary but for the Home Office itself to be changed. Rumours had been circulating that he, as well as Clarke, harboured thoughts of succeeding Blair as Prime Minister, but the suggestion that he would be staying at the Home Office until the next election seemed to indicate that he would not be challenging Gordon Brown for the leadership – an assumption he duly confirmed. Intriguingly, in the absence of a 15% reduction in the prison population through the courts, Michael Spurr, before he became Chief Executive, had led a team in NOMS which came up with a plan to achieve the same effect with legislation to reduce the length of time spent in custody – although it never reached the statute book. Spurr told us that Reid had agreed the plan on a Friday but instead announced the removal of prisons, probation and criminal justice from the Home Office the following Monday.

As part of his Home Office Reform Action Plan, Reid wanted to see a 50% reduction in headquarters staff over the next few years with a shift of resources to the front line. He gave a strategic plan to his Junior Ministers – Gerry Sutcliffe and Patricia Scotland – and allowed them to get on with it. It certainly kept a distance between him and the operational chaos of overcrowded prisons and foreign national prisoners. In Parliament, he was proposing that a new contract between Ministers and officials would clarify their 'respective roles and expectations in relation to policy, strategic decisions, operational delivery and management' (Hansard, HC 19.7.06). His ideas about a new contract seemed to involve a version of *agency status* that was close to that espoused in the Fulton Report of 1968. By the end of the summer recess, there had been a further steep rise in the prison population which only accentuated the desire for reform. However, the probation service was also under severe strain. In July, he had claimed that NOMS was only meeting 22 of its 33 performance targets and in November 2006 he made a speech at Wormwood Scrubs in which he argued that probation was not working well. The Offender Management Bill that replaced the Management of Offenders and Sentencing Bill, aimed to replace local Boards with independent Probation Trusts and to remove the public sector monopoly by bringing in the private and voluntary sector. He also proposed taking back powers to 'deal with' failing trusts and during the second reading he said that 'almost regardless of the amount of resources the reoffending rate had stayed obstinately high.' The opposition accused him of 'setting up the probation service to fail – reorganising it to death' (Hansard, HC 11.9.06). But it was also a period which Chris Grayling, some years later, was able to cite in support of his proposed split between the NPS and his Community Rehabilitation Companies.

The most immediate issues, however, as far as Reid was concerned, were related to immigration, the deportation of foreign national prisoners and the need to develop counter-terrorism. He asked his Permanent Secretary for his views on the immigration department. He was told by David Normington that 'it was not fit for purpose'. When Reid used that phrase publicly, he was widely criticised for blaming his civil servants, though we understand that he took the phrase as his own in order to protect his Permanent Secretary. His solution to the problem of the complicated range of departmental responsibilities within the Home Office was formally announced in March 2007 at the same time as he told the Commons that the Prime Minister had asked him to undertake a review of counter-terrorism. It involved transferring the responsibility for criminal justice, prisons and probation to the Department for Constitutional Affairs, which already housed the Lord Chancellor, Charlie Falconer, and turning it into the new Ministry of Justice. The Liberal Democrats had, in fact, challenged him to do just that, or something very like it, during the debate on the Home Office Reform Action Plan. Evidence that the plan was perhaps not fully thought through came when the opposition expressed concern that Falconer was in the House of Lords and this would be inappropriate for a Minister of Justice. Reid was forced to concede that this might be a temporary arrangement.

Although Reid's plan for a Ministry of Justice apparently reflected his long-standing view that the countering of crime should be separated from the application of justice and that it may have been discussed in Cabinet, others have gone on record with different accounts. Jack Straw relates how in late January 2007, as part of his preparation for a Sunday morning TV appearance, he called John Reid to see whether there were any Home Office issues which might be bowled at him.

> 'John told me that the Sunday Telegraph would be running a story by him proposing that the Home Office be split in two, so that it was likely to be a big story. ... Charlie Falconer, then Lord Chancellor ... only learnt of John's intentions through a phone call on the Saturday night'.

Nor had the senior judiciary been given any warning, and according to Jonathan Powell, who had been Blair's Chief of staff, that avoidance of consultation with the Judiciary had been deliberate (Powell, 2010, p 153). We discuss the judicial response to all this in Chapter 6. Charles Clarke was understandably miffed at having his previous domain described as 'not fit for purpose', and David Blunkett, thought the change diminished the role of the Home Secretary. Nonetheless, the change was hastily pushed through and the new Ministry of Justice was born in May 2007. By then Reid had announced that he would resign from Cabinet when Gordon Brown took over from Tony Blair as Prime Minister. He was succeeded as Home Secretary by Jacqui Smith though she no longer had any role in prisons or probation. These were now the responsibility, albeit briefly, of the new Secretary of State for Justice, Charlie Falconer.

Charlie Falconer (May 2007–June 2007)

We interviewed Lord Falconer at his London office at Gibson Dunn, the US Law Firm he had joined on leaving office and he was happy for everything to be on the record. Charlie Falconer was not a career politician but had spent much of his professional life practising law, some of it alongside his friend Tony Blair. He failed to gain a seat as an MP but was created a life peer by Blair, after the 1997 election. He served first as Solicitor General, then had an unfortunate period in charge of the Millennium Dome, served briefly as Minister for Housing, Planning and Regeneration before arriving in the Home Office with responsibility for criminal justice, sentencing and law reform. Falconer had become Lord Chancellor, in the newly created Department of Constitutional Affairs in 2003 to which the Courts Service was transferred from the Home Office. Initially, his appointment was for an 'interim period' until Tony Blair's intention to abolish that ancient office was brought into effect. In May 2007, he became the first person to occupy the combined role of Lord Chancellor and Secretary of State for Justice. But the process of getting from one position to the other was messy, with the Prime Minister and his advisors seeming to flounder in a sea of ignorance and incompetence. Nevertheless, Falconer initially thought he would be Lord Chancellor and Minister of Justice for the long term.

Falconer told us that he agreed with John Reid's assessment that the Home Office wasn't fit for purpose: 'It was doing very badly'. So when John Reid gave him the opportunity he 'very enthusiastically took prisons and probation and all penal policy off the Home Office' into the Ministry of Justice. However, he told us that he took it on against the advice of his Permanent Secretary, Alex Allen, not to do it 'in part because of the money issues.' The judges were concerned that prisons would absorb more and more of the budget but Falconer thought that 'the legal aid and courts budget is tiny by comparison to the prisons budget … [so] … stealing from the court and legal aid budget … would never make any difference to the scale of problems that we had got.' The process of resolving matters with the judiciary had begun before he took on the responsibility as Secretary of State for Justice, and Falconer was probably right in his assessment of the budget at that time, though real problems were to occur under the next two Governments. All told, Falconer spent just six weeks as Secretary of State for Justice although he 'was very much hoping to be involved in it forever … or not forever … but for a longer period than six weeks.' Tony Blair had told him that 'if you agree to take on the prisons, it'll be almost impossible for you to stay, because it's so much a thing that's got to be in the Commons. I was saying …. I'm sure I can manage it.'

When we explored with him the relationship with the judges at the time of the break-up of the Lord Chancellor's Department and the creation of the MoJ, he agreed that

> 'they were very, very against it because they hadn't been consulted. They thought it hadn't been thought through properly, and, you know they had a point in all of that. But they changed because … with the Lord Chancellor no longer Head of the Judiciary they had to take on much more responsibility about the role of judges, which they didn't initially want to do. And then they grasped it pretty firmly and pretty warmly'.

Indeed, Falconer told us the changes increased the power of the judges vis-a-vis the Executive, and that the 'cosy relationships between the Prime Minister and the person who appoints all the judges' was no longer appropriate. However, he had consulted with both Harry Woolf and Nick Phillips who asked whether he was going to remain Head of the Judiciary and he said that he wasn't. He told us 'there was a tricky struggle going on between me and the judges about what powers I am going to keep during the interim period.' In fact, he kept control of the appointment of judges during the interim period despite hostility from the judges. In his view

> 'the original reforms were about the Lord Chancellor no longer being the Chief Judge and Speaker of the Lords; once the Lord Chancellor ceases to be the Head of the Judiciary, the Speaker of the House of Lords and a member of the cabinet as the Lord Chancellor, then the role, in effect, goes away. It survives in title, but basically the Lord Chancellor is the Minister of Justice'.

His final judgement on the matter was that it 'was the right thing to do' but it was done 'in a cack-handed way'.

The mission set for him as Justice Secretary was 'to deliver a world-class justice system that has the protection of the public and the reduction of reoffending at its heart' (Hansard, HC 29.5.07). If New Labour did regard that as a serious aspiration, they were no longer willing or able to provide the resources to deliver it. Things were certainly not world class when he took them over: 'people were circling the M25 in prison vans while they were trying to find them somewhere to go.' His spokesperson in the House of Commons was David Hanson whom we interviewed in Portcullis House. He gave a similar account: 'We had people walking round prisons trying to find places that could have been used' to accommodate prisoners. Hanson, had been asked by the Prime Minister to be the Commons representative for the Justice Secretary as well as the Junior Minister for Prisons and Probation and he remained in the latter role under Falconer's successor Jack Straw. On appointment he 'met with the senior officials and Charlie Falconer, and was given the outline of what the Prime Minister wanted'. There were four big things to do: 'get more prison places; modernise them; reduce the number of people going to prison where we could; and strengthen community sentences' by getting 'more flexibility in the work of the probation service.'

Two early papers produced from the new MoJ – *Justice: A New Approach* and *Penal Policy: A Background Paper* promised to protect the public by ensuring there were enough prison places. The plans to provide 8,000 more prison places by 2012 would continue but by June 2007 the relentless rise in the prison population led to a Treasury announcement of additional funds to provide places for a further 1,500 prisoners. Meanwhile Falconer authorised a controversial, albeit very modest, scheme whereby prisoners could be released up to 18 days before the end of their sentence which offered some slight relief. There was further promotion of the sentences of IPPs – although Falconer later came to regret that – as well as support for the greater use of community sentences; and concerns as to whether the Sentencing Guidelines fully reflected the greater use of suspended sentence orders envisaged in the CJA 2003.

New plans were to be introduced, in the *Criminal Justice and Immigration* Bill, for a fixed recall period of 28 days for non-dangerous offenders who breached their parole, which would relieve pressure both on accommodation and the work of the Parole Board –which had become so inundated with recommendations for recall that special one person panels had to be convened in order to review them. However, Falconer rejected calls to review Blunkett's IPP measures, and it was left to Jack Straw to effect their partial reform. Also rejected was the idea of the courts being run as a separate agency because it might endanger their budgets and the independence of the Judiciary. Falconer commissioned a review of how the approved premises, which housed parolees who had no suitable accommodation, were financed. Finally, in June 2007 just before his departure, he and the Treasury commissioned a new review by Lord Carter on how best to provide enough prison accommodation for the longer term, and how prisons and probation might be better managed, because NOMS, the product of his first report, was not functioning well and its existence was increasingly being called into question. But Falconer promised a renewed commitment to the end-to-end management of offenders and the commissioning model embodied in NOMS, during the passage of what was now just the *Offender Management* Bill (the *and Sentencing* having been dropped by Clarke). Carter's second Report was produced with the same speed as his first and was published in December 2007, by which time Jack Straw had been installed as Lord Chancellor. Falconer told us that his hope had been that 'Carter would set standards and give us a shopping list for the Treasury … this is what Carter has said we need to do in the long term.' However, he distanced himself from Carter's recommendation to build Titan prisons, telling us 'that was a big mistake' and he told us that he thought that 'Carter would not have deviated from what Jack Straw wanted.' That view was strongly contested by Martin Narey, and indeed Pat Carter himself. In fact, Straw was not at all keen on Titan prisons, the idea for which came out of a workshop organised by Carter, and represented a businessman's idea of the cheapest way to increase the supply of accommodation. As Martin Narey put it 'the emphasis was on what could be done to lower costs because NOMS needed to tighten its belt'.

In our interview Falconer was scathing about Grayling's subsequent policies on both prisons and probation, but he also argued that government policies had to be set alongside real changes in attitude to criminal justice and in the seriousness of cases coming before the courts. He thought Blair was right to change the perception that 'the Labour party … always took the side of the defendant against the victim or the community'. He suggested that there had been a change in cases coming before the Crown Courts since the 1980s from 'domestic burglaries and quite a lot of street robberies, serious but not that serious. The diet now is of serious sex abuse and serious sexual violence cases, violence short of murder'. In retrospect he told us

> 'I think the indeterminate sentences, which I take full responsibility for, were a total disaster. One of the reasons the prison population went up was because people were coming in at the beginning of their sentence and not leaving [on their tariff dates]'.

He thought that judges had to take their share of the blame because they are 'the people who have most determined the length of sentences' whereas, without exception, the judges told us that they had no choice but to raise other sentences in line with the minimum sentences introduced by politicians, in order to maintain proportionality with regard to the gravity of the offence.

Falconer believed that 'society's demand for the length of prison sentence has gone up' and that research showed that 'the general public are tougher than what the courts are in fact doing.' In fact, research evidence, from regular sweeps of the Crime Survey for England and Wales, formerly known as the British

Crime Survey was summarised by the MoJ (2013), and showed that 'most people underestimated the severity of current sentencing practices' whilst nevertheless believing that 'the courts were too lenient' (p2). Overall, the public seemed generally satisfied with the 'fairness' of the criminal justice system but were less satisfied about its perceived effectiveness. Falconer was genuinely 'surprised' by this and said that it 'undermines my basic theory'. Of all the politicians with whom we discussed these issues, only Rory Stewart claimed that he was familiar with that research. In our long discussion Charlie Falconer told us he had changed his mind on drugs policy so that 'I am in favour of de-criminalisation right across the board because it's so obvious that we've failed in our "war" against drugs.'

Looking to the future, Falconer expressed some hope that the publication of the Sentencing Code, which had been entrusted to the Law Commission in 2014, would give clarity over sentencing for the Judiciary, politicians, the Press and the Public. The Sentencing (Pre-consolidation Amendments) Bill, which at the time our interview was then in the Commons, was intended to pave the way for that. But, alas, a considered view from one of our legal colleagues was that the resultant 'Sentencing Act 2020 is not really a code but a consolidation of the previous messes into one very big mess!' At the end of the day Falconer's main concern was that there had been a failure to put in the proper resources to provide decent conditions. He would have liked to see much more expenditure 'on really intensive interventions for people on the cusp of a criminal career.' He told us that 'we trailed off incredibly badly after a very good start, particularly in the youth justice area.'

Both Falconer and his Junior Minister David Hanson agreed that there was a real problem in British democracy about the politics of churn although for slightly different reasons and they also differed about what could or should be done about it. Hanson's concern was that 'churn of ministers is not a good place to be because that gives power to officials.' He told us that he 'walked into the prison service and probation … and met with officials' who had been in prisons and probation for 30 years 'so you have got to have focus and drive to get your points across … because they're professional people with lots of experience.' This was very reminiscent of what Michael Howard had told us. He recognised that 'it doesn't give continuity of political discussion' and that 'it's very important to give people a good run at it' but he knew that 'in the nature of this place that's not going to happen'. We got the feeling that he rather enjoyed the cut and thrust this involved. He strongly disagreed with our search for ways of finding continuity and compromise within and between parties in order to get more reasonable policies. Again, like Michael Howard, he fiercely argued 'that's democracy' and that he was accountable to his constituents for his policies: 'politics is about priorities in public spending.' Falconer recognised the need for better ways of governance, and initially wasn't at all sure about what they might be. But he went on to think aloud about a possible way forward, one initially put to us by Peter Lloyd, and we return to this in our conclusions.

Falconer had been involved in the setting up of further pilot studies of drugs courts and although he was in favour of them, he thought their main targets were 'people who are not going to be in custody' and who may be 'on some kind of journey' and could benefit from an array of services under the supervision of a judge. When we raised with him the possibility of extending the idea to those in custody, he paused to give the matter some thought, after which he said 'it should be.' We wondered whether IPP sentences might have been the ideal situation in which judges could have become involved with the supervision of the sentence – especially given the impasse that had been reached whereby prisoners had to demonstrate that they were no longer a risk but were unable to access the programmes that might provide appropriate evidence. Falconer agreed that 'in relation to the IPP, that would have been a good idea'. In general, he would not 'be averse' to working towards such a process, but said

> 'it's so difficult to imagine it happening in our current system. It would need a different cadre of judges … the guy who did it in the Liverpool court did it brilliantly although he had been just an 'ordinary judge' … so that supports your view that they would learn how to do it. If judges got engaged in that sort of process it would inevitably have an effect on the way they sentenced at the beginning'.

That 'ordinary judge' was Judge David Fletcher who presided over the North Liverpool Community Justice Centre for eight years and who had helped many offenders to turn their lives around in what, admittedly, was a time-consuming and often frustrating, but ultimately very rewarding process. The Centre had been visited by Blair, Brown and Straw among many others but was eventually closed by Grayling in 2014. Although Falconer could clearly see the benefits from the judges becoming more sympathetic to the problems people faced, and more understanding about their lapses, he saw it as a 'bit of a non-starter at the moment because of financial problems'. But just as he had become more enthusiastic the more he thought about ideas for overcoming the politics of churn, so he did about extending the role of judges into the supervision of custodial sentences.

He greatly regretted that he did not get a chance to implement policies as Justice Secretary. He had tried to persuade Tony Blair that he could manage things from the House of Lords, but Blair was no longer in charge. 'I was fired by Mr Gordon Brown in June 2007, so my opportunity to do anything was rather cut short. I wanted to stay but he didn't want me to.' He was succeeded by Jack Straw.

Jack Straw (June 2007–May 2010)

Jack Straw had been in charge of prisons and probation as Home Secretary at the beginning of the New Labour years and was back at the helm at the end – now 'in tights' as he put it in his memoirs (Straw, 2012), as Lord Chancellor and

Justice Secretary. David Hanson remained as Prisons and Probation Minister until 2009 when he was succeeded by Maria Eagle.

Jack Straw's time at the Ministry of Justice has to be seen against the background of the collapse of the sub-prime mortgage market and the ensuing banking crisis of 2007–2008. Although Charlie Falconer had secured a good settlement from the Treasury, there was a tightening of the purse strings. In December 2007, the Government denied that the cuts were affecting prisons or probation, but almost immediately the prison service had to introduce the Standard Core Day across the prison estate to deliver efficiencies and improve the consistency of regime delivery as part of saving £16 million. After the collapse of Lehmann Brothers late the following year, the financial pressures on NOMS increased. By the end of 2008 it had made further cash savings amounting to £52 million and in 2009 it was announced that under a NOMS prudent-efficiency programme, the probation budget would be cut by 2.2% and all non-urgent maintenance in prisons would be deferred. It is not clear, either from his memoirs or from our interview (which had to cover both periods in office) how hard Straw fought against these cuts, nor is there anything to help us in Gordon Brown's memoirs.

In our interview he drew attention to the major differences in his approach to work in the Home Office and the MoJ.

> 'When I first got into government I had a clean slate. I had done a huge amount of work with my team in the three years that I had been Shadow Home Secretary and we had really developed and stress tested the policies we were going to use. There was a huge amount of legislation, most of it positive, much of it still there. When I came back, and others had been responsible for the system for the last six years, you just had to pick up where others have left off'.

In his second term of office, he quickly found that the Prison Officers Association were still as capable of de-stabilising not just a single prison but the whole system as they had been in his first. Almost immediately the POA had given 24 hours' notice of a national strike and Straw successfully applied for a High Court injunction requiring them to return to work. Shortly afterwards he added a provision to the *Criminal Justice and Immigration Bill* to renew the comprehensive ban on strike action by prison officers, which had been invoked by Michael Howard, but subsequently withdrawn in return for a voluntary non-strike agreement. This did not settle matters, however, and Hanson told us that the POA were advising members not to accept a 'workforce reform changing the terms and conditions for new staff' even though it did not affect existing staff. Straw had little choice but to threaten that 'the Government would pursue a competition agenda'. Michael Spurr, by this time was having regular meetings with Straw as they 'were constantly under pressure'. Spurr told us that 'Straw didn't want to put prisons to the market … but he was frustrated'. The decision was taken to go for the poorest performing prisons – Leeds or Birmingham. 'Leeds overwhelmingly accepted the deal' but Birmingham did not and 'Birmingham went to the market'. This initiated a competition programme that was continued by Straw's Tory successors. Much of what Straw had to say about prisons in his memoirs was about his conflicts with the unions, and there were, surprisingly, no indexed references to NOMS or even probation. Though these omissions may be indicative of Straw's priorities whilst in office he certainly had other things on his mind, including the ramifications of the MacPherson Inquiry into the police handling of the murder of Stephen Lawrence, and the protracted attempt to extradite General Pinochet to Spain.

He did not allow those matters to get in the way of other business and he announced that Lockyer would undertake an urgent review into the problems which the introduction of David Blunkett's IPPs had created. He described the IPP sentence, somewhat flippantly given the numbers involved and the lack of *any* reliable method of telling whether risk had been reduced, as 'a good idea that went slightly wrong'. In the first year after the IPP sentence had come into effect in April 2005 there were already about 1,000 prisoners so sentenced and by the time Straw came back into office, there were almost 3,000. By October 2007, there were 6,740 lifers, by far the highest in Europe, plus 3,386 serving IPP sentences – altogether some 12% of the prison population. IPP sentenced prisoners had increased at an annual rate of 111% or 150 a month. It was becoming clear that NOMS could not provide such prisoners with the necessary interventions required to demonstrate that the risk had been sufficiently reduced for them to be released by their tariff date. The Lockyer (2007) review recommended that IPP prisoners 'should be moved quickly to establishments that can offer appropriate assessment and interventions.' But prison reform groups as well as academics and practising lawyers were concerned at the inherent injustice, substantially new to the criminal justice system, that offenders could receive an indeterminate sentence not for what they had done but for what they might do, under the guise of public protection. It was a concern greatly exacerbated when it became clear that the threshold for entry into an indeterminate sentence had been pitched so low and the bar for getting release was set so high. Much debate centred upon the very concept of 'dangerousness' and the dubious assumption that the only evidence of the reduction of risk, and which could justify release on licence, was the completion of some form of treatment intervention. As Lord Phillips had told us 'almost anyone in prison is a risk'.

During the debates as the 2007 Bill passed through Parliament to become the Criminal Justice and Immigration Act 2008, there were constant references to lurid events which purported to indicate the need for greater public protection. In relation to IPPs, however, the Act attempted to mitigate some of Blunkett's errors by introducing a new 'seriousness threshold' before the court could impose an IPP sentence – essentially either a prior conviction for a listed offence or where the current offence would warrant a minimum prison term of two years. It also changed the wording of the CJA 2003 so that, if the stipulated conditions were met, the Court *may* rather than *must* impose the sentence and removed the presumption of dangerousness in the case of those with previous convictions. But although the changes slowed the rate of growth of IPPs in the prison population they were not retrospective, thus creating a further injustice for those already in custody. Moreover, the concerns over prisoners being held substantially beyond their tariff date did not go away.

The Bill had been introduced just as Tony Blair gave way to Gordon Brown as Prime Minister and was widely seen as an attempt to reinforce the trajectory of criminal justice policy which Blair had established. Although Straw had previously argued against an apparently endless stream of legislation reacting to events he was now overseeing a Bill which included a further extension of the use of civil orders. These had been introduced with ASBOs from Straw's first term at the Home Office, and had continued through the Parenting Order, the Control Order and the proposed Serious Crime Prevention Order (in a separate Serious Crime Bill going through at this time). What was now advocated was the Violent Offender Order 'intended to fill a gap, providing a tool for the management of risk posed by those violent offenders who have not been awarded a public protection sentence'. The Bill envisaged a wide range of restrictions and obligations that might be imposed by an order. These civil orders served both to widen the net and narrow its mesh so that more people got caught up in the criminal justice system, because *breaching* them constitutes a criminal offence. Although the Act gave back some discretion to the Judiciary which Blunkett's IPP sentences had taken away, in other areas discretion was removed. Thus, the Act sought to restrict the power of the Court of Appeal to quash convictions because of serious lapses of due process if there was sufficient evidence to indicate guilt. It was a measure which rather implied that large numbers of serious criminals were 'getting off' because of procedural matters whereas the actual number of such cases was small. In pursuing its own perceived need for speedy, simple and summary justice it seemed that the Government was losing sight of the basic values underlying the criminal justice system – the presumption of innocence and the right to a fair trial before an independent court.

The Criminal Justice and Immigration Bill was one of two dubbed as *Christmas Tree Bills* by the opposition because of their eclectic mix of provisions. The other was the Coroners and Justice Bill which included among other things a number of reforms to the Sentencing Guidelines Council, henceforth to become the Sentencing Council, intended to improve consistency whilst avoiding the straitjacket of American-style grid systems.

To some degree both these bills rested upon recommendations from Lord Carter's Review of Prisons which Falconer had commissioned. Carter had been asked 'to consider options for improving the balance between the supply of prison places and the demand for them and to make recommendations on how this could be achieved'. When we interviewed Pat Carter, he told us his 2007 report was based on the premise that 'we couldn't get sentencing to work' given the impasse between judges and politicians who each blamed the other for the prisons being so full. He agreed with Straw that what was needed was 'a rational debate on sentencing that recognises, as with any other public service, that resources are finite' (Hansard, HC 5.12.07). But the so-called 'artificial' ways of cutting the prison population were ruled out by parliament, with the new Sentencing Council required to assess what works in sentencing and the resource implications of proposed legislation but not permitted to link sentencing ranges to penal resources post legislation, as Carter (2007) had proposed, noting the rejection of his capacity clause in the Offender Management Act 2007. The key recommendations taken forward for achieving a better balance and better value were therefore heavily weighted in favour of increasing the supply. He proposed a much expanded prison building programme with an increase of 6,500 places on top of those already planned to be in place by 2012. Most of those places would be in large complexes of 2,500 places, so-called Titan prisons, based on similar schemes in the United States. These would permit the closure of old, inefficient prisons and still leave 5,000 new places offering improved chances of reducing reoffending.

The demand side would depend upon the success of the Sentencing Council in improving the transparency, predictability and consistency of sentencing. He told us that he had wanted to end 'a policy of ridiculous catch up' which used substandard cells in remote places. His solution was simply to 'get some headroom' and he defended Titan prisons as being, potentially, just like four or more smaller prisons but sharing the same site and some central facilities under the leadership of a single governing governor. Although Charlie Falconer had thought that Carter would only have written things that Straw would want to see, Carter told us that 'Jack wasn't interested in big prisons.'

The report by Carter (2007), however, fell far short of the comprehensive review of sentencing policy which John Halliday (2001) had called for several years earlier. It was greeted by Anne Owers, then HM Chief Inspector of Prisons, as 'a missed opportunity', and with dismay, even incredulity, by Penal Reform groups and members of the Justice Committee. In April 2009, Titan prisons were duly renamed 'cluster prisons' and it was announced that 7,500 extra places would be provided in five new prisons, two of which would be in the southeast and privately constructed and run. In a nod towards their critics, each prison would accommodate 1,500 prisoners rather than the 2,500 planned for the three original Titans. It was claimed they would be more versatile than the large Victorian local prisons they were intended to replace, although academics and prison reform groups complained that the large locals tended to be in large conurbations where they were needed whereas the new cluster prisons would likely be in remote locations difficult to visit.

The Offender Management Act 2007 was viewed by civil servants as the 'culmination of New Labour's frustrations over probation.' Jack Straw told us that he had to 'pick up' the implementation of the provisions of that Act, although he paid tribute to David Hanson for overseeing most of the changes, involving the move from Probation Boards to Probation Trusts and the contracting out of some services. But Straw was convinced that probation wasn't working effectively and that there was a continuing lack of public and judicial confidence in community sentences. Probation Boards were reluctant to put any of their own services out to tender. Carter, called in Phil Wheatley and Michael Spurr, then Chief Operating Officer, to ask their advice about how 'to sort out the system' in the face of spiralling costs, and they persuaded Straw of what was 'the right thing to do'. In 2008, in line with Carter's recommendations, it was planned to streamline the MoJ and for NOMS to become an Executive Agency with Phil Wheatley as the Chief Executive. He was to be responsible for running public sector prisons and commissioning services as well as managing performance across NOMS, Probation Trusts and Boards, private prisons and other providers. In April 2009 new Directors of Offender Management (DOMS), replaced the former Regional Offender Managers (ROMS). The Permanent Secretary at that time, Suma Chakrabarti, was keen to make appointments from outside the prisons and probation services in order to bring fresh thinking to meet new challenges. In the competition which followed three Directors were appointed who had governing or operational experience in prisons (Trevor Williams, Steve Wagstaffe and Phil Copple); one was the former Director of the National Probation Service (Roger Hill) and three were mainstream career civil servants. The remaining three had either private sector or local authority experience. Some functional areas, including the management of the high security estate, remained under the management from Headquarters, but the streamlining produced savings of £40 million by eliminating duplication. Straw had to reassure Parliament that Probation Trusts would remain the lead providers of the service so long as their performance was acceptable, and Hanson told us that he gave a commitment to the Commons that the Act would not be used to privatise the probation service, though nothing was written on the face of the Act. And he was frustrated because 'the probation services were independent bodies that I didn't have direct control over'. By 2009 Straw had become more confrontational threatening marketisation of those Boards that had not acquired Trust status.

Another of those things he had to 'pick up' concerned the flak about the 18-day early release scheme introduced by Charlie Falconer. Straw knew perfectly well that 18 days was neither here nor there in terms of a prison sentence but also that there would be a bad press reaction when, inevitably, some early release prisoners committed further offences. Accordingly, he resolved 'to collect as much data as possible and publish it each month' in the belief that openness was the best policy. He had already explained to the BBC the day after his appointment that the policy would continue 'for some time' and indeed it did. Hanson told us that although 'we always took the view that we're not going to be run by the *Daily Mail*,' the Press had made a fuss over what they claimed was public concern and this was exaggerated by MPs in opposition day debates. In reality the proportion of releases that result in SFOs is quite small – although a few of them will have tragic consequences – and Straw was well aware of that. The conviction of Sonnex and Farmer in June 2009 for the murder of two French students the previous year brought widespread criticism upon the probation service even though failings by the prison service, the police, the crown prosecution service and the courts had also played a part. Sonnex, at the time of the murders was on licence from an eight-year sentence for violence. He had been classified as a medium risk rather than high risk, which would have warranted supervision under MAPPA. Instead, he was assigned to a young probation officer in Lewisham as part of her caseload of 127 – more than three times bigger than the average for the Lewisham office. He had already committed a further offence and should have been recalled to prison but there had been delays in locating and apprehending him. It was deemed that there had been a senior management failure in that caseloads were not monitored so that resources could be moved from the least pressed offices to the most pressed. The decision was taken that David Scott, who had taken over as Chief Probation Officer for London following the murder of John Monckton four years earlier, would have to go. Scott accepted that he was accountable and resigned before he was sacked and then highlighted the problems of probation, disputing Straw's claim that resources were not an issue (*The Guardian*, 10.6.09).

In spite of the extraordinary pressures which the rising prison population placed on the prison service, Straw did not believe in attempting to control the size of the prison population.

> 'If you've got a crisis as we had you've got to manage it down – but in the long term my view is that it's an error in policy to have a target for the prison population which trumps other considerations like levels of crime. But if your policy of dealing with the causes of crime works then numbers will come down anyway'.

As we have noted such a hope is wildly optimistic, but he thought there had been some progress in relation to specific groups of offenders, particularly women, and he paid tribute to Baroness Jean Corston for her admirable report (Corston, 2007) and to the work of Maria Eagle in carrying forward the government's response. The government had immediately accepted most of Corston's recommendations and developed a small pilot study to test the merits of a multi-functional, custodial centre for women. We interviewed Jean Corston in the House of Lords on 30 October 2018 and she, in turn, was very grateful to Straw, who went on to fund the setting up of the women's centre network to the tune of £15.6 million at a time of impending financial crisis. She was also very positive about Maria Eagle who got reluctant officials onside and whose efforts enabled the system to grow from 'a handful to 51 centres in no time'. With a strong push from the centre, she told us, sentencers' confidence in women's centres as a disposal had increased to the point where it became possible to take two women's prisons out of use. Within six months of the publication of Corston's report, philanthropic investors, with the support of former Junior Minister Fiona McTaggart, had set up the Corston Independent Funders Coalition (CIFC) to support her recommendations.

He was also at least somewhat hopeful that the review by the former Home Office Minister Lord Bradley, which he had commissioned in December 2007, would eventually divert more offenders with mental health problems away from prisons. We interviewed Keith Bradley in the House of Lords tearoom on 20 June 2018 about his report (Bradley, 2009). Given that as many as 70% of the prison population suffer from multiple psychiatric problems, and that prison conditions and regimes could only make those problems worse rather than better, the question for Bradley was 'why did so many people with such conditions end up in prison?' His hope was that if one could prevent them going to prison, or remove them, one could then be more effective about what is done with those who really have to be in custody. In all, his report made 82 recommendations, all of which were accepted in principle. We wondered how he felt about the fact that after ten years there was still comparatively little to show for his efforts. He told us that 'I'm not going away until they're all implemented. I've been through four governments in that ten year period' and he kept going back to make sure they sign up, and importantly to keep the Treasury committed. He 'put so much emphasis on health' because that was more likely to get money into the system, but the main problem in the way of progress was the short political cycle which meant that one government, or even one Minister, cannot commit the next. However, he was able to claim some success in that 'liaison diversion teams' enabled psychiatric nurse assessments to inform the charging officer, or magistrates on first appearance to avoid delays of 6 to 8 weeks waiting for a psychiatric report. Other modest successes included 'preventive measures such as street triaging' and the use of 'section 136 suites' instead of police cells if vulnerable people were removed from the streets for safety reasons. Asked about the situation in prisons for those with vulnerabilities he said 'it remains pretty dire … the prison officer is the principal carer for vulnerable prisoners' and without the right 'support on the wings to recognise the first signs of vulnerability, it escalates before anyone intervenes'.

Lord Bradley lamented the fact that there continued to be no coherent policy about transfer to NHS facilities and the fact that there would probably always be a proportion of mentally disturbed offenders who had to be held either in prisons or the high security hospitals. A major programme of joint funding enabled the NHS and the Prison Service to develop four pilot projects, two in high security hospitals and two in prisons, for persons said to be suffering from Dangerous Severe Personality Disorder (DSPD). DSPD is essentially an administrative category rather than a clinical diagnosis. It had long been thought that people with personality disorder, previously known as psychopaths, had been beyond the reach of psychiatric treatment. The results of the evaluations of these pilots were inconclusive, but it seemed that prisoners held in the bespoke secure hospital units – at double the cost of prison facilities – were more hostile about their experience than those held in the prison units. Leaving aside issues about the definition and the success or otherwise of treatment, the attempt to devise individualised regimes for very difficult offenders provided a welcome opportunity for prison staff to involve prisoners in a joint enterprise. The DSPD experiment was replaced by a joint NHS and NOMS initiative – Offender Personality Disorder (OPD) Pathways – which transferred the secure hospital money to the cheaper prison and probation services.

When Straw had been in charge at the Home Office, he had adopted a consultative, collegiate stance and enjoyed the confidence of his civil servants. As Justice Secretary, though he was still prepared to listen, he had to pay more attention to detail perhaps because money was now much tighter. Hanson told us that Straw was 'very hands on ... a finger in everything' and Hanson himself talked to directors 'every day' and received 'lots of blunt advice' from Phil Wheatley. Gordon Brown also took a close interest in things because of the financial situation and Straw knew he needed to keep the Treasury on side if he was to make headway over the accommodation crisis. When Wheatley and Michael Spurr told Straw that they had achieved all the economies they could, Straw refused to accept that and effectively forced them into the first version of benchmarking. Nevertheless, Straw wrote in his memoirs that 'Gordon could see the big picture. Complete meltdown in the prison system would not be clever'. Although initially the Treasury was 'unkeen', after much wrangling, and in the light of Carter's report on the need to build more prison places, 'I got my money' (p 507). But Straw had seen what meddling too much had done for Michael Howard and, as he told us, he recognised 'that prisons are really fragile institutions and if you've not got enough stable staff the prisoners will take over .... it is a really difficult job being a prison officer'. During his time as Justice Secretary, he continued the New Labour policy of providing more resources for the development of offending behaviour programmes.

Although Straw told us he had no problem with the notion that the main function of imprisonment was punishment, like many of the politicians we interviewed he argued that this was not inconsistent with rehabilitation. He certainly endorsed the prison service policy of seven pathways to reducing reoffending, which had been developing under Charles Clarke, and focussed on the problems surrounding accommodation, drugs, debt, family, employment, numeracy and literacy. Whilst the famous aphorism of our most influential Prison Commissioner, Alexander Paterson, that 'You cannot train men for freedom in conditions of captivity' may no longer hold sway there seems little doubt that each of those seven pathways would be easier to pursue in the community. Nevertheless, some 700 employers were recruited to work with the open and resettlement prisons in the Reducing Reoffending Corporate Alliance to help with employment and employability among prisoners. However, Straw also gave a speech to the RSA in October 2008 in which he criticised 'the criminal justice lobby' for failing to consider victims who should be at the heart of the justice system. He remained concerned to bolster the confidence of the Judiciary, the Press and the Public in community sentences and, two years after an incognito Lord Phillips had done his day on unpaid work, there was a campaign for persons sentenced to community payback to wear high-visibility clothing. This was fiercely attacked by the late Harry Fletcher, then Assistant General Secretary of

NAPO, and others, as an attempt by the government to show they were tough and which was demeaning to those required to wear them. Senior members of NOMS had sought to make the design as discreet as possible and Straw vigorously defended their introduction.

By the end of Jack Straw's time at the MoJ, some 13 pilots had been established of what were now called Dedicated Drug Courts. Preliminary process evaluations seemed to show promise of increased completion rates for the sentences imposed and reduced reconvictions.

On 6 May 2010, the General Election saw the end of New Labour in government and Jack Straw handed over the Ministry of Justice to Ken Clarke.

Part two: The Directors of Prisons and Probation

Richard Tilt

Richard Tilt's period as Director General had started under the Tory Government and continued under New Labour. He had found Michael Howard 'courteous and willing to listen' and so they had 'a perfectly reasonable relationship … even though we disagreed on many things'. He found Anne Widdecombe difficult, largely because she was so busy with her own battles with Michael Howard to the 'detriment of her responsibilities' as a Prisons Minister. Straw had a very different style and was very good 'to work with or for,' and had 'the normal considerations for the people around him'. In any event, Tilt 'didn't have any trouble talking Jack Straw out of paying too much attention' to the Learmont Report. He also thought himself fortunate to have later worked with Joyce Quin and the late Lord Williams. But he thought that the underlying problem was that successive Home Secretaries were nervous about delegating. He could not remember 'any significant issue that could be dealt with without the Home Secretary's involvement'.

However, it seemed to Tilt that whereas Howard was obsessed by his prospects of getting into No 10, Straw was too deferential to its new occupant, Tony Blair, who was 'against doing anything radical in the prison service.' Since Straw 'would not countenance any move towards reducing the prison population', Tilt faced the perennial dilemma: 'we didn't know whether to just simply keep doing more overcrowding, or whether to try and build some new prisons.' He was determined not to return to the use of police cells at a cost of £500 or more a night but continued with Lewis's strategy of 'building new cell blocks in existing prisons,' something the Treasury was prepared to fund. Although this was quicker and cheaper than building new prisons it usually 'meant there were not enough accompanying facilities to go with the accommodation'. He was well aware that the problem with 'building new accommodation is that the courts simply fill it up'. However, he told us that prior to his departure, 'we got to a position where we had hardly any overcrowding'. That assessment did not entirely square with the position described by the PRT but there had been some improvement and in any case it did not last for long. Ultimately, Tilt would like politicians to decide on 'what is a reasonably sized prison population' similar to other western European countries with similar crime rates, whereby 'you could halve the prison population'. Tilt described working through the Woolf recommendations to implement as many as they could but told us how the Treasury held sway, 'blocking attempts to introduce a code of standards' and refusing to countenance 'limiting population to CNA'. He remained convinced, however, that 'with the right politician taking a lead' and strong support from No 10, this could yet be done.

Towards the end of Tilt's time in charge, there was a significant investigation into bullying and racial abuse of prisoners by officers at Wormwood Scrubs. However, although he acknowledged it to be a problem, he didn't believe it was 'systemic' and felt that 'once you got the evidence' there were clear pathways for dealing with it. Regrettably, the unions had been obstructive about this with threats of industrial action but he thought that over time 'the POA had got better on this front'. As early as 1982, when he was seconded to headquarters and working on staffing issues, he proposed that 'we should apply the principles of what was then called "Work and Finish" to prison officers so as to remove the incentive to create work in order to maximise overtime opportunities'. Although it was initially regarded as too complicated to be introduced, it was eventually taken up and became the precursor to Fresh Start which was introduced under Chris Train in 1987. Tilt, unlike his predecessor 'wasn't a huge enthusiast for private prisons'. But he regarded 'the introduction of the private sector' as the biggest game changer 'in relation to the POA'. He never believed 'it would go anywhere very much' and reminded us that it still only accounted for 'about 10% ... it was that 20 years ago'. It had in his view failed to bring the promised innovation, other than poaching some of the 'best people' from the public sector. He still found it 'slightly distasteful'. Although an early supporter of offending behaviour programmes, he had come to the conclusion that 'none of us, probably, has much idea what the answer is ... to stopping someone reoffending'.

Tilt was in favour of prisons and probation people gaining a better understanding of each other's roles and to that end he had been an enthusiastic supporter of secondments between the two services. Indeed, as we discussed in the previous chapter, he was an early advocate for bringing prisons and probation together. However, he identified the almost inevitable swamping of the probation service by the prison service and the potential tensions arising from the superior levels of education and professional training of probation officers. He was certainly keen for aspiring future prison managers to be exposed to the findings from research in criminology, penology and management, and negotiated the creation of the Master's degree at the Institute of Criminology at Cambridge in which both the present authors have been involved for many years. The course later became open to probation officers, and other criminal justice professionals, including those from other countries, and has enjoyed the support of all Directors of both services to date.

Richard Tilt is an essentially modest man and not one either to blow his own trumpet or to welcome the limelight. After four years at the top, including his one year as Acting Director General, he decided not to seek an extension of his contract. But, unlike other Directors, he did 'leave happily'. He told us 'I had achieved my main objective of getting the service back on an even keel' after the upheavals surrounding the sacking of Derek Lewis. It cannot be emphasised enough that this was no mean task, albeit one which was helped by the fact that he was the first Director of Prisons to be appointed from within the service and he was well liked and respected by his colleagues. It was a time when governors had greater confidence in the way in which they were led in mutually supportive ways. He could look back on having overseen 'the end of slopping out' and was on a path towards 'eliminating overcrowding.' He had an excellent record on escapes, and was able to see off the over-reaction proposed by Learmont. Among his many achievements, which were lauded in the *Financial Times* (2.2.99) was a large expansion of offending behaviour programmes, especially for sex offenders. The Sex Offender Treatment Programme (SOTP) initially was highly regarded, although as he ruefully told us 'doesn't look so good twenty years on'. He was replaced by Martin Narey.

Martin Narey

We interviewed Martin Narey in a relatively quiet corner of the foyer of a hotel near Liverpool Street station. He told us that like Richard Tilt, he took up his post knowing that 'no one else would do it', after New Labour had failed to find someone through a 'major head-hunting exercise'. He had been inspired to train to become a prison governor after watching Rex Bloomstein's 1980 television documentary series on Strangeways which exposed the fundamental indecency of prisons and the appalling things that could happen there a decade before the riots. It was around that time that the prisoner, Barry Prosser, was kicked to death by prison officers at Winson Green, but who were never successfully brought to justice. 'I just had to go and look at a prison … I went to Lincoln on Christmas Eve 1981, saw it was more than true … I was desperately keen to help to change it.' It was to become his mission, indeed 'a noble challenge in itself, treating people, who've done terrible things, with decency'. He knew well enough that 'this was something that had to be addressed the whole time … it's not just an add-on thing'. Narey soon found this kind of message was unacceptable to the majority of Ministers then as it is now. He had seen how Michael Howard's focus on austere regimes 'gave licence to people to interpret it in a very bad way.' But then later, in the period of New Labour, he found that Bev Hughes, failed to see the 'symbolic' importance of calling people by their first names. Her response was 'this is not enough if we can't rehabilitate people'. Austerity and rehabilitation both trumped decency in the political lexicon.

After a brief spell 'at Lincoln as an officer', he quickly moved on to Frankland, 'the No.1 dispersal prison at the time' by way of career progression. Joe Pilling, then Director of Personnel and Finance, co-opted him into his first Headquarters position, managing the changeover from 'prison regions to area management'. After this he 'left the prison service' and entered 'the civil service fast-track'. He returned to the service as Head of Security and Director of Regimes, and was 'very quickly promoted to the Prisons Board as Director of Resettlement'. Then 'Richard Tilt very, suddenly said he wasn't going to apply for an extension to his contract … and I found myself in the top job … the job nobody wanted'. Eventually, he ruefully continued, 'I left the job unhappily … as did Phil Wheatley.' He could have added Joe Pilling, Derek Lewis and his sometime counterpart as Director of Probation, Roger Hill although at the time of our interview Michael Spurr was yet to suffer the same fate. The 'relationship between Director General and Ministers has always been a troubled one'.

Nevertheless, Narey had entered the job in the spirit of 'great optimism' because under New Labour it was a time of enthusiasm for new initiatives and there was 'more money than you could ever imagine.' He and Peter Dawson, helped to change the narrative from Howard's 'Prison Works' by crafting Straw's *'Making Prisons Work'* speech in December 1998. Crucially, Tilt had rebuilt 'ministerial confidence' post Lewis, 'the population in historical terms wasn't too difficult' and the Treasury was pouring money into 'offending behaviour, literacy and numeracy programmes'. Narey was not responsible for answering parliamentary questions, as Straw had fulfilled a manifesto pledge 'to take back proper ministerial responsibility for the Prison Service'. However, there was no doubt that 'they were concerned about prisons', from the Permanent Secretary at the Home Office all the way to No10 and he kept 'quite a lot of freedom' to 'speak up' and 'defend operating decisions', in part a result of Straw's fresh memories of what had happened to Howard. Even so, he told us, 'I don't think you can de-politicise prisons'.

In retrospect, Narey said 'I got a bit carried away with some of that optimism. The in-house research suggested the premium on offending behaviour programmes could be simply huge'. But, despite making 'reductions on reoffending, albeit at huge cost', he had to concede that academic criticism of that research as unreliable was correct and he had now come to the conclusion that 'our scope for reducing crime is genuinely very, very limited'. He was accused of being 'defeatist' during a Home Office Select Committee review. Ministers, he told us, were either simplistic or deceitful to insist that a short treatment programme 'will change 18 years of neglect and abuse' and that one could 'then send them back to exactly the same disadvantage that they came from.' This 'lack of honesty about what prisons can achieve is at the centre of the unhappy relationship between Director Generals or Chief Executives of NOMS and Ministers because Director Generals can never deliver what they want'. This situation was made worse by the churn of Ministers who wanted different things. A 'combination of fast-moving Junior Ministers' filled with political ambition, and the fact that 'no Minister is ever interested in the initiatives of his predecessor' prevents 'any real attempt to deal strategically, or deal with issues in the long-term'. He had to deal with at least 14 Ministers during his seven years in office. He contrasted that with his six years at Barnardo's after he left the service, and where he had only to deal with one chairman, which meant that 'we could make long-term decisions .... we knew we had to see things through.'

Like Richard Tilt, he enjoyed good relations with Jack Straw who seemed to have some understanding of prisons and 'was always willing to listen and was very supportive'. In Narey's earlier role as Director of Regimes, he had urged Straw 'to put more TVs into cells' telling him that 'Michael Howard would be very critical' but making the argument 'it would reduce isolation and it might reduce suicides'. Straw agreed saying, 'well it's the right thing to do', something which Ministers 'very rarely say'. Narey believed 'the Prisons Minister is an important person' if they are around for long enough. He told us that 'in the '80s, the Prisons Minister ... was a Minister of State ... and crucially a House of Lords post ... as opposed to a Parliamentary Under-Secretary in their first government job'. The brighter Parliamentary Under-Secretaries were destined for quick promotions, the less bright to parliamentary oblivion. The House of Lords, moreover, was less given to making idiotic decisions. Narey was fortunate to work with one such well-regarded minister, the late Lord Williams of Mostyn, whom he described as 'a very good, thoughtful man' but on whose death Paul Boateng was appointed in his place. Boateng had refused our request for an interview, but Narey told us that they had a tumultuous relationship. At one time, Boeteng insisted on 'vaginal searches of women coming to Holloway' as his solution to the problem of drugs getting into the prison. 'I was telling him that, not least for moral reasons, he could not do that. We bawled at each other'. When Zahid Mubarek was murdered by his cellmate at Feltham, Narey told us that 'Paul would have burnt me for that without any hesitation'. Boateng used agency status to get Narey 'to do a lot of the public stuff, so whenever there was a critical report on anything, it was me who was on the *Today* programme or *Newsnight*'. But Narey saw the advantages of speaking out just as Joe Pilling had done. 'When you're talking to the media ... about decency and keeping places clean ... you're really sending a message to your staff and your governors'. He had no hesitation in backing up words with action when he removed 'the governor from Dartmoor', whose prison was 'dirty' and who 'couldn't find the main recess on his wing'. Narey similarly got rid of

> 'staff who abused prisoners ... you can change the minds of some people by convincing them that they should act in a more moral way, and others you change their minds because they think if they don't they'll get sacked'.

In this way, he claimed to have taken 'some of the anger out of prisons', finding it 'no coincidence' that there was only one riot – oddly enough at Lincoln – over the time that he and Phil Wheatley were in charge of prisons. Narey got more support from both Hilary Benn and the late Paul Goggins as Prison Ministers, both committed to getting things done. Unfortunately, Benn was 'promoted very quickly'. Goggins was 'genuinely interested in the virtue of small incremental improvements to make things a little bit better. We got a lot of day to day things done'. Other Junior Ministers had resisted the proposal to make condoms available to combat Aids and Hepatitis, for example, but Goggins approved it.

Although Narey 'didn't get on' with Blunkett, he nevertheless respected him as 'a Secretary of State of real courage. Harry Woolf and David Blunkett ... got on well, and just agreed that' the capping of the prison population 'could be done'. Woolf ensured buy in from the Judiciary through the mechanism of the newly created Sentencing Guidelines Council. Narey

> 'was absolutely convinced as the prison population slowed down ... we had a mechanism for not allowing the population to grow ... we'd stop it at a much lower point. And I believed those resources would go ... to improve support and supervision in the community'.

The mechanism of prison population management was trialled as a 'shadow process'. If there were any proposed changes to sentencing legislation, the Home Office statisticians would calculate how the Sentencing Guidelines would increase the prison population and the Sentencing Guidelines Council would 'tweak the guidelines' to ensure 'the increase was zero.'

Narey was to become the Chief Executive of the NOMS which was introduced by Blunkett following the recommendations in Pat Carter's report of 2003. In this new role the Chief Inspectors of Probation, first Graham Smith and then particularly Rod Morgan, helped Narey 'to understand the challenges facing the probation service'. Their advice on caseloads and other matters fed into his ideas that under the NOMS framework more resources could be diverted into probation. However, he believed that the prison inspectorate could have been more supportive by discussing what should be prioritised within existing 'resource constraints'. Too often Ramsbotham 'exhausted Secretaries of State' by saying 'everything is awful' rather than differentiating between the good and the bad and advising 'on how to make the system better'.

Carter's five-year plan for a fully contestable NOMS fell far short of the 25 years it had taken the Canadians to integrate their prison and probation services and which had so impressed Richard Tilt. Narey told us he was 'not opposed to NOMS, but it was pushed on us ... and it was going a bit too fast. We were trying to change two difficult operational services'; however, 'I believed passionately that ... I would be able to move investment from prisons to the community'. Initially 'the Home Office, No.10 and the Treasury' were very engaged, 'the meetings to discuss NOMS were chaired personally by Tony Blair'. However, 'it quickly began to disintegrate' with the loss of 'David Blunkett who had ownership of it ... Charles Clarke just wasn't prepared to pursue ... the propositions on which it was founded'.

'There were three essential elements to the NOMS I believed I was creating' he told us. 'One was making probation officers the managers of prisoners in prison'. Within constraints, they would manage them through sentence and preparation for release. 'Second, that there would be more competition. I became a convert because private prisons just did some things which public sector prisons were slow to do, particularly on decency and dignity'. He thought the threat of competition would also drive improvement in the public sector.

> 'And the most important one, for which we had a bill in the Commons, (the Management of Offenders and Sentencing Bill) when David had to … resign … which would have capped the prison population at 80,000'.

But then 'Charles Clarke, seized with the belief that he was going to succeed Tony Blair, literally and metaphorically, tore up that bill'. Clearly, relations between Narey and Clarke were strained. When Narey had first become Director General of the prison service, he had made a point of cultivating John Gieve, then Head of Public Spending at the Treasury, 'getting them to see us as a viable place to invest public money'. Later, Gieve was promoted to Permanent Secretary at the Home Office and whilst Narey valued his operational independence, he still saw prisons as part of the wider Home Office. As Chief Executive of NOMS, Narey became a 'principal advisor on sentencing policy' bringing with him 'a tranche of the Home Office' whilst Phil Wheatley took responsibility for day-to-day management of the prisons. Narey did not view this in terms of agency, because agency status remained with prisons not NOMS at that time. 'NOMS was about much more than running the prison and probation service, it was about policy', he told us, and 'because it was acknowledged that my job was as big as many people running departments I was made a Permanent Secretary.' He became a central Whitehall figure speaking out on behalf of prisons and spent 'a lot of time in the Treasury' and 'Downing Street', getting 'money for suicide prevention', by describing 'how awful … it was to be phoned and be told that someone else had killed themselves.' He recalled giving 'the first of what was very briefly known as the Downing Street lectures' with 'the Prime Minister sat in the front row' of a lecture on 'penal policy'. By this time, Narey was not only in a position to liaise with the judiciary but also to speak out both on sentencing matters and prisons policy. According to Wheatley, Clarke resented Narey's high public profile, objecting to 'celebrity civil servants'. Clarke told us that he was glad when Gieve was moved to another post. But he was also apparently threatened by the close relationship between Narey and the Junior Prisons Minister Paul Goggins. According to Narey, 'the new Secretary of State' believed that 'we agreed on too much' and therefore 'I was dominating the Minister', and so Goggins was moved on. Eventually, Narey told us, that Clarke 'retreated on competition and had no truck with capping the prison population …. and that's when I resigned'.

After Martin Narey stepped down from his post, Helen Edwards took over as Head of NOMS and 'did a little of my job for a while', and then 'Phil (Wheatley) took over' and 'just became an operational head' without a policy role. The Sentencing Guidelines Council continued but without any requirement to match the prison population with the level of resource. That fleeting 'acknowl-edgement you would never get anywhere until you control the prison popula-tion' was lost and with it the 'strategic five year plan agreed with the Prime Minister'. Charles Clarke published his own 'Five Year Plan' in 2006 but it was for 'Reducing Reoffending and Protecting the Public.' The change of minister meant NOMS, like agency, was not implemented as it had been envisioned or by those who had envisioned it, with two of its three founding propositions gone.

Martin Narey briefly stepped back onto the stage as an advisor on the Prisons Board several years later at the behest of Michael Gove and with the support of Michael Spurr. He hoped it would be an opportune time to make a difference because Gove, at that time, had a close relationship with David Cameron.

Roger Hill

We interviewed Roger Hill at his office at Sodexo Justice Services, one of the largest private companies responsible for running 122 prisons world-wide at the time of our research, five of them in the UK. It went on to own six Community Rehabilitation Companies (CRC) introduced under Grayling's *Transforming Rehabilitation* (TR) agenda. The interview took place on 24 June 2019, by which time this latest phase of probation's chequered history was being brought to an end following the devastating critique by Glenys Stacey, HM Chief Inspector of Probation, in her final Annual Report. Hill had lived through much of that his-tory and was the third, and longest serving, of the three Directors of the National Probation Service (NPS) which was founded in 2001 and lasted in that form until 2009 when the post was abolished.

Hill joined the probation service in 1978 with a professional social work training, and worked as a probation officer rising up the career ladder in sev-eral local areas before becoming a Chief Probation Officer, first in Lincolnshire in 2001 and then in London in 2004. By the time he worked in London, he had seen what he called 'a significant change' under which Chiefs, at one time accountable to their local probation committee had become 'Statutory Office holders – not quite civil servants' as he put it, line managed by and accountable to, the new Director of the NPS. In April 2005, he was himself appointed to be the National Director by Martin Narey and worked closely with Phil Wheatley to bring prisons and probation together in 2008. He held that post until 2009 when, under a third iteration of the NOMS, ROMS were replaced by DOMS. In that reorganisation, he became the DOM for the South East.

With so much experience of this extraordinary history of change, Roger Hill was able to give us a unique insight into the advantages and disadvantages these brought for the work of probation officers. Here we are mainly concerned with the changes wrought under New Labour. Crucially, he thought it a mistake to try to push the probation service into closer relationship with the prison service, since as a locally based service the more natural partners were the courts and the police. 'As an operational Chief' he told us 'the courts were a very signifi-cant body with whom … we had a relationship' and for whom the provision of reports containing the necessary information to pass a fair sentence was a prime function. Thus, when he became Chief Officer of London, he had some sym-pathy when the judiciary 'were hopping mad' about the apparent inability of the London Probation Service to provide pre-sentence reports following the standard three-week adjournment. He agreed to put matters right and the ser-vice released resources to provide timely reports to the Crown Court by creating 'the same day report … in magistrates courts.' Theoretically, these were hand-written but often 'in reality they were a probation officer standing up in court and talking to the magistrates.' The system was later rolled out nationally and Hill remains convinced that in the interest of speedy justice, this kind of 'local dialogue' between probation and the courts is essential.

Hill explained that when the NPS was established the number of probation areas was reduced from 54 to 42 and were coterminous with police areas thus emphasising 'the importance of the relationship between them.' Both were 'pre-dominantly community-based organisations … dealing with … the same people in the same environment, experiencing similar problems' and so 'it was very easy to …. talk on the same wavelength. Sharing information, sharing intelligence on some of the most difficult cases' was producing 'some great results'. Strong enforcement and public protection arrangements, and a closer working relation-ship with the police, were in place although he said that some of the blanket inclusions in the public protection arrangements, 'all sex offenders', for example, were 'surprising', given their relatively low likelihood of reoffending. He gener-ally regarded the establishment of the NPS 'as a good thing' transforming the pre-2001 'patchwork of uncoordinated probation services delivering different things in different places and in different ways' into a service that was 'held to account' for delivering the National Standards which had been first set in 1992 and were periodically revised.

Although, like others we interviewed, Hill thought that Jack Straw seemed to adopt a 'pretty balanced' approach to things, he viewed New Labour's obsession with enforcement and public protection as essentially 'a lever … to make the changes they wanted to make with the service.' Ultimately, it became up to the probation service to 'take out a warrant' if an offender failed to come in: 'there are not going to be blue lights flashing around looking for them'. Accountability shifted from delivering national standards to a situation whereby probation, like prisons, were 'measured by failure, not by success. If you've done everything right there isn't anything to put in the newspapers' but it is quite the reverse if 'somebody who the probation service is working closely with commits some heinous crime … which they do sometimes'– albeit rarely. But as a newly nationalised service without agency status the NPS had little opportunity to justify or explain its actions and was more frequently subject to ministerial calls for change 'and at a greater scale than any other part of the criminal justice system'.

By the time he was made Director of Probation in 2005, he viewed the latest political rhetoric of 'reducing reoffending' as 'the next stick with which to bash the probation service'. Accountability now translated into 'constant bureaucratic demands'. Rather than helping and managing 'those people who are in crisis out in the community' staff were spending 75% of their time in front of a computer demonstrating their accountability through written records and completing the 'hugely time-consuming' offender assessment system (OASys). OASys, so Phil Wheatley told us, had started out as a paper system long before NOMS, but there were also two existing assessment systems, ACE (Assessment, Case recording and Evaluation) and LSI-R (Level of Service Inventory – Revised), and a working party had been established to choose between them with the aim of standardisation. In the event they chose neither but instead computerised OASys into which elements of both the other systems were fed. What was intended to become a comprehensive and universal tool to assist probation, prisons and the Parole Board in assessing, among other things, risk was then installed on an inappropriate computer platform. It was inordinately complex, not user-friendly and worked to nobody's satisfaction. According to Hill these problems were exacerbated by 'an inspectorate at that time saying if it's not recorded it didn't happen'. He regarded this as inevitable – 'scrutiny just brought with it a tyranny' – but unhelpful. Whilst he thought it would take a 'brave government' to 'slash the expectation to record … by 80%', he argued that 'a more active approach by probation staff, alongside offenders in the localities in which they live, would have more impact than typing up computer notes.' He also suggested that a wider staff base, with a better gender balance, and more people with much wider experience might be significantly more effective. He thought that body video cameras might provide some protection for probation officers as an alternative way of demonstrating accountability if things went wrong.

Hill had some real concerns when NOMS was established with a brief 'to align probation with prisons … in … just three years' and with probation managing offenders throughout their sentence. Whilst he recognised that this was not 'entirely illogical' he also thought that 'the critical bit' of managing offenders 'is immediately prior and immediately after release'. For someone on 'a 15-year tariff', the prison service might as well manage 'for 14 of those years, because what's the probation service going to do? Not very much'. For Hill the problems for the first iteration of NOMS were more operational than political. The idea of ROMS, whether from prison or probation backgrounds, was not welcomed by the prison service. He thought that Phil Wheatley was overprotective of prisons, and that whilst he may not quite have used such a blunt term as 'get your tanks off my lawn' that was what it seemed like from a probation perspective. Consequently, it was virtually impossible for Martin Narey to go where he wanted to go with NOMS. The ROMS were not given the budgets for probation and did not manage the prison service area managers, who continued to hold the budgets for prisons as they'd always done. When we confessed that both of us came from a research background in prisons and not probation, he forgave us but declared that 'in terms of people who make significant decisions, who are able to protect organisations. It's always prisons … probation is a rarity in all this'. In the third iteration of NOMS, when ROMS were replaced by functional DOMS Roger Hill was the only one drawn from a probation background.

In 2007 he 'had the misfortune to inherit the role of Senior Responsible Officer (SRO) for NOMIS', when it was delegated to him by Helen Edwards after the departure of Christine Knott. NOMIS was the IT system which Carter envisaged would be shared by the joined-up services, and became one of the blunders described by Antony King and Ivor Crewe (2013) as well as the subject of an incredulous report by the National Audit Office (HC 292, 2009). As far as Hill was concerned 'it was a poisoned chalice'. The original budget had already been spent and at one time he had to go to David Hanson, the Prisons Minister to ask for more money. The project was finally brought under control but ended up being for prisons only. The budget he had as DOM for the South East was over half a billion but of that 'you might have only a million' over which there was any flexibility – the rest was all committed. Since he could hardly say 'well, I'm not going to run that prison' there was, in reality, very little scope for him to make choices or innovate. But it did give him time to 'think a lot about what mattered about public service' and he concluded that it was 'what was delivered' and how effective it was, rather than 'who delivered it'.

Whilst still Director Probation in 2008 Hill had worked with Louise Casey after her advocacy of 'visible community payback' which he saw as a 'very big potential lever' to regain public and judicial confidence in community sentencing. 'The probation Chiefs were much more sceptical and a significant number worked actively against that agenda,' he told us. His personal view was that all community sentences could and should have a strong element of punishment, and public confidence and awareness of that was 'raised if you can see it and that it is doing something useful'.

Hill saw the 100% funding of prisons and probation by the central government as flawed because they become 'essentially a free service' as far as local authorities are concerned and who therefore have 'little interest in who gets sent to prison – and who returns to crime afterwards … because they don't have to pay for it'. Until 2001, probation had been funded 80% by the government and 20% by local authorities and so there was some sense of local accountability at least for probation. He would wish to see some real financial incentives to local areas in the way in which the courts use prisons and probation. Martin Narey had the transfer of more resources from prisons to probation as one of his central ambitions for NOMS. Hill's solution went a stage further by giving communities incentives to invest in early interventions as well as probation and thereby trying to reduce the numbers going into prisons. He recognised that transferring resources would be complex, involve risks for all concerned, and could not be done quickly. What Hill had in mind was a 'gain-share arrangement'. His idea was to 'keep the central funding of the prison service for a fixed period' but to run a 'shadow budget' to explore over a five-year period what savings could be made if local areas sent fewer persons to prisons and dealt with them in the community instead. We could then say to a local authority 'if you can reduce the number of people you send to prison over the next five years, then we set the budget for real in five years' time'. The savings central government made from the improved management of prisoners, over what would have been the case had they continued to send people to prison at the previous rate, could be used 'to spend on local services but you'd obviously have to come up with some incentives to bring this about'. Whereas Narey's hopes for redistribution of funds from prisons to probation were constantly frustrated by ministerial churn or political timidity, Hill's proposal places matters in the hands of local authorities, with their knowledge of local issues. Hill developed the idea through a worked example, which he led in 2010 and was based on the city of Brighton, to produce a notional figure of 'what Brighton spends on imprisonment.' The preliminary work identified a number of complex issues including the possibility that once started, the approach might be 'hard to pull back from.' He also recognised that much detailed research and development would be needed. Although he discussed it with Michael Spurr, Brighton Council officials and the local Police Divisional Commander, from all of whom he got encouragement, his departure from office meant that it was never put to ministers.

Hill's pursuit of this idea, was echoed in the work of the Justice Select Committee (2010) at this time with their all-encompassing report on 'justice reinvestment.' This sought to address the 'crisis of sustainability' of the criminal justice system post-crash, pre-austerity. They agreed prison, whilst a national resource was a 'free commodity' locally, whereas the array of social, educational, treatment, employment and housing services needed to support offenders and others away from offending, are all subject to local budgetary constraints, limiting their availability to the courts. Their report challenged the Government better to invest limited resources based on the available evidence, rather than focus on which services could sustain the biggest cuts. They recommended that the prison population cap should be instated and prison building funds invested elsewhere. This, they suggested, in language reminiscent of that used by Lord Woolf, would only be possible if criminal justice was removed from party politics and repackaged to the public.

Phil Wheatley

We interviewed Phil Wheatley at his London flat on 21 June 2018. He had joined the prison service as a graduate in1969, initially working the landings as a prison officer, before becoming an assistant governor, then deputy governor at Gartree and Governor at Hull. In 1992, he moved to Headquarters as Assistant

Director of Custody and from then on he had, 'a ringside seat' to see 'what was going on at the centre' when Joe Pilling was replaced by Derek Lewis, under Ken Clarke. By 1995, he had become a member of the Prisons Board as Director of Dispersal Prisons and worked alongside both Richard Tilt and Martin Narey, before becoming Director of the Prison Service in 2003, and finally Director of NOMS from 2008 until he retired in 2010. His appointment as Director of Prisons came after Martin Narey left the prison service in the run up to the establishment of NOMS and he served alongside successive Directors of Probation – Eithne Wallis, Steve Murphy and Roger Hill. When Martin Narey resigned from NOMS he was succeeded by Helen Edwards and by 2008 when she moved on it was clear that NOMS wasn't working in the way intended. Wheatley told us that 'Pat Carter expressed disquiet … and thought that the operational leadership needed sorting out and told Jack Straw and senior officials that the only viable solution was to give the task to me and the senior HM Prison Service team'. Straw agreed with this, as did the Permanent Secretary, Alex Allen and Wheatley was duly appointed albeit 'with some hefty supervision from an external oversight group' to ensure that the prison service 'would not shaft the probation services'.

But during the run up to the general election in 2010 it was clear that times would be hard whichever party won. 'By the end of the Blair era,' he told us 'Ministers pushed very hard for prisons to pack all comers in like sardines' whereas earlier under New Labour, 'if prison numbers were likely to exceed the maximum safe operating capacity emergency money from the Treasury could be secured for quick build accommodation and matching regime facilities'. He had taken 'a very firm line that HMPS would not hold more prisoners than we could safely accommodate … and that approach came to be accepted as a way of life.' However, when Suma Chakrabarti had replaced Alex Allen as Permanent Secretary shortly after Wheatley had been appointed as Chief Executive of NOMS, they had a difficult relationship from the outset. Chakrabarti quickly decided that Wheatley was too powerful and difficult because he was inclined to tell 'either him or Ministers about the operational realities of prisons and probation and the risks we were trying to manage' that they did not want to hear. Gus O'Donnell (then Cabinet Secretary and Head of the Civil Service) was persuaded by Chakrabarti that Wheatley's appointment should be regarded as a two-year temporary appointment after which it could be externally advertised, although it was hinted that Wheatley might serve longer if he became 'more corporate'. His post was to be re-advertised in early 2010 although Wheatley made it clear he would not apply under such circumstances. When the post was advertised he resigned.

Wheatley's time at the top of the Prison Service and NOMS meant that he worked under six Home Secretaries or Lord Chancellors: David Blunkett, Charles Clarke, John Reid, Charlie Falconer, Jack Straw and briefly, after the change of government, Ken Clarke, as well as at least eight Junior Ministers. He was in as good a position as any to give a view on the politics of churn. In his time it was bad enough, even though it was possible to make some progress in spite of ministerial interference. But it was a great deal worse for his successor Michael Spurr, and after a decent interval following retirement Wheatley was more than ready to speak out about it, knowing that 'those who are currently doing the job can't do so'. But it was important for everyone to understand that 'a succession of Secretaries of State have made it almost impossible to do our job' (*The Guardian*, 12.12.16). Wheatley recalled a time, from his early career, when politicians listened to their civil servants if and when they 'said something wasn't a good idea.' There was a 'bipartisan approach' to even the highest profile disasters from the escape of the 'great train robbers' in the 1960s right up to the Strangeways riots of 1990. The Mountbatten and Woolf Reports, were not greeted with 'party political point scoring' but an 'acknowledgement that we failed to invest' and a desire to do better. He singled out Whitelaw, Hurd and latterly Ken Clarke as the Ministers who encouraged prison leaders to speak out on issues like 'underfunding' and 'overcrowding'. In part, this enabled them to 'put pressure on the Treasury' for more 'money to make things better … and probably also to keep the pressure off … the demand on prisons'. At this time, Ministers and prison leaders were united in their view that prisons were 'fairly unpleasant places' and in their desire 'to make sure the truth about prison was outed'. He also recalled a productive relationship with the Treasury over Fresh Start which was very 'expensive' but they supported it because they believed 'that would help prisons to work better'. Although Fresh Start was useful in turning the prison officer into a more professional salaried employee and temporarily at least ending overtime working it did not produce the hoped for enhancement of regimes and nor did it end problems with the POA. Later, when Wheatley was 'responsible for capacity planning' and the need to find prison places, the Treasury, at least initially 'were not unreasonable' as long as they believed 'we used our money properly.' With their help, Wheatley was able to put systems in place that demonstrated that the service knew exactly the condition of the prison estate and what maintenance was required so that 'we could spend money much more intelligently'.

However, it was during this time when he was 'responsible for policy on security and the size of the estate' that 'the system tilted' and 'the prison service became overwhelmed by increasing numbers.' Then the Treasury 'were no longer keen on investing in prisons to create more places, because it didn't look like a good investment'. They were not prepared to support the political ego of the Home Secretary and so began what Wheatley called

> 'a game of dare … the Treasury doing their best to constrain the money … the Home Secretary allowing the population to increase … then the Prime Minister (he had in mind both John Major and Tony Blair) would intervene somewhere nearing the election to say actually, we can't be letting prisoners out early. We'll lose votes so you're going to have to put money in'.

This resulted,

> 'at the last minute, in some very fast building, of accommodation that wasn't as good as it should have been, in the wrong places. Ministers, loved a quick fix, because it made them look as though they'd done something. They didn't like strategic, long-term planning, which meant their successor might get the credit'.

This meant that it was not really possible 'to develop the right prisons in the right places' with the 'the right sort of security that matched the people we'd got'.

Wheatley claimed, that the tipping point came with the killing of James Bulger in 1993. The unholy trinity of populist mantras – Blair's, 'tough on crime', Major's 'condemn a little more' and Howard's 'prison works' – all served to politicise criminal justice to a degree never seen before. Even Woolf, when he spoke to the Service, talked of the pressure to respond to sustained media criticism of the judiciary to 'up sentence lengths, without there being any change in legislation' for fear 'they would undermine respect for the law.' Michael Howard, more than any other minister before him, placed prisons in the political spotlight. Wheatley regarded many of his initial interventions as 'unreasonable', although he found that so long as 'you knew your subject' it was possible to 'argue back.' He found Anne Widdecombe a welcome counterweight to Howard. Wheatley told us that she obviously 'cared' but had a 'sense of grip' and always tried to be 'supportive.' He said she was 'the nicest minister I've ever worked with'. But it was soon to become difficult for 'senior civil servants' who were 'not specialists, or confident in their authority and position,' to take a stand. Increasingly, over the years, civil servants began feeding Ministers 'what they wanted to hear', agreeing 'impossible' targets and failing to point out potential pitfalls. Politicians were only 'interested in announcing the change' in policy or organisation, and 'getting the credit for it'. They were not really interested in the difficulties of 'delivering it'.

For Wheatley, the New Labour era was a mixed experience in terms of ministerial support and political direction. Whilst he found Boateng to be someone who 'wouldn't want to be told that's not possible' other Junior Ministers, Hilary Benn, Paul Goggins and Fiona McTaggart were 'determined to be helpful'. But their power remained insufficient to limit ministerial interference in operations. He described one stand-off with David Blunkett, whom he regarded as a bully, when 'prisoners got on the roof at Rudgate prison. Blunkett didn't like this … and sent word that we must get them off the roof.' When Wheatley resisted and explained that they had the situation well contained Blunkett dispatched Paul Goggins 'to tell me the error of my ways', as well as his private secretary to remind him 'that the minister's political reputation was on the line. I had to point out that the lives of my staff and prisoners … trumped his political reputation. Goggins didn't push further and the prisoners came down peacefully so it was a 'non-event'.

New Labour introduced massive changes for prisons and probation through the introduction of Carter's NOMS. Phil Wheatley accepted that 'ministers are there to decide things' and 'politically they will go in a different direction' but they need 'to pay attention to the practicalities of running something'. NOMS, he thought, was a prime example of failing to think things through and civil servants giving poor advice to Ministers. In his view, Pat Carter's report was the 'answer to the Treasury' to find a way to stop the 'game of dare' and find ways of reducing the prison population. He told us that Carter was 'full of big ideas' but he didn't 'do details'. NOMS was predicated on underestimated workloads and costs, and overestimated outcomes. Wheatley thought the idea of end-to-end management of offenders by probation offices was 'fairly facile'. Caseloads split between the community and a number of prisons wasted valuable time in travel, and 'access to courses' in prison was beyond their gift. Treasury money for offender behaviour programmes was still available, thanks to a successful pitch by Martin Narey about how they would reduce reoffending. Carter had said that we would 'only buy what works' but the 'solid research' needed to 'know whether it worked or not' didn't match Carter's short timescales. In time, data did show 'improvements in reducing reoffending' but the numbers were insufficient to make 'a big dent in the prison population'. In any case, courses were only one part of prison regimes and new money for other matters had dried up by 2003 and was replaced by an expectation of 'year on year savings'. This aspect of the first iteration of NOMS was a predictable failure.

A second element in the NOMS agenda was that services should be subject to competition. Like Pilling, Tilt and Narey before him, Wheatley recognised the usefulness of the threat of privatisation for driving up performance in public sector prisons. The prison service had already developed a workable model: they had the data for identifying the worst performing prisons and often they could be persuaded to improve without having to carry out the threat of contracting out. This, he told us, was just as well because 'contracting out is an expensive process … a million pounds doing it for … a decent sized prison'. It also 'causes disruption'.

The third element was to be the implementation of measures to help 'manage the prison population down'. The Judiciary had 'made it clear that they were not prepared to take the hit for reducing sentencing while politicians criticise them for making light sentences'. Despite Blunkett's agreement with Lord Woolf and Derry Irvine about tweaking the guidelines, he went ahead with the amendments to the CJA 2003 introducing 'mandatory life sentences because he was worried about losing the political say on when lifers were released.' The judges understandably took the view that 'if you say that a life sentence is no longer going to be 15 years but it's going to be 30 years, then that will up our view about … what a determinate sentence prisoner gets, because' they had to make sentences for different offences proportionate to one another. Since Wheatley's time in office, he had watched sentences having at least 'doubled' with no apparent political gain.

After Narey resigned over Charles Clarke's refusal to contemplate any attempt to control the size of the prison population, NOMS was pretty much a dead letter, although it continued to tick over with Helen Edwards at the helm. But a new iteration of NOMS resulted from Carter's (2007) second review of prisons. Wheatley told us that 'when it was plain the whole thing was a cock up and costing a fortune, Pat Carter came back ... and said ... they're not doing what I wanted them to do.' According to Wheatley, Carter suggested to Straw that the prison service should effectively 'take over the probation service and run the whole system.' They decided to keep the name of NOMS so they wouldn't 'lose face'. Thus, Phil Wheatley duly became the new Director of NOMS and Agency status effectively passed from the prison service to NOMS. He almost persuaded Straw to change the name to Her Majesty's Prisons and Probation Service until Straw realised it would look 'as though he'd changed his mind'. The new arrangement meant that 'the prison service got the whole of the train set to play with for two years ... and we did manage to make it make more sense'. However, towards the end of New Labour, populism had begun to trump *doing the right thing*, and on several occasions Straw interfered with operational decisions contrary to the new framework agreement. He vetoed Wheatley's plan to compensate prisoners for a reduction in the time they could spend out of cell, by a modest increase in wages. And amidst much media publicity, demanded a 'ban on all parties in prison', when photos were leaked to the media of light relief organised for deeply damaged female prisoners at Holloway prison. He also insisted on ending a 'clowning programme', designed to fill a regime gap at Whitemoor prison. Such incidents 'could have been ridden out' by a more resilient and supportive minister.

Within prisons, day-to-day management changed little under the early versions of NOMS. Wheatley had been relentlessly cost-cutting for years to cope with a rising prison population but without extra money. 'We were constantly having to make two, three percent savings out of our core custodial business.' This essentially translated into making savings through more efficient use of staff. There was plenty of scope because the prison service still carried a legacy of the past excesses of the POA in negotiating 'differential staffing levels, many of which didn't make any sense whatsoever'. Now that the POA had been faced down over their threats of industrial action, Wheatley was quickly 'able to get in reasonable staffing levels, and reasonable shift patterns', which meant that 'we could begin to make places work better'. Wheatley continued Narey's 'decency agenda', putting his own 'definition on it', speaking out about 'a whole series of practical things that prison officers could understand'. This, together with the threat of market testing had 'gradually changed the culture' so that prison officers no longer felt that they could 'just thump people if we want to.'

By the time of the latest iteration of NOMS, Wheatley told us they had reached what 'we thought was our achievable staffing levels ... without taking a hit on performance and safety' and he and Michael Spurr, then his Chief Operating Officer, so informed the Secretary of State. Straw wasn't 'prepared to accept that' and so they had to go 'through a process of benchmarking ... which with the benefit of hindsight' greatly oversimplified prison life. Breaking down the daily regime into individual processes, they looked for the places where these were accomplished with the tightest possible staffing ratios and used 'the best' as the benchmark across the estate. But the process failed to take account of the fact that the best was often achieved by exceptional staff in favourable circumstances and could not be replicated across the board. 'Adding together all the leanest possible systems', Wheatley told us, left them 'in a very unstable place'.

Once he was in charge of both prisons and probation, Wheatley was better able to compare and contrast their operations. He understood why 'the probation service was rightly wary of us because we looked at them and thought they'd never really become more efficient' without 'the pressure of competition'. Different practices had developed in different services, 'some services used probation officers for just about everything, and others used' the lower qualified grade of 'probation service officers for a lot more.' There was much time wasted in meetings and money lost on administration. In Wheatley's view, theirs was a world previously unbothered by 'politicians and the centre', and had been protected by their secret weapon, the 'very good lobbyist' the late Harry Fletcher, the assistant general secretary of the NAPO. But 'having taken most of what we could out of the prison service ... the pressure to make savings' now hit probation. Wheatley wanted to use the option of some degree of competition to encourage efficiencies within the service. Subjecting 'a couple of the smaller probation services that were under performing' to the threat of marketisation might encourage them to use 'PSOs a bit more' and probation officers 'more effectively'. 'It would have woken them all up,' he told us. This option had existed from the beginning of NOMS but was removed by Charles Clarke, reinstated by John Reid and finally quashed by Straw, although he threatened its use to exert pressure on the Probation Boards to become Trusts. The probation service did eventually begin producing similar performance data to the prison service 'comparing their reconviction rate with their predicted reconviction rate'. Wheatley found it bizarre that this didn't already exist for a service whose very 'reason for being is to reform people'.

References

Auld, Sir R. (2001) *Review of the Criminal Courts*, London: The Stationary Office.
Blair, T. (2011) *A Journey*, London: Arrow Books.
Bradley, Lord K. (2009) *Lord Bradley's Review of People with Mental Health Problems or Learning Disabilities In The Criminal Justice System*, April.
Carter, Lord P. (2003) *Managing Offenders – Reducing Crime*, The Strategy Unit.
Carter, Lord P. (2007) *Securing the Future. Proposals for the Efficient and Sustainable Use of Custody in England and Wales*, House of Lords.
Corston, J. (2007) *A Report by Baroness Jean Corston of a Review of Women With Particular Vulnerabilities in the Criminal Justice System*, Home Office.

Halliday Report (2001) *Making Punishments Work. Report of a Review of the Sentencing Framework for England and Wales*, July 2001.

King, A. and Crewe, I. (2014) *The Blunders of our Governments*, London: One World Publications.

Lockyer Review (2007) *Service Review – Indeterminate Sentence Prisoners*, Ministry of Justice, August 2007.

Ministry of Justice (2013) *Attitudes to Sentencing and Trust in Justice: Exploring Trends from the Crime survey for England and Wales*.

National Audit Office (2009) *The National Offender Management Information System* (HC 292), London: HMSO.

Powell, J. (2010) *The New Machiavelli: How to Wield Power in the Modern World*, London: Bodley Head.

Straw, J. (2012) *Last Man Standing: Memoirs of a Political Survivor*, London: Pan Macmillan.

4

THE COALITION GOVERNMENT 2010–2015

Introduction

After the election in 2010, Liam Byrne, the outgoing Chief Secretary to the Treasury, left an ill-judged note for his successor, the Liberal Democrat David Laws: 'Dear Chief Secretary, I'm afraid there is no money. Kind regards and good luck, Liam Byrne.' Later, according to his memoirs, Laws (2016, p 33) 'inadvertently' paraphrased that note as follows: 'I'm afraid there is no money **left**' (emphasis added). That additional word made it possible for New Labour to be painted as responsible for the economic situation through profligate borrowing and spending, thus diverting attention from the excessive sub-prime lending by the big financial institutions. In fact, New Labour had been cutting public expenditure before the 2008 collapse of the Royal Bank of Scotland and Lehmann Brothers and had planned a drop in public investment from £69 billion in 2009 to £46 billion by 2014–2015.

In his budget statement, Osborne claimed, 'The country has overspent; it has not been under taxed' as though these were objective facts rather than political judgments. He set himself targets for bringing public expenditure into line with income by 2014–2015 in a process of 'consolidation' by adopting the IMF's formula. This dictated that 80% of the burden should be borne by public expenditure cuts, and only 20% come from increased taxation. Osborne wanted additional cuts of £30 billion by 2014–2015 and also proposed the disposal of public assets which, according to him, 'should **rightly** be in private ownership' (emphasis added). He then asked spending departments to come through with their proposals for cuts to meet these objectives. If no departments were protected, this would amount to a 20% cut across the board. But once protection was given to the NHS and International Aid budgets, the cuts for unprotected departments would be closer to 25%. Thus was ushered in a decade of austerity

DOI: 10.4324/9781003201748-5

pursued with little regard to the damage to public services and the social fabric. The rejection of an alternative formula allowing borrowing at historically low rates of interest the better to maintain those services owed much more to a Conservative determination to 'roll back the State' than it did to economics.

Cameron, taking a leaf from Blair's playbook, encouraged the use of political advisers and brought Francis Maude into the Cabinet Office with a brief to make the civil service more efficient, but which may well have further eroded the availability of well-informed expert advice generally. On criminal justice, Cameron vacillated and allowed Ministers to do the same – but austerity overshadowed all. There were continuities with New Labour, but there were also changes of direction. There was political intrigue and a falling out over Clarke's plans to reduce the prison population and a further example of the dangers of speaking truth to power when Nick Hardwick rightly assumed that Grayling would not extend his contract as HM Chief Inspector of Prisons. Phil Wheatley's resignation – consequent upon his refusal to reapply for his post after his criticisms of cuts under Straw – took effect soon after the election. He was succeeded by Michael Spurr upon whom the ideological commitment to producing more for less placed increasingly impossible demands. The prison service was stripped to the bone, and the probation service part privatised in a fruitless attempt to demonstrate the effectiveness of payment by results (Table 4.1).

Part one: The politicians

Ken Clarke (May 2010–September 2012)

Ken Clarke told us in our interview at Portcullis House that he was back in the Cabinet because David Cameron had promised to find him a place in the Government after the election. He had expected to become Secretary for State for Business, but in coalition negotiations that went to Vince Cable and Cameron unexpectedly suggested that he become Justice Secretary and Lord Chancellor. It thus fell to Clarke to start the process of cuts that would impact most severely upon prisons, legal aid and the courts. Laws wrote in his memoirs, 'I managed to persuade Ken Clarke, the Justice Secretary, to settle first to encourage the others … I had got my first contribution of £325 million from the Justice Department' (2016, p 33). It amounted to 23% of the Ministry of Justice's (MoJ) budget.

Clarke's preparedness to contribute his full share of savings to the Exchequer, without the usual fight expected of the head of a spending department, was not just because he thought that was the right thing to do in light of the Conservative Party's version of the national interest. It was also importantly predicated upon his belief that the savings could actually be made by reductions in the size of the prison population through legislative action and by persuading the courts to make better use of community penalties for less serious offenders. Clarke had initially responded to challenges by Jack Straw and Sadiq Khan, then shadow Justice Secretary, that these cuts would result in the loss of between 11,000 and 14,000

TABLE 4.1 Coalition Ministers, Directors of Service(s), Key Legislation, Department and Service Reorganisation 2010–2015

Year/month (general election in bold)	Justice Secretary & Lord Chancellor	Key prisons and probation legislation	Prisons & Probation Minister	Director of Her Majesty's Prison Service (HMPS)	Director of National Probation Service (NPS)	DG/CEO of National Offender Management Service (NOMS) agency	Department and Service Reorganisation
2010 May	Kenneth Clarke		Crispin Blunt	N/A	N/A	Phil Wheatley continued	
2010 Jun		**Legal Aid Sentencing and Punishment of Offenders Act 2012** new sentencing		2010-2015 no separate director of HM Prison Service, instead functional directors within the NOMS agency.	2010-2015 no separate director of probation.	Michael Spurr	2nd **NOMS agency**, regional layer removed; continue to commission & provide offender management services in prisons & probation.
2012 Sep	Chris Grayling	framework to increase use of community sentencing, end IPP sentencing & custody plus, new powers to amend parole test & presumption against bail; unable to reverse the burden of proof for parole, simplify schedule 21 & increase sentence discount for early pleas.	Jeremy Wright				
2014 Jul		**Offender Rehabilitation Act 2014** extends post release supervision and therefore recall to all prisoners for a period of 12 months (previously rejected in the shape of custody plus Criminal Justice Act 2003 owing to cost).	Andrew Selous				
2015 Feb							2nd **NPS** created alongside 21 Community Rehabilitation Companies (split possible under the **Offender Management Act 2007**) to separately manage high risk, and medium and low risk offenders; replaces 35 probation trusts; situated within NOMS agency.

prison and probation staff, by saying that the bulk of the cuts to the MoJ budget were falling upon 'administration and legal aid' both of which he described as 'bloated.' He had to survive criticism over his intended closure of more than a hundred 'underused' courts. However, as time went on, he became increasingly concerned that it would become harder to maintain good order within the prisons. According to Laws, Clarke became tougher in his negotiations with the Treasury and pointed to the danger of prison riots if he carried out all the cuts he had originally offered. Or, as Clarke put it, the 'Prime Minister's entourage suddenly became less zealous than they had been in pursuit of the headline figure'.

Clarke told us that when he became Justice Secretary, he had been

'astonished to find that the prison population had almost doubled ... since I had been Home Secretary. and for no serious reason except I'd been succeeded ... by a series of Ministers playing to the gallery and trying to show they were tough on law and order'.

He singled out both Michael Howard and David Blunkett who introduced

'dreadful things like mandatory sentences which I totally disapprove of so it struck me that what I had to do was get rid of mandatory sentences and try to influence the Sentencing Council ... to get penalties down to a more justifiable level. The other thing I was anxious to do was to get out of prison the wayward, vulnerable and mentally ill and other waifs and strays who shouldn't be there. When I was Justice Secretary the state of overcrowding and the state of most of our prisons had got worse than it had been when I was Home Secretary and I tried to reverse it'.

In these aspirations, he was joined by his Parliamentary Under Secretary for Prisons and Probation, Crispin Blunt, who had equally unexpectedly been appointed to that post in the share-out with the Liberal Democrats. We interviewed Blunt at Portcullis House on 20 June 2018. Blunt explained to us that the cuts were somewhat less severe than they might have appeared because they had been calculated on the basis that the population would rise to 96,000 by the end of the budgetary period when in the event it remained stable at around 85,000.

Clarke recognised that it would be important to keep the judiciary on side if he was to bring the prison population down. He had seen that 'judges unfortunately respond to the newspapers and their political masters ... by putting sentences up.' In June 2010, he courageously delivered his first major speech as Justice Secretary aimed at judges, magistrates and the Parole Board, announcing a major change of direction. As Blunt put it in our interview, that speech in effect told them 'that they would not be shouted at by politicians if they did not sentence people to custody or actually released people from prison'. The speech seemed to have some impact in holding off further rises in the prison population. A month later, this was followed up by a speech by Blunt which almost cost him his job. It was given to mark the 100th anniversary of Churchill's great Prison Reform Speech as Home Secretary but Blunt's talk was written up by Jack Doyle as 'parties for prisoners and the public are paying' (*Daily Mail* 23.7.10). A copy of the *Mail* was apparently thrown down in front of the Prime Minister by Andy Coulson, who 'had obviously been appointed as Rupert Murdoch's representative in Number 10' according to Clarke, demanding that Blunt be sacked. But Coulson had not actually read the speech which, in fact, had been cleared by Blunt's private office through the usual channels and had received the full approval of Ken Clarke.

That month, Clarke announced a review of the sentencing framework which already had a familiar New Labour ring to it – the need for tougher community penalties in which the courts and the public had confidence. Whilst he agreed that 'there is a case for some short sentences' for minor but relentlessly recidivist offenders, which was always a bugbear for the courts, he argued that their use 'where a really effective and convincing community penalty is available should be avoided.' The Green Paper, *Breaking the Cycle: Effective Punishment, Rehabilitation and Sentencing of Offenders* (Cm 7972) was then published in December and called for a 'revolutionary shift in the way that rehabilitation is delivered and financed' if reoffending was to be reduced. These arguments in the Green Paper had been taking shape under Dominic Grieve when he was shadow Minister of Justice. Crime rates had been falling, but custodial sentences had become both more frequent and longer. Moreover, the use of fines had been falling and was being replaced by community sentences, thus imposing more demands on the probation service. Clarke envisaged the opening up of all rehabilitation services to competition from potential providers in the private, voluntary and community sectors, and proposed a shift of emphasis from the mere *provision* of programmes – it was thought much of New Labour's spending on programmes had been ineffective – to *outcomes* through the introduction of pilot schemes for 'payment by results' as measured by reductions in reoffending. By these means, prisons and probation could be held to account. In fact, pilot schemes had been introduced under New Labour at the behest of Jack Straw but the best-known pilot, the Social Impact Bond scheme at HMP Peterborough – in which social investors would be paid on the basis of observed improvements in reconvictions of released prisoners – did not begin until September 2010. Phil Wheatley recalled from memory that the scheme was quite sophisticated and delivered statistically significant results, although the published data, in what is a methodologically problematic area, were largely observational and the results somewhat mixed.

The vehicle that Clarke hoped would sort out the 'mess of Byzantine complexity' that sentencing policy had become, and thus deliver the reduction in the prison population, was the *Legal Aid and Sentencing of Offenders Bill* which had its first reading in July 2011, and during which time he held many discussions with the Judiciary to allay their doubts. But by the time it became the *Legal Aid, Sentencing and Punishment of Offenders Act (LASPOA) 2012*, most of the wheels had fallen off. There were lengthy debates on both the Green Paper and the Bill in which it was mooted that sentences be reduced by half in return for early guilty pleas, that Imprisonment for Public Protection (IPP) sentences be replaced by determinate sentences, reserving indeterminate sentences only for those who posed extreme risks and the abolition of minimum sentences – all of which were opposed by New Labour. Both Clarke and Blunt ran into predictable difficulties with the Press in defending the possibility of reducing the sentences of persons convicted for rape in return for guilty pleas. The Bill also proposed reducing the number of short sentences of imprisonment and remands in custody, the increased use of restorative justice and a new focus on helping offenders with drug and alcohol problems and getting the mentally ill out of prisons, following Lord Bradley's Report published the previous year. But as the proposals were debated in Parliament, various amendments were introduced and although Clarke got the Bill through the Cabinet Committee, chaired by Nick Clegg who basically shared Clarke's views, Cameron got very cold feet. In our interview, Clarke told us that

> 'Cameron had once told me that he wanted a liberal Justice Secretary but he didn't want anybody to know that or see that. But now Cameron was terrified that we were going to be seen as soft on crime … accused of taking away tough sentences and letting people out of prison … and I'm afraid David got it all thrown out'.

Clarke (2016) wrote in his memoirs (pp 448–50) that Cameron, like Blair before him, had surrounded himself by a 'huge entourage' of special political advisors (so-called SpAds) in No 10, most of whom tried 'to second-guess and direct the work of Cabinet ministers', but he refused 'to be part of that system.' He wrongly assumed that his 'veteran status' insulated him from such interference. Cameron suggested that he should meet Rebekah Brookes, 'Rupert Murdoch's representative on earth' who tried, but failed, to convert him to more prison ships and military boot camps. She had obviously become 'accustomed to meeting with Home Secretaries and Justice Secretaries and having her advice taken seriously.' New Labour Ministers had paid 'unbelievable deference' to her creation and use of 'celebrity victims' and produced absurdities like making the 'minimum sentence for murder with a knife … significantly higher than … murder with a poker.' When he became aware that his own advisers and civil servants were being approached by Cameron's aides with similar ideas for unacceptable policy proposals, he instructed the Permanent Secretary that departmental civil servants were not to hold meetings with them without his consent. Blunt told us that Clarke 'gave terrific protection to the department and everyone working within it essentially telling No 10 officials to take a hike.' But in the end, it was to little avail and the advice that Cameron got from his SpAds trumped the advice of his Justice Secretary and the Cabinet Committee's considered approach to criminal justice policy. In an extraordinary *volte-face*, Cameron insisted on the inclusion of yet more mandatory minimum sentences, a measure to criminalise squatting and the extension of the potential date of release for sexual and violent offenders from the halfway stage to the two-thirds point. And, in an effort to emphasise the appearance of toughness, the word Punishment was added to the title of the Bill.

In the end, Clarke had to come up with proposals for new minimum sentences but asked his officials to draft the threshold so high that few, if any, offenders would ever be likely to meet them. He also took the precaution of consulting his old friend and adversary from earlier years at the Bar, Igor Judge, who by then was Lord Chief Justice (LCJ), about the matter. Clarke told us that Judge had no problem with minimum sentences so long as they had the usual get-out clause, namely, 'unless it would be unjust to do so in all the circumstances.' A similar clause had been inserted into Michael Howard's mandatory sentences at the insistence of the judiciary and which made some of them 'a dead letter' although others continued to have 'a marked effect ... and sometimes caused injustice'. This was not quite how Igor Judge recalled the matter when we put this to him, but the difference may not be worth a dispute. In our interview with Clarke, he gave vent to his anger and frustration with Cameron for undermining his attempted reforms in no uncertain terms. However, greatly to his surprise, but only after lengthy horse-trading, he had got the Prime Minister to agree to the total abolition of the IPP sentence, which was replaced by extended determinate sentences and the wider use of discretionary life sentences. Unfortunately, the abolition of IPP was not retrospective, and so has left large numbers still in custody well beyond their tariff dates, in part because Clarke could not get Cameron to agree to reversing the burden of proof in parole decisions whereby the onus is placed on IPP prisoners to show that they are no longer a risk before they can be released. The possibility that this could at some point be changed by Statutory Instrument was, however, written into the Act and the matter was taken up again by Michael Gove in the next government. New Labour's sentence of 'custody plus,' which had never been brought into force because of costs, was also abolished.

Although his failed attempt at sentencing reforms represented a clear change of direction from New Labour, there were other matters where Clarke told us he was 'proceeding on a very similar basis to the previous Government.' He agreed with Straw's encouragement of 'honesty in sentencing' which required judges to explain prison sentences, and their implications for the amount of time actually served, in 'plain English'. This fitted with a wider rhetoric, shared with New Labour, about the place of victims in the criminal justice system in a new Green Paper *Getting it right for victims and witnesses* (Cm 8288). On 27 March 2012, Clarke published two consultation papers, confusingly titled *Punishment and Reform: Effective Probation Services* (CP7, Cm 8333) and *Punishment and Reform: Effective Community Sentences* (CP8, Cm 8334). The first envisaged a lighter touch performance management with less prescriptive National Standards, and antici-pated private sector involvement in supervising low-risk offenders; the second proposed a real element of punishment in every community order – more rigor-ous community payback, tagging and longer curfews. These broadly followed up on a strategy developed in New Labour's Offender Management Act (OMA) 2007 except that New Labour would have kept core tasks of offender manage-ment and supervision within the public sector and only interventions would have been opened up to competition. The consultations led to the *Crime and Courts Bill* though this was not to become law until Chris Grayling had become Justice Secretary. It was another step on the road towards the setting up of Community Rehabilitation Companies (CRCs) and compulsory post-release supervision of all short sentence prisoners, although Clarke and Blunt might have done things differently. Blunt wondered whether, had they stayed in office, they would have ended up by linking the probation service to Police and Crime Commissioners who would then be 'less obsessed with arresting people' and more concerned about 'what came out of the system at the other end'. Clarke, however, was more inclined to try and improve the existing Probation Trusts through competition in line with the previous New Labour policies rather than embark on more organisational change.

Clarke was greatly enamoured of the virtues of private enterprise and had led the way in the process of privatisation in the prison system, which had contin-ued under New Labour, and now seemed set to flourish. Jack Straw had cho-sen Birmingham, over other potential candidates, to be put out for competitive tender, because of its poor performance and earlier threats of strike action by the local Prison Officers Association (POA). In 2011, the public sector put in a strong bid to continue running Birmingham prison but lost the 15-year contract to G4S. Blunt had told us that 'the winning G4S bid had 150 more staff than the public sector bid' which he took to be 'an example of the impossibility of the public sector to compete against the private sector'. Five years later, Birmingham was moved into special measures following a major riot in 2016 and adverse reports from the Inspectorate, and G4S was stripped of its contract the following year when an Urgent Notification (UN) procedure was invoked by HM Chief Inspector of Prisons. Michael Spurr gave a different version to Blunt's appraisal of the bids. But it is important not to oversimplify the pros and cons of public versus private provision. We were assured by Peter Dawson, for example, that initially Birmingham 'was transformed by privatisation very much for the better' and that its subsequent decline 'owed much more to pressure to expand, overcrowd and take on courts from further afield'. He told us that 'Clarke was committed to competition across the board to include all public sector prisons' a policy which he found coherent because 'there were still lots of absolutely embedded practices and attitudes which were not going to change without that'. He thought there was also a sense in which the public sector tended to promise 'things they have never done before in order to win the bids'.

Clarke had initially been opposed to building more prisons but eventually became converted by Blunt's argument that it would be easier, and much less expensive, to put new prisons out to tender rather than existing ones, and that by closing old prisons it would be possible to make the prison estate more fit for purpose. A programme of replacing new for old prisons had begun under Jack Straw and continued, albeit in fits and starts in line with the changing pressures on prison places. Blunt told us he had a vision of getting 'roughly 50% private, 50% public sector' with an expansion and improvement of training and leadership skills for both prisons and probation staff. Clarke, however, did not vouchsafe any such figures in our interview and nor was he forthcoming about his intentions when Spurr directly sought clarification. Nine further competitions were announced, Lindholme, Moorland, Hatfield, Wolds, Acklington, Castington, Durham, Onley and Coldingley, with a strong warning from Clarke to the POA to learn the lessons from Birmingham. He told us: 'I have no idea why my eventual successor Chris Grayling promptly cancelled this policy upon taking office.' Blunt was quite explicit, however, when he described Grayling's cancellation as part of his 'Faustian pact' with the prison service over the latest round of benchmarking of staffing levels, which precipitated the prison service more deeply into crisis.

When he was at the Home Office, Clarke had established the prison service as an arms-length Next Steps Agency under Derek Lewis and then very much left him to it. So, it was no surprise that he took a 'hands off' approach to the management of the Justice Department. Clarke set the direction of travel and the priorities, but as he put it to us 'I've always run departments rather like a debating society. … You've got to have respect for the expertise of your officials.' This style of management was certainly appreciated by those in day-to-day charge of implementing policy. It also enabled Blunt to tell us that he and Clarke were in 'almost complete alignment.' Blunt was rather less well aligned with prison officials, however, when they thought he unfairly blamed them for failing to provide sufficient accommodation in a timely manner. According to Blunt, he and Clarke had three priorities: 'work for prisoners, restorative justice and payment by results' on which he focused most of his attention. They never came remotely close to their goal of establishing a 40-hour working week for prisoners, but they were successful in attracting some private companies to get involved in training and employing prisoners. The pioneering figure in that area had been James Timpson, who since 2002 had employed many ex-prisoners and established a number of training academies inside prisons. Expansion of these, Clarke noted, was difficult because of the lack of space for workshops in many prisons. Blunt developed what he called the 'One3One Solutions' initiative, which sought to involve businesses in partnerships with the 131 prisons which had scope for employing prisoners whilst in prison or training them for employment on release.

Clarke and Blunt continued New Labour's promotion of restorative justice and launched a Restorative Justice Register and encouraged training in restorative justice skills in prisons and juvenile institutions. Crispin Blunt maintained a profound belief in the concept of payment by results and pilot schemes were started in one public and one private prison. Many overtures had been proffered in response to his calls for potential models for effective rehabilitation and he was keen to test them against reoffending rates. When we pointed out that there could be no clear way of linking the 'results' to any programme offered by the providers, or even, as Richard Tilt reminded us, of linking any individual's response to any particular prison. Not to mention that there is no way of measuring *reoffending* – 'reconvictions' being as much a measure of victim, police and prosecution activity as it is of criminal behaviour. Or that whether or not someone reoffended would depend upon so many other factors in their situation post-release. He brushed such considerations aside saying 'I don't care. I'm just interested in outcome'. By the time Clarke and Blunt were moved on from the MoJ, there were 28 pilots running for payment by results. Clarke was more cautious on these and was still waiting for the evidence from the pilots. He told us 'I don't think we ever got so far as having a properly worked up system which I was prepared to implement'.

Blunt clearly thought that his approach of wanting to 'let a thousand flowers bloom,' as he put it, was difficult for National Offender Management Service (NOMS) to take on board. In his view, NOMS was struggling to absorb probation and anyway their officials much preferred a more prescriptive model both of what they should provide for prisoners and by way of offender management in the community.

After two years and four months in office, Clarke was surprisingly offered, and gladly accepted, the position of Minister without Portfolio in the Cabinet. Blunt was effectively sacked and did not get another ministerial role. Inevitably, the politics of churn would overtake some of their initiatives. One of Clarke's regrets was that he hadn't been able to do more by way of implementing the recommendations of the Corston Report on women in the criminal justice system. But the prison population had remained stable and the support for officials had helped the prison service to improve or maintain standards: as Nick Hardwick, then HM Chief Inspector of Prisons reminded us, 'if you look at all the data, up until 2012 things were improving.' He also noted that the probation service had won a national award for excellence in 2011. Peter Dawson reflected that Clarke was the last Minister who 'was prepared to say that reducing the prison population was a worthy end in itself' and to argue the case intelligently. Ken Clarke told us that 'Grayling arrived at the Justice Department saying that he'd been ordered to be a tough law and order justice secretary'. Hopes of a reasoned approach to prisons and probation had been dashed.

Christopher Grayling (September 2012–May 2015)

Our interview with Chris Grayling eventually took place in the House of Commons on 10 January 2019. It was our fourth attempt. Throughout much of our interview, Grayling struck a confident pose leaning back in his chair until it was balanced on its two back legs. He described the thinking behind his appointment by David Cameron in the following terms:

> 'the remit I had was basically two-fold, strengthen the rehabilitation revolution and to get rid of the narrative surrounding the Government around soft justice'.

He had previously been Minister of State at the Department of Work and Pensions (DWP) where he told us he had 'masterminded the Work Programme,' which he claimed had produced 'a massive fall in long term unemployment' through 'the largest Government scheme of payment by results'. Not everyone was impressed by the Work Programme which seemed to be no more effective than ordinary job centres, and was described by Richard Whittell, of Corporate Watch, as more 'concerned with slashing benefits than getting people into work' (*The Guardian*, 30.6.12). Richard Tilt told us that he had been Chair of the Social Security Advisory Council during Grayling's tenure at DWP and 'we were in a perpetual state of disagreement with him'. Grayling had expected to be promoted to Secretary of State at the DWP, but his boss, Duncan Smith, had turned down the job of Lord Chancellor preferring to stay where he was and Cameron offered the Justice Department to Grayling instead.

Grayling told us that he believed that Ministers should give direction but leave it to officials to get the job done on the ground, though that was not always what it seemed like to the officials to whom we spoke. Indeed, he made several direct interventions in prisons and his hands were all over the probation 'reforms'. His Junior Minister of State was Jeremy Wright, who did much of the heavy lifting on prisons and probation and whose official title also included rehabilitation and sentencing. Grayling thought highly of him describing him as 'very able' and encouraged us to talk to him. Unfortunately, Jeremy Wright, who by that time had become Attorney General, declined to be interviewed. On 2 July 2018, however, we did succeed in talking to Andrew Selous in Portcullis House. He had become Parliamentary Under Secretary in July 2014 when Wright was promoted.

One measure of Grayling's self-confidence came when he told us that on taking over as Secretary of State, he gave himself 'two weeks in which to get around the task' before making 'decisions about anything.' He obviously thought of himself as a quick learner. Thereafter decisions came thick and fast. It had taken New Labour's Charles Clarke a year to understand the workings of the admittedly much larger Home Office. Selous told us that 'new Secretaries of State … have their own agendas and priorities and the department, quite properly, bends to that.' Selous, as a new Junior Minister, confessed that it took him about a year to get his head around everything, in part because he found that career civil servants were often only in post for two or three years, so that there was a lack of corporate memory as to what had been tried and what had worked. He found the best sources of information were directly from senior prison and probation staff. Although Grayling saw himself as continuing from where Ken Clarke and Blunt had left off – he inherited the Crime and Courts Bill from them as well as ideas concerning reforming rehabilitation and payment by results – as usual, there was very little contact between successive regimes. Grayling 'went out for dinner' with Clarke, and Blunt had a brief discussion with Wright 'on the terrace.' But whilst there are superficial nominal continuities, it is clear from the comments by both Clarke and Blunt that they were alarmed at the way things developed under Grayling, including his cancellation of pilot projects and his rolling out of untested schemes, his abandonment of privatisation by cancelling the proposal to put nine prisons to the market, and his determination not to reduce the prison population at any price.

Four months into his term of office, Grayling published a landmark consultation paper, *Transforming Rehabilitation: a revolution in the way we manage offenders* (Cm 8517) arguing that the spending of £4 billion on prisons and offender management and the wider economic costs of offending estimated at £13 billion were no longer acceptable. He wanted to achieve 'more for less' and this was to become the watchword underlying Grayling's approach to both prisons and probation. It provided a sharp contrast with what had gone before. Grayling told us 'Ken focused on more work in prisons and did a very good job of that within the constraints imposed by the prison estate' whereas 'I focused on through-the-door and post-prison rehabilitative support.' His proposals involved changing the role of some prisons to assist the resettlement of prisoners towards the end of their sentences and the delivery of community sentences and rehabilitation services by a range of providers in the private and voluntary sector who would only be paid in full when they could show that they had reduced reoffending rates.

Let us start with the prisons not least because the view from inside the prison service was that Grayling had no interest in them whatsoever and very little understanding of what they were about or how they worked. Although Grayling inherited from Clarke what he called 'a really challenging set of finances,' he told the House of Commons that

'prisons must cost less and do more' (Hansard, HC 8.11.12).

According to Grayling, it had been Clarke's 'intention to privatise the whole of the prison estate' because 'private prisons are cheaper to run than public prisons,' Blunt had said that he and Clarke would have been content with 50% private prisons, but Clarke had not given any figure in our interview and his officials in NOMS were certainly unclear as to his actual intentions. Grayling's immediate problems were how to respond to the bids already received in regard to the nine prisons which had been put out for competitive tender following the privatisation of Birmingham, and to determine what the extent of future outsourcing would be. Initially it had been intended to privatise five of the nine prisons – two, Castington and Acklington, to Sodexo and three in Yorkshire,

Moorland, Lindholme and Hatfield, to Serco. But it then emerged that G4S, and Serco had been deliberately overcharging for electronic monitoring contracts and were to be subject to a Serious Fraud Office investigation and so the Serco bids were put on hold until there was clarity about the outcome. With conditions in the three Yorkshire prisons deteriorating, Spurr successfully argued for the abatement of the Serco bids, and given that the investigation dragged on for over five years before Serco accepted culpability, Spurr considered that had been 'a good call'. Serco and G4S eventually repaid £179 million. Castington and Acklington, which had been awarded to Sodexo, were on adjacent sites and were merged into a single establishment, Northumberland. The main attraction for privatising Northumberland, Grayling told us, was the opportunity to create 'a campus with a strong education centre and do something very exciting on the education front.'

In our interview, Grayling told us that he decided to abandon the competition, with the exception of two prisons, 'for two reasons. First, it didn't deliver savings till the mid-2020s ... and second, I wasn't convinced that the market could cope with this scale of privatisation'. In light of the situation at Serco and G4S, that assessment of the market was almost certainly correct. He also told us that an alternative was 'already emerging' in the form of

> 'an in-house bid which had been designed by prison governors themselves which introduced benchmarking and which basically took the most cost effective way of doing things across the prison estate and applied it to these nine prisons'.

Benchmarking had begun under New Labour when Phil Wheatley and Michael Spurr (then Chief Operating Officer) had to respond to Jack Straw's refusal to accept that the service had achieved the lowest staffing levels beyond which safety would be compromised. Wheatley had spoken out so forcefully about this that he was invited to become *more corporate* and reapply for his post when it was advertised in June 2010. That first version of benchmarking, Wheatley told us, had put the Service 'in a very unstable place' by the end of Clarke's time in office. Grayling expected the Service to do even more for even less and the pressure was on Michael Spurr to deliver. The POA had been softened up by the privatisation of Birmingham and the process of tendering for nine further prisons, and the possibility of yet further benchmarking offered an alternative to further widespread privatisation. Michael Spurr told us that he accepted responsibility for initiating the *Prison Unit Cost Programme*, as the new version of benchmarking was called. Although it offered lower savings than could have been achieved through competition, they could be gained much more quickly 'enabling the service to live within the allocated budget over the remainder of the Parliament'. The programme had the support of both governors and the POA as 'the lesser of two evils' compared to further widespread privatisation. But, as Wheatley and Spurr had warned, the price was indeed 'a hit on performance and safety'.

Whereas Nick Hardwick had been able to point to improvements in most areas of performance up until 2012, thereafter things deteriorated rapidly.

Grayling put it to us that 'the decision was there to take and I could not see the benefit of rushing down the privatisation road. From my point of view, it meant we could deliver savings, not on the same scale as privatisation, but much quicker.' He did also enjoy the irony that the so-called 'Faustian pact,' in which an end was called to privatisation in return for major cuts in staffing, actually resulted in 'the POA in my office describing it as a great victory.'

Once upon a time, prisons had their own works departments which theoretically could quickly respond to local problems, including damage caused by prisoners, as well as provide useful employment for some prisoners. Peter Dawson told us that in reality, they were often 'slow and unreliable' and that when the first-ever market test was aborted at Brixton, the 'one element that was successful, and continued, was contracting out of works'. That may have been a one-off. Be that as it may, Grayling insisted that the prison service put the cleaning and maintenance of the estate, as well as *all* ancillary services from the management of stores to waste disposal, out for tender to the private sector. Although there could be possible advantages in centralising some of these services, New Labour had taken the advice of Phil Wheatley and regarded such matters as just too complicated to be worth the effort. In 2014, with little experience of outsourcing, difficulties in calculating estimated future costs over such a complex range of activities and the pressure of having to deliver more for less, the prison service awarded contracts to Carillion and Amey to run these services over four geographic regions. But the companies had put in massively underfunded, and essentially undeliverable, bids. Although Amey fared a little better, Carillion collapsed at the beginning of 2018 and a new government company had to take over and deal with a £900 million backlog of repairs. None of the anticipated savings from the outsourcing were achieved: instead, the prison service ended up paying much more. Andrea Albutt, Chair of the Prison Governors Association, told us that Carillion had left the prisons in 'a terrible state', and the Prisons Minister, by then Rory Stewart, found it difficult to contain his anger, which he directed at the prison service, about the broken windows at Liverpool and elsewhere, and the generally poor state of many prisons.

Both women's prisons and the high-security estate were to some degree protected under benchmarking, but the newly 'agreed' reduced staffing levels were rolled out in stages across local and training prisons effectively locking in restricted regimes for the great majority of prisoners. There were undoubtedly serious reductions in staffing as the service sought to make ends meet. A temporary freeze on recruitment was put in place as were arrangements for redundancy, euphemistically called the Voluntary Early Departure (VED) scheme. In future, there would be different contracts for new staff with lower pay and conditions, and some changes were introduced to the roles of existing staff, relieving some senior officers of line management responsibilities. Moreover, as the quality of life in prisons deteriorated with increasingly squalid conditions and rising levels of violence against prisoners and staff, drug abuse and self-harm, there were more officers reporting sick and many deciding just to leave. In a nice understatement, Andrew Selous told us there was a 'slight mismatch between officers and the number of prisoners.' He thought that the 'recruitment freeze a really stupid thing to do' and that 'a major recruitment drive' was needed, because in addition, those taking the VED route 'we lost about 90 officers a month just through retirement or ill health or whatever.' Andrew Selous told us that he had been there for several months when Spurr first warned him of 'the link between spice and violence' but that his private secretary warned him against making that public too soon.

Nick Hardwick, had become HM Chief Inspector of Prisons just as the new government ushered in its rehabilitation revolution. Hoping for the best but fearing the worst, he had prudently taken the precaution of laying down a baseline in his first annual report (HMCIP, 2011) 'to provide a useful point of comparison as the work of the Inspectorate develops … and the Government's reforms take effect.' He became increasingly critical in his subsequent reports laying the blame for the deterioration of regimes and increasing levels of violence more on government policy than prison management. Hardwick told us that in 2012

> 'with the loss of experienced staff, that's when the safety issues started to go through the roof … this was not due to poor performance by anyone but was due to political decisions about resources … the staff being insufficient for the numbers of prisoners they were holding … and Grayling didn't like me saying that'.

Indeed, Grayling took great exception to Hardwick's criticisms and tried to persuade his independent Chief Inspector to emphasise the positives instead of the negatives. As Hardwick put it:

> 'He was pressurising me quite hard to change what I was saying, which I wouldn't do. … Grayling made it clear to me, through officials, that I would have to reapply to be reappointed and my chances weren't good'.

Nick Hardwick served out the remainder of his term, somewhat outlasting Grayling, but although he thought that Michael Gove, with whom he had a good relationship would have reappointed him, he had already decided to leave. In his final report, for 2015–2016, he complained that:

> 'Assessed outcomes in the prisons we reported on in 2014–15 fell sharply across all areas, and overall the outcomes we reported on were the worst for ten years. Our own assessments about safety were consistent with the data that the National Offender Management Service (NOMS) itself produced'.

Whilst there were many factors that contributed to the decline in safety in prisons, it remained his view 'that staff shortages, overcrowding and the wider policy changes described in this report have had a significant impact on prison safety' (p 10). The number of full-time equivalent staff, of all grades and roles, who were in post in public sector prisons, had been reduced by 29% between March 2010 and December 2014, from 45,080 to 32,100 and in evidence to the Justice Select Committee, NOMS reported that staff in post were 8% or 2,481 below the agreed benchmarked levels (Justice Committee, *Ninth Report*, p 39). Hardwick endorsed the Justice Committee's conclusion that

> 'the key explanatory factor for the obvious deterioration in standards over the last year is that a significant number of prisons have been operating at staffing levels below what is necessary to maintain reasonable, safe and rehabilitative regimes'.
>
> *(p 10)*

Hardwick was later appointed by Michael Gove as the new Chairman of the Parole Board.

Grayling told us that he accepted that 'the budget problems were always there' but didn't 'buy the argument that the increased levels of violence had anything to do with money'. He argued that 'there was no difference in the changes in the levels of violence and assaults between the prisons which had to introduce change' to staffing levels 'and those that did not' although, not surprisingly, Michael Spurr disputed that interpretation. So too did Peter Clarke, who succeeded Nick Hardwick as HM Chief Inspector of Prisons: when we spoke to him on 16 November 2018, he told us that 'the women's estate by and large works well, the open estate by and large works well, the high security estate to an extent works well. They didn't suffer the staff cuts'. In Peter Clarke's opinion, 'benchmarking was not based on sensible numbers. They went too far down'. He pointed out that if you looked at the system over the decade since 2008, in the first half

> 'the violence levels were stable or even decreasing very slightly. In the second five years, when the cuts really took effect, you had double digit increases in almost all categories. Common sense tells you that if you take 30% of the staff out of a people hungry business … there's going to be an effect'.

Grayling had never had any 'plans to reduce the prison population' other than by the removal of foreign prisoners – a repeated area of failure for successive governments. Intriguingly, given the fate of Ken Clarke's eviscerated LASPO Act, the Criminal Justice and Courts Bill 2014 was loudly proclaimed as the Bill that 'draws a line under Labour's soft justice culture.' It proposed the ending of automatic release at the half way point for extended determinate sentences and Grayling would have liked 'to do away with all automatic release' (Hansard, HC 24.2.12) but could not do so because of the pressure on prison places. In the face of mounting criticism that the prisons were in a state of crisis, he vigorously denied that but admitted that 'a few more prisoners will have to share cells'. He claimed that nobody had been able to give him a clear answer when he asked 'who are the people who are currently in our prisons whom you don't want to be there?' Whilst almost everyone could point to one or another individual who met their criteria, he argued, 'I have not found thousands of people whom one should just release.' Echoing Michael Howard and others he claimed that 'almost everyone in prison has committed dozens of crimes before, maybe had lots of community sentences before, been through the courts many times and eventually someone says enough is enough send them to prison.' In his judgement, he said, in the by now well-rehearsed argument of successive Ministers, a better way of reducing the prison population 'is by preventing people coming back to prison' – reducing reoffending through the so-called rehabilitation revolution. Never mind that that was never likely to happen: if only because the prison and probation services could not deliver rehabilitation in the circumstances in which they found themselves as a result of increasing cuts to the budget which made it difficult to deliver the basics. That alone made the argument the bane of the lives of Directors of Prisons and Probation. But of course, there are much deeper reasons why such a policy could not succeed, being based on a false premise that there is a finite number of criminal individuals who could be treated and cured or otherwise turned away from their wicked ways. Grayling's Criminal Justice and Courts Bill 2014 was set to make matters worse by creating new mandatory minimum sentences, which had been such a *bête noir* for Clarke, for the possession of offensive weapons and introduced a new parole test of public protection, which undermined Clarke's hopes for changing the burden of proof in IPP cases. It was, said the Opposition, another *Christmas Tree Bill* filled with goodies at Cameron's request to win the election. It was thought it would require a further 1,000 new prison places.

The consequences which flowed from *Transforming Rehabilitation* for a long-beleaguered probation service brought morale to an all-time low. We have set out in detail in previous chapters the history of changes that had been made to probation. It began with Michael Howard's removal of professional training but went on through a forced marriage with the prison service under Blunkett, and threats of privatisation to persuade Probation Boards to become Trusts under Straw, and then Clarke and Blunt looked to put interventions out to tender whilst keeping offender management and supervision in the public sector. These developments set the scene for Grayling's *Transforming Rehabilitation* agenda, quickly known to all in the field by its initials, TR. But Grayling's TR introduced privatisation in what might be seen as the worst possible way – organised around the slippery concept of risk. He proposed a split between the NPS which would be in charge of MAPPA and other high-risk offenders on the one hand and 21 CRCs which were to be responsible for supervising lower-risk cases in their areas, on the other. The CRCs would be paid for the services they provided, partly by a down payment upfront and a payment by results element at the end. These changes were actually made possible through John Reid's OMA 2007. Although Straw and Hanson had offered reassurances to Parliament that the 2007 Act would not be used as a route to privatisation, this was not written into the Bill, as Straw admitted in our interview, so there was no need for further legislation. The arbitrary split between public and private sectors on the basis of risk was hotly contested at the time, not least because risk is not a static concept. But concern was also expressed at the prohibition of prize-winning probation trusts from competing for contracts; at pressing ahead without proper piloting and evaluation; the lack of clarity over contracts and payments, and at the undermining of local relationships and existing voluntary arrangements.

Grayling had noted that there were some 50,000 short sentence prisoners who were released every year 'with literally no support, no guidance and no one knew where they were going' and that 60% of them re-offended. He was determined to do something about that – albeit it in a totally untested way because Cameron had become impatient with Clarke's evidence-based approach. It had profound consequences for probation. His Offender Rehabilitation Act (ORA) 2014 imposed a mandatory 12 months post-release supervision for all offenders. It was pointed out that a similar provision had been proposed under New Labour's sentence of *custody-plus*, but had never been implemented because of the cost – £194 million at 2004 prices – which illustrates the sizeable gamble of Grayling's strategy of 'more for less.' However, it has to be said that this part of the TR package was widely welcomed, including by some of our judges, apparently without recognition that it also introduced the possibility of recall to prison for breaches of conditions and adding further to the prison population.

As Andrew Selous told us, under the TR agenda, the 'engine was turning over at quite a high rate of revs with all sorts of deadlines' met at considerable cost. As contracts were let for rehabilitation and supervisory services, in 21 geographical contract areas that had been planned within the MoJ, a lot of the Department's resources went 'into running the competition.' Peter Dawson described the competition, in which he had been involved, as a 'miserable, dismal process'. The 35 recently created Probation Trusts were swept away and the staff working within them were assigned either to the NPS or to whatever CRC was awarded the contract for the former Trust area. Glenys Stacey, HM Chief Inspector of Probation, later noted in her annual report (HMIP, 2017) that the 'teething problems' were 'largely resolved. More deep-rooted problems now prevail.' The system had been developed, she said, 'quickly and within costs and time scales set by Ministers but its implementation left difficult issues to manage.' A major problem was that the numbers on community sentences had been going down since well before the introduction of TR and continued thereafter. Caseloads for CRCs declined whilst those for the NPS, dealing with higher risk offenders, and a heavy burden of making reports to courts, increased. Michael Spurr had warned the Secretary of State of the potential consequences of this for the contracting process but Grayling continued, with the belief that the market should work this out for itself. The problems were further exacerbated by a change in the mix of cases from the courts – with fewer offenders sentenced to designated offending behaviour programmes (OBPs) and many more to the new Rehabilitation Activity Requirements (RARs) attached to community orders. CRCs received lower payments for RAR cases than they did for OBPs because, under the former, they were expected to develop new initiatives which, if successful, would enable them to earn more from the payment by results element of the contract. The end result of rolling out this programme of Byzantine complexity without piloting was disastrous. CRCs received much less money up front than the government had expected; so they had less to invest in activities to reduce reoffending. Although this resulted in windfall savings for the MoJ, this was a false economy because it meant that the CRCs could not deliver a decent service and eventually their viability was undermined. It was always going to be difficult to get the voluntary sector involved with the CRCs because they would not have the upfront money to work on a payment by results basis. Although Grayling would have liked to believe that TR had produced measurable reductions in reoffending, the reality is that it is impossible to say with any certainty what the effects were on re-offending, or if there were any apparent changes in offending rates, then of attributing them to any particular cause. Among many other factors, there had at this time been changes in police practice, driven by their own budget reductions, which would be likely to have changed the chances of some crimes being reported or detected and brought to justice.

LCJ Thomas thought Grayling's privatisation of parts of the probation service 'had been a disaster' and he had real concerns about the blanket provision of supervision for short-sentence prisoners. We discuss the views of the Lord Chief Justices we interviewed on this, and other matters in Chapter 6. Grayling, however, had few regrets and no apologies. It was not his decision, which so angered the judges, to 'cut their pensions' or to slash 'legal aid' which infuriated solicitors and barristers – that was where Clarke had intended the cuts to fall. Indeed, in our interview, he argued the case that although he had to take the flak, most of it would more properly be aimed elsewhere. He told us that he was simply trying to live within the budget that Osborne and Ken Clarke had bequeathed. As he put it to us, he did not have to 'impose' benchmarking on the prison service because that was planned by 'prison governors' and was greeted as a 'victory' by the POA. No, he didn't constructively dismiss Nick Hardwick – 'he just reached the end of his term and I didn't reappoint him'. What became known as the books ban, he claimed, 'was a complete fabrication' by the prison reform lobby and the Press. What actually happened, he told us, was that he and Wright requested a review intended to standardise Incentives and Earnt Privileges (IEPs) across the prison estate, so that prisoners could no longer complain that what they were allowed in one prison was disallowed in another. It was left to 'prison governors' to standardise the rules. There had always been rules about the number of parcels prisoners could receive. When books were sent in, they came in parcels, and when someone tried to exceed the parcel limit, which just happened to contain a book, the 'Howard League and others' turned it into a ban on books, but 'no Minister had ever had a conversation about sending books into prison'. It is conceivable that the story about a book ban came about in the way he described, although Richard Tilt, who had written to Grayling to complain about the matter but never received a reply, certainly contested it. Grayling's review of IEPs was clearly linked to what he told Parliament was 'a tougher and more Spartan regime' (Hansard, HC 16.6.14) – a change from 'decent but austere' in the political lexicon. He struggled to recall using that language when we taxed him with it, but he did concede that 'I did not want, for practical or political purposes, prison to be seen as a comfortable environment … prison should not be a place that people want to go back to.'

Although he was proud of the fact that he was 'actually the person who had closed the most prisons', Michael Spurr told us that Grayling closed some of the better small prisons and replaced them with cheap monstrosities. Grayling told us that he was mostly opposed to the idea of selling off city-centre prisons not just because they were in the place where they are needed, but because 'the cost of building a new place is little different from the amount you get from selling the land.' The North Liverpool Community Court, presided over by Judge David Fletcher and which sought to bring local community services together in the same building as both Magistrates and District Courts, was closed on Grayling's watch but we were unable to explore this in our interview.

After the general election of 2015, Cameron had more cabinet posts to fill and needed to find a space to bring back Michael Gove, and it was Grayling who had had a bad Press throughout his time in the Justice Department, who had to make way.

Part two: The Directors of Prisons and Probation

Roger Hill

Roger Hill had become Director of Offender Management (DOM) for the South East in 2009 when NOMS underwent a reorganisation which did away with his former post as the National Director of Probation and replaced Regional Offender Managers (ROMS) with new functional Directors. In 2011, in a further iteration of NOMS, he reluctantly decided not to apply for the newly created position of Director of Probation Contracted Services because of potential adverse consequences for his pension and he retired. We said a good deal about his public career in the previous chapter and he had told us that the day he retired had been 'one of the saddest days' of his life. However, he was immediately offered a post with Sodexo Justice Services, the largest private-sector provider of probation services, running six of the 21 CRCs. He thus bridged the changeover from New Labour to the Coalition government and, indeed, was still working part-time with Sodexo when we interviewed him.

We can now turn to his views on developments under the coalition, first from his position as a National Director and then from the private sector. Roger Hill told us that, by 2010, there was increasing recognition, both under New Labour and the Coalition, that the probation service was essentially local and that centralisation had not worked well. There was some support for that view from the All-Party Justice Unions group which represented staff views on NOMS, which challenged the imposition of more bureaucracy into essentially professional services. Debates in the House of Lords showed strong support for probation as a local service. Hill had not been averse to private sector involvement in probation but thought that artificial divisions between public and private domains were not helpful. In the light of his experiences at Sodexo – contracted to provide supervision and intervention services to medium- and low-risk offenders on a payment by results basis – he could see many ways in which the private sector could do what the public sector could not, if only they were given the opportunity. But the split whereby NPS retained operation of offender management, court services and high-risk provision, left CRCs 'unable to form relationships with the courts' which would be central if you wanted to encourage them to use CRC interventions. 'The way to do it' would have been 'to have allowed CRCs to go to court, talk about their innovations … their alternatives to custody'. That, he thought, would have been a better way to reduce the number of short sentences, which at the time of our interview, both David Gauke and Rory Stewart were committed to doing.

Hill laid the blame for the final format of the contracts with the CRCs as much 'at the door of senior civil servants', including 'senior operational people' rather than entirely on Grayling himself. 'I don't think there's any way in the world a Minister could have dreamt up something so complex, convoluted, and difficult'. True there was a strong political component in the form of 'payment by results' but the contracts themselves were 'process heavy' and actually limited the 'scope for innovation.' In his experience, they bore all the hallmarks of 'operational probation managers'. A better balance was needed, he thought, between the ambition of Ministers and the overcomplication of civil servants. But Hill listed many reasons for the failure of the CRCs being able to deliver. One was the more or less complete failure of the MoJ to deliver IT systems that enabled the various parts of the system to communicate with each other. Another was that the MoJ often failed to deliver its side of the contract so that cases arrived without assessment, late or sometimes not at all, yet nevertheless wanted to micromanage the delivery of the contract by CRCs through contract management teams. Nor was the MoJ able to find a way of dealing with the changing pattern of cases coming from the courts as the number of community sentences declined. The contracts were also so short-term that there was insufficient time for things to bed down before they were evaluated.

The way the contracts were drawn up was very problematic for the CRCs because the Inspectorate, under Glenys Stacey, insisted on measuring them 'against a set of expectations … which we were not contracted to deliver', and yet objected to innovations that had been 'a very deliberate part of the bid'. He looked back, nostalgically, to a time when he was a Chief Officer and the Probation Inspectorate, then under Rod Morgan, had been constructively helpful to the service. He believed that 'the government wanted outcome-based contracts' which would be 'the right way to drive innovation'. But he recognised that payment by results is problematic in that it assumes that you are actually 'able to measure things somehow'. In fact, he knew well enough that there are not only problems in measuring reoffending but it is extraordinarily 'difficult to attribute cause and effect or why reoffending has increased or decreased'. There *were* outputs from supervision that could be easily measured, for example, getting someone into employment or decent housing, but these were not taken into account.

Phil Wheatley

As we reported in Chapter 3, Phil Wheatley did not leave NOMS happily. Although his actual retirement officially took effect from 30 June 2010, he stood aside from the beginning of the month to give his successor Michael Spurr, with whom he had worked closely over the last several years, a free hand. He nevertheless remained keenly interested in the fate of both prisons and probation. As things were, Wheatley believed that there was precious little his successor could have done to avert the current crisis in our prisons.

Like Roger Hill, Phil Wheatley wanted to use the option of competition in probation, as he had in prisons, not *en masse* but to encourage efficiencies within the service. Like Hill, he recognised the need to keep the services intact, not split management from interventions, and wanted to put 'a couple of the smaller probation services that were under performing' out for tender. He hadn't been able to do this but had made incremental improvements which were lost, 'when Chris Grayling decided he wanted to totally reshape the probation service in a way that's destroyed its cohesion'.

Wheatley told us that when Clarke had 'committed to the much tighter budget', he had hoped to mitigate the consequences somewhat by reducing the prison population, but he was 'stopped by David Cameron from doing it. Sacked'. According to Wheatley, by the time that austerity was kicking in, NOMS had already responded to cuts in the last years of New Labour by making changes to the organisational structure and by starting a process of 'benchmarking' staffing in poorly performing prisons against those in better performing prisons. As a result, it was already running 'reasonably efficiently … most of the savings that were possible … had already been made. If you were efficient being hit by a 25% cut was very painful' and, of course, 'nobody at the centre of Government actually knew what was efficient'. Clarke's second line of defence, the 'rolling programme of market testing was never going to deliver the savings to live within the money' that was available. In any case, Grayling cancelled that programme.

In this situation, Wheatley's successor, Michael Spurr, was left with no choice: 'you can only spend what money parliament votes for you … the only way he could live within that… was to lose lots of staff, very quickly'. The

POA 'cheerfully' signed up to the latest round of benchmarking because 'they got rid of privatisation and got loads of pay out for their most experienced members'. However, 'the new terms and conditions', which were also part of the agreement to replace those 'expensive, experienced' officers who were lost, were so poor that it was a struggle even to meet the lower staffing levels. Given the

> 'complexity of a prison officer's job, if you replace the people who can do that quality work with people who can't do it, you'll have a problem'.

The result was a very unstable situation where prisoners stepped into the 'vacuum' left when there were fewer experienced staff on the wings.

Wheatley noted that 'control and order deteriorated in nearly all local prisons and there were other riots, including a serious incident at HMP Bedford'. The main problem was not a question of public or private but 'implementing cost savings which meant having fewer staff, a reduction in the proportion of more expensive experienced officers, and a radical thinning out of management and supervisory grades'. The government 'wanted to buy cheap prisons', giving no credit for delivery over 'very basic contract specifications' and it was notable that 'older, well-funded contracts at Altcourse, Parc and Dovegate, continued to operate reasonably well. Freshly let or refreshed cheap contracts like Birmingham and Doncaster got into difficulties'.

Towards the end of his time, according to Wheatley, Grayling, rushed through 'some privatisation' to ensure he looked like a 'proper Conservative' prior to the election. Contracting out all prison maintenance and ancillary services for an estate then comprising 117 prisons, an Immigration Removal Centre and three Secure Training Centres, some purpose-built in bygone eras others repurposed from military uses, housing men, women and children in high-, medium- and low-security conditions was, to say the least, a 'complicated' matter. It required 'skilled procurement people', but these had already been lost to austerity cuts. Speed and lack of expertise resulted in contracts that were 'too tight so the people you've contracted to are in danger of going bust'. The sensible option would have been, 'a slower process, probably a region at a time, not a great big national scheme'.

Michael Spurr

Michael Spurr became Chief Executive of NOMS in June 2010, having until then been its Chief Operating Officer. It would be hard to imagine a more difficult moment to take command. It was just a month after the general election, austerity was in the air and, as he told us, Phil Wheatley 'was being forced out, effectively.' Spurr thought twice about throwing his hat into the ring, knowing that the Permanent Secretary, Suma Chakrabarti, wanted a non-operational leader to run things differently but also wanting 'to make sure the organisation was in as good a place as possible'. He told us he was totally committed to the 'decency agenda' which had been 'driven by Martin Narey's vision' and 'enacted by Phil Wheatley's utter clarity about what was required'. Like both his predecessors, he believed 'we were beginning to tackle long-standing problems in local prisons, the systemic brutality … and the poor conditions'. So, after due consideration, he applied and 'in the end they decided I was the safer pair of hands'.

He had told us that, by then the newly united NOMS had already made savings with '40 million pounds taken out of duplication'. The agency had gradually been streamlined to the then 'Government's preferred … regionalised model … with directors of offender management (DOMs) … responsible for prisons and probation in each region'. Probation boards had been pushed towards gaining Trust status, although with fewer mergers than Spurr would have liked. Prisons, apart from the functionally managed estate, were also similarly placed under Directors of Offender Management. The regions (North East, Yorkshire and Humber, North West, West Midlands, East Midlands, East of England, South East, South West and London) were all mapped on to 'the nine government regions plus Wales' and it all worked 'in a single system.' Although the model attracted 'a lot of dislike across the sector', Spurr believed it was the right approach.

However, the model had little chance to take root, because 'the moment the Coalition Government came in … they abolished government officers for the regions … on the basis we don't need this extra layer' – thus eliminating DOMS. Spurr described this as a 'classical political divide' between political regimes but conceded that one just had 'to live with those sorts of things'. Ken Clarke's agenda had 'two main … objectives … we will tackle the deficit … and would put public services to the market'. The Treasury immediately curtailed 'capital expenditure' on prison building, and so a replacement for Liverpool prison was cancelled. As a 'non-protected department', Clarke took the 'expected reduction … about 23%' and that was passed on to prisons and probation which accounted for well over half the Ministry budget. This was huge, Spurr told us, 'because … we, unlike most departments … actually do deliver direct services. My budget was about £4billion and we took a reduction of £893 million'. Clarke 'didn't discuss' the cuts but did 'plan … to reduce the prison population' in the hope of balancing the books. Spurr believed that Straw 'would have fought much harder against' the cuts, because 'he didn't believe you could reduce the prison population'. The cuts had to be made over the five years 2010–2015 and initially, Spurr told us, he was able to make manageable savings whilst maintaining performance. Even so, this involved reducing headquarters costs 'primarily by taking out those regional layers. I took £96 million out' by making 'a 42% reduction in head count.' Central management bore the brunt of savings – '37% costs above establishment or probation area level. Headquarters functions were reduced and combined, paring down frontline support. Some sensible savings' were taken out of the probation trust programme, making 'them focus on how they were deploying their resources better'. Area management teams were stripped back to 'basic coverage … one manager for a larger area with about three people supporting them … with similar oversight of probation trusts' leading to an inevitable loss of 'grip'. This was all classed as 'admin', despite their role in keeping operations going. Oversight and support for frontline work was significantly reduced.

However, the main way in which Clarke thought costs could be driven down 'was through competition' with Spurr 'managing the nine prisons competition process' and 'a separate bid team … putting the public sector bid together'. Spurr asked Clarke how far he intended to go down his preferred route of privatisation because he needed 'to plan a strategy' and know whether Clarke had any red lines. He was particularly seeking reassurance around the high-security estate because he thought that privatising high-security prisons would be 'too risky'. But he also strongly argued for a large, strong and viable public service provision 'because if things go wrong, you need an ability to step in'. Clarke's response 'was that there was such a small proportion of the estate that had been privatised, that we didn't need to get into that conversation at this point. Now, that made it very hard in planning terms.'

In the event, the only major upset was the loss of Birmingham to G4S, who were 'desperate to win', following the loss of two big government contracts and recent reputational problems, although Spurr conceded they submitted 'the better bid at the time.' The prison service bid team wanted to keep it in the public sector and the 'the competition drives you to be as tight as possible. That's … what it's designed to do. And at this point it was designed to reduce cost. It wasn't designed to improve quality' although 'nobody wanted it not to be safe.' Spurr expressed his concerns to Clarke having noticed that 'some of the providers for the nine prisons … were proposing staffing levels and ratios we weren't delivering anywhere. … If everything ran smoothly, every day, then you might just about get away with it.' But things don't always run smoothly. Clarke told him not to 'second guess the private sector' but nevertheless allowed him to take matters up with the companies concerned. In the process, he told us, 'we exposed significant issues. The thing about Ken Clarke was he would have taken on any advice that came out. As it happened, we never got there, because other things intervened, including his removal from office.' What had become clear was that bids, including in-house bids, with staff complements calculated on a best-case scenario, as Phil Wheatley had told us, was an over-simplification of prison life which left prisons very vulnerable if anything went wrong.

Spurr told us that Clarke 'wanted a mixed market model' for probation and after a period of consultation, they agreed on a 'workable model' which involved 'a further reduction in the number of probation trusts' and a requirement for them 'to outsource some of their services'. A stronger 'threat' of greater privatisation was applied to encourage Trust cooperation. Spurr was a convert to the value of a mixed market. Whilst he thought Clarke was 'overly positive about the private sector' as well as a fiscal hawk, Spurr welcomed his pragmatic approach which left him, as Chief Executive, in charge of the commissioning, provision and management of offender services – somewhat comparable with the situation in the NHS.

On operational matters, Spurr found Clarke to be 'a fantastic Secretary of State to work for … who wasn't swayed by the media.' So when Spurr had to apologise because 'we'd had the first Cat A escape in about fifteen years … he was measured and sensible' and said 'what are you apologising for? These things happen.' Clarke was also 'more than happy to hear' and to respect opinions different from his own in a joint attempt to 'work through policy … and that's all you can ask for as an official.' Both Clarke and Blunt were keen on 'getting people into more productive work with more activity in prisons, and then into employment afterwards,' engaging private business in the process. Both also 'believed in the potential for payments by results' and several pilots were set up as envisaged in the rehabilitation revolution laid out in the Green Paper (Cm 7972) *Breaking the Cycle*. Two pilots were in resettlement prisons, and Spurr recalled them as 'proving you can't do it in the public sector … Leeds … working … with social providers … was really good … but it wasn't really fundable … on the basis of reducing reoffending'. Further pilots, including two in Manchester and London, 'with local authorities and other agencies,' potentially sharing 'any benefit that came from trying to reduce reoffending', were based on the justice reinvestment model. However, whereas the Green Paper and Ken Clarke had strongly advocated the need for 'piloting', this was deemed unnecessary by No10: Cameron wanted it delivering now, 'during this Parliament'.

The Green Paper had also looked to simplify the sentencing framework, and Spurr obviously regretted that Clarke was unable to get his proposed reforms, which could have delivered a reduction in the prison population, past the Prime Minister. But he was pleased that Clarke had fought for 'and won the argument about abolishing IPPs, which, actually, was absolutely driven by him'. Although Blunt was very much in agreement with Clarke on policy, Spurr regarded him as 'ineffectual' as a Junior Minister and 'not politically savvy'. His desire to get the arts into prisons and his 'admirable' view that 'we're not going to be hounded by *The Sun*' put him so publicly at odds with the Press that he was unable to do what Junior Ministers do best, 'deliver things … quietly without anybody noticing it'. His 'very unhelpful and unnecessary' discussion of 'rape cases in Parliament' and the proposed 50% discount in relation to 'guilty pleas' contributed, in Spurr's view, 'to Ken Clarke's demise.'

'Mr Grayling came in … and I remember going to this meeting and slightly being taken back' at his 'three point agenda from Mr Cameron: one, keep the judges onside; two, toughen up prisons; three, deliver payment by results by the end of the Parliament for probation'. Although Grayling had suggested to us he was a 'hands-off' minister where operational matters were concerned, Spurr saw things differently. In terms of TR, Spurr told us that Grayling had his 'hands all over it'. Spurr was told, rather than consulted, on who was going to head up 'the departmental priority' of 'delivering payment by results to the probation service'. Grayling's choice of Senior Responsible Owner (SRO) for the programme, was Antonia Romeo, who was a senior civil servant within the MoJ but not part of the NOMS agency. Spurr recognised this as a 'classic problem of democracy' with which one had to live: as a civil servant his job was to follow orders but it was also his job as a civil servant to give honest advice and 'you'd hope people would … be prepared to, actually, learn a bit' before they acted. Spurr's position, as Head of NOMS, was technically that of 'Senior Business Owner', giving him the right to say 'yes or no we can or can't implement this' but no involvement in 'developing the contracts'. However, he did manage to exert some influence by transferring 'trusted … staff' across to help.

Grayling 'saw himself as a commercial person' and got involved in details about 'performance targets where he wanted 90 per cent achievement' despite Spurr pointing out that some of the assumptions underlying the contracts were wrong. Grayling's decision, however, was that 'the market' could 'look at the data' and work this out for themselves. Equally, the private sector providers were not aware of how efficient the public sector probation now was and assumed there were greater savings to be made. Both these factors were apparent in the failure of TR. Other unwelcome interference came from Paul Kirby, 'a special adviser to David Cameron' and Head of the Policy Unit at No 10. He apparently believed that one could effectively do away with probation as it then existed. Instead, he would have 'advice to court given to the court service, supervision of those on license post-release given to the police, and community interventions given to the private or public sector'. Spurr successfully argued against that, his view being 'much like it was on prisons … if we're going to marketise any of this, you need a strong public sector provision in case it doesn't work, and to maintain expertise'. On this, he had the support of Grayling 'who was worried about the political risk about high risk offenders … which is why we ended up with a national probation service'. 'High risk' in this debate had little to do with statistically reliable risk assessments because sex offenders, for politicians, constitute a very high risk even though comparatively few sex offenders actually re-offend. Given that all sex offenders fall under MAPPA, 'we ended up with the definition of who are the high-risk offenders being, effectively, all MAPPA cases'. Alternative splits between the public and private sectors for probation were possible. The unworkable split on the basis of risk was a populist decision.

According to Spurr, Grayling 'didn't care about overcrowding in prisons' and was content to leave much to his Junior Minister Jeremy Wright. Spurr told us that Wright was a good Minister who provided strong support on day-to-day operational issues during a highly pressured period under Grayling. However, they disagreed on changes to the IEP scheme. Spurr 'strongly believed that IEP is something we should have dealt with operationally' as it had been, more or less without political interference, since Howard's time. 'It did need some tightening and sorting out' but Spurr would have preferred 'to do that' himself. However, Spurr came to believe that Wright was given a very clear brief by Grayling to toughen things up and thus went 'through the whole privilege list himself about what should be on it or not.' This may have served to earn Wright his 'credentials on the Conservative right' but Spurr also thought Wright believed that tightening things up on privileges might 'give one permission to do a whole range of other progressive work on rehabilitation'. Wright certainly reintroduced the notion of 'starting people on basic' rather than standard, a 'tougher entry' which had been tried before and which led to 'some really bad experiences'. This policy disappeared with Grayling's departure and was, in any case, more 'rhetorical' than reality as Wright, more reasonably, had agreed to access to televisions 'which was the big thing' on the introductory two-week basic regime. However, Spurr agreed that the book ban furore 'was completely unfair on Grayling,' and recalled that when he was a governor, he 'didn't allow things to be brought in through visits.' How on earth, he asked, could 'you run an IEP scheme if you just allow people to bring in things through visits?' Spurr described Wright's successor Selous as someone who 'cared an awful lot' but did not have the power to 'really operate at a ministerial level' by confronting the Secretary of State.

Grayling would have been happy to put more prisons 'out to the market' but 'the G4S, Serco electronic monitoring scandal got in the way' and there simply wasn't a market available. Grayling 'wanted to concentrate on probation' so was open to suggestions as to how in prisons there could be a 23% reduction in costs and still maintain industrial relations. Spurr came up with the 'alternative' to 'attempt to take that money out internally, through what became the Prison Unit Cost Programme' another round of 'benchmarking, effectively'. The Treasury and Grayling 'pressed very hard for the outsourcing of other stuff, like facilities management' and Spurr agreed to go along with it, against his 'better judgment.' He had successfully 'stopped' similar proposals under New Labour in 2007. But now his options were limited and he believed that additional benchmarking, based on the 'public sector bid for Birmingham,' was 'the least worst option' and the 'only way of achieving the savings within the timescale'.

There was also to be a 'programme of twenty prison closures.' Two of New Labour's privately financed prisons, Thameside and Oakwood, were coming on stream providing 3,000 new places. These would allow smaller, 'good quality' but very expensive prisons like Kingston, which housed 350 prisoners at £38,000 a head compared to Oakwood's £12,000 per place, to be removed from the system. However, the new 'larger prisons' were much 'harder to run'. Making compromises like this, but with the agreement of the POA and the PGA, they could take another '£300 million' out of the system. Half of that was on staffing, and half of it was on closing the smaller prisons.

'I genuinely believed at the time that there was the potential for it. ... I remember having this conversation during the day when Grayling came to see me that we'd see a dip in performance [but then] we would adjust to be able to bring performance up'.

The reality was that benchmarking, outsourcing and prison closures could not deliver 'more for less'.

Spurr described benchmarking as a three-stage consultation process with governors who were allowed 'to make decisions about their prisons' and there were some 'eleven different benchmarks' for staffing. However, some establishments were so worried about the threat of privatisation, that they pre-empted the process and stripped staffing levels to below the proposed levels. Some 'governors' went 'too hard' and 'too fast'. In hindsight, Spurr told us, 'my failure was not holding it tight enough at the centre'. And of course, many staff 'were fed up with the system' and 'lots of people wanted to go'. The problem was, 'not the people going under the VEDS, it was loads of people going in addition to VEDS'. 'What we hadn't anticipated was the numbers of people going because they didn't like it'. This meant that the service 'never operated at benchmark staffing levels' but instead we were '2,000 below'. 'The areas where that didn't happen are, interestingly, the places where we've had the least problems'. Grip was retained in the centrally managed high security and female estate but elsewhere, things were done at a 'regional level' where 'I didn't have the capacity to hold all of it tight'. Spurr's intention was to stop the 'process of reducing cost' through staffing 'if it was clearly getting to a point where, actually, we couldn't manage that'. His first sight of the effect of 'psychoactive drugs' and the 'changing behaviour in prisoners' was 'at Ranby in 2014'. However, because of the time lag between events and their appearance in the statistics the '2014 data ... were not looking too bad'. It wasn't until 2015 that things really showed up, but by the time he was able to put on the brakes and then get the money to reverse the process things 'had gone too far'. It was a problem destined to continue as the churn of Ministers under the next government became ever more frequent, with predictable consequences for both efficiency and effectiveness.

References

Clarke, K. (2016) *Kind of Blue: A Political Memoir*, London: Macmillan.
HMCIP (2011) *HM Chief Inspector of Prisons for England and Wales*, Annual Report 2010–11, London: The Stationary Office.
HMCIP (2016) *HM Chief Inspector of Prisons for England and Wales*, Annual Report 2014–15, London, The Stationary Office.
HMIP (2017) *Her Majesty's Inspectorate of Probation for England and Wales*, Annual Report 2017.
Justice Committee (2015) *Prisons: Planning and Policies Ninth Report, 2014–15*, House of Commons.
Laws, D. (2016) *Coalition: The Inside Story of the Conservative-Liberal Democrat Coalition Government*, London: Biteback Publishing.

5

THE CONSERVATIVE GOVERNMENT 2015–2019

Introduction

In May 2015 the Tories surprisingly won an overall majority but then had the highest rate of churn of any of the governments covered in this book with four Ministers occupying the role of Secretary of State for Justice and Lord Chancellor – Michael Gove, Liz Truss, David Lidington and David Gauke – in just four and half years. In 2016 David Cameron called for an in-out referendum on Europe, backing remain, but lost and resigned. He was replaced by Theresa May and the rest of the Parliament was dominated by Brexit. When Theresa May called a snap election her hopes of an increased majority did not materialise, and her resignation led to a leadership election and the assumption to the Premiership of Boris Johnson prompting the resignations of several of the politicians who have figured in our story.

Three of the four Lord Chancellors were non-lawyers following in the footsteps of Chris Grayling, the first Lord Chancellor with no legal training or expertise. It was a period in which there was the beginning of a recognition of the damage done to prisons and some attempt to repair it, but it was too little, too late and some initiatives made matters worse. What had started out under Ken Clarke as agency status for prisons and then for the National Offender Management Service (NOMS) was systematically reversed under Liz Truss for what became HM Prison and Probation Service (HMPPS) with many important operational functions returned to the Ministry of Justice (MoJ). It was left to David Lidington to steady the ship. There had been a sense in which Ministers initially steered clear of probation because Grayling had 'done that' although eventually, it became apparent that the situation in probation was untenable. David Gauke, who had at one time practised as a solicitor, recognised the need to control the size of the prison population although his proposals

DOI: 10.4324/9781003201748-6

targeted the group that would make the least difference – short sentence prisoners who account for only a small part of the daily average population. He also looked towards reforming the situation in regard to Community Rehabilitation Companies (CRCs) (Table 5.1).

Part one: The Politicians

Michael Gove (May 2015–July 2016)

Like many of his predecessors, Michael Gove had not expected to become Minister of Justice. Before the election of May 2015 he had been Chief Whip and before that Secretary of State for Education where he had enjoyed a ring-fenced budget and controversially wrought major changes to the education system. His rapid extension of New Labour's self-governing academies, encouragement of Swedish-style free schools and his changes to the examination system and the National Curriculum, from which academies were exempt, had all incurred the wrath of one or another section of the educational establishment as well as Opposition politicians. After the Trojan Horse scandal, involving alleged attempts to develop an Islamic ethos in some schools, Cameron took him out of the frontline. Grayling told us that Cameron 'felt badly about side-lining his friend' and after the election brought Gove back into the Cabinet as Justice Secretary. In just a few years the vacillating Cameron had moved from wanting 'a liberal Justice Minister' (Clarke), whose liberalism 'he didn't want anybody to see'; to appointing another (Grayling) to 'be tough on law and order' and to 'get rid of the narrative around soft justice'; to appointing Michael Gove with a brief to confirm Cameron's new-found wish to be seen as a reformer.

We interviewed Michael Gove at his office in DEFRA on 21 August 2018 (in the presence of his SpAd who had been with him at Education). He told us that Cameron had three things in mind when he was appointed: first, that his 'experience of public sector delivery problems … as Education Secretary' would be useful at the MoJ; second, he wanted 'a better relationship with the judiciary'; and third, he wanted someone to 'find a way through the challenges of replacing the European Convention on Human Rights with a British Bill of Rights.' However, once in office he had to 'deal with concerns over legal aid and the transformation of the court estate, but the biggest single issue was the prison system.' Within days of his appointment, he invited Martin Narey to give advice on how he might reduce the prison population – an invitation which Narey readily accepted. Somewhat to the chagrin of his predecessor, Gove managed to persuade Osborne to put an additional £500 million into the MoJ budget, which went up from £16.2 billion to £16.7 billion.

A few months after Gove's appointment, Cameron gave a major speech on prison reform at the Policy Exchange about which Nick Hardwick, the outgoing Chief Inspector, told us:

TABLE 5.1 Conservative Ministers, Directors of Service(s), Legislation, Department and Service Reorganisation 2015–2019

Year/ month (general election in bold)	Justice Secretary & Lord Chancellor	Key prisons and probation Legislation	Prisons & Probation Minister	Director of Her Majesty's Prison Service (HMPS)	Director of National Probation Service (NPS)	CEO of National Offender Management Service (NOMS) agency/ Her Majesty's Prison and Probation Service (HMPPS) agency	Department & Service Reorganisation
2015 May	Michael Gove		Andrew Selous	N/A	N/A	Michael Spurr	New reform prison model fitting academy school/ NHS trust model for prisons to be run as autonomous entities.
2016 May	Liz Truss	**Prisons and Courts Bill** intended to place four purposes of prison in statute to hold the Secretary of State accountable to Parliament & to remove requirement for Secretary of State to report to Parliament on operational matters; Secretary of State in turn to directly hold prison governors to account.	Sam Gyimah			continued	**1st HMPPS agency** replaces NOMS and is embedded in the Ministry of Justice (MoJ) in line with the new functional model of government, eroding operational autonomy; commissioning and other agency functions (future policy direction, setting standards & scrutinizing performance) gradually removed from the agency & placed in the MoJ; some budgets devolved to governors now empowered *not* autonomous, academy model lost (see Prison Safety and Reform White Paper 2016).
2017 Jun	David Lidington	**Prison and Courts Bill** falls in part owing to negotiations over resource.	Rory Stewart				
2018 Jan	David Gauke						
2019 Apr				Phil Copple	Amy Rees	Jo Farrar	**2nd HMPPS agency** negotiated by Michael Spurr; separate Director Generals of services reinstated; more operational functions removed from the agency and placed in the MoJ (HR & finance transactional services, procurement services & transactions, IT, estates capacity function & services); operational policy, commissioning and interventions returned to the agency.
2019 May	Robert Buckland						Unified Probation Service to manage all probation services by 2021.

'if you compare it with the inspectorate report, if he was a student he'd be done for plagiarism. I think the inspectorate can claim some credit for eventually getting additional resources for the changes that happened.'

One element of Cameron's reform programme involved 'plans to give governors complete control over the way they run their prisons' which had obviously been worked through with his new Justice Secretary. When we asked how this came about Gove, glancing at his SpAd, told us 'I think we converted him. David was looking for things that would confirm his agenda as a domestic reformer.' In fact, according to one of our contacts, Gove had actually written the speech.

More than most Justice Ministers or Home Secretaries, and second only to Grayling whose policies had such an impact on both prisons and probation, Gove brought with him a belief that the policies he had adopted in his previous role could be adapted and applied to prisons. He had given comparatively little thought about either prisons or probation before his appointment although he had visited HMP Coldingley, which was in his constituency, and Wormwood Scrubs, to try 'to understand the context of prison education.' He was shocked 'by the tolerance of drug use … and the disgusting conditions' at the Scrubs. He spent time listening to prison officers, for whom he developed 'enormous respect', although he thought that the Prison Officers Association (POA) poorly represented their views. He also became 'intrigued by the backgrounds' of the prisoners to whose stories he listened intently, and he was inspired by the documentary about Jimmy Boyle at the Barlinnie Special Unit. He came to believe that such backgrounds could be overcome if staff had the freedom to give prisoners more responsibility. He recognised that not all prisons could be run like therapeutic communities but he also believed that prisons should not just be 'human warehouses'. He thought that the best way to achieve 'effective rehabilitation' was through 'specialist prisons … which focused on the needs of particular sets of offenders' with more autonomous governors able to 'shape the appropriate policies' for their prisoners. The model he had in mind 'was similar to the model we had in academy schools.' He also thought it would be easier to do this in criminal justice where there was 'not so much division between parties on the issues … and the public aren't as concerned … as they are about others' in education or health. He fully realised that 'not everyone is a fan of academies' but he seriously underestimated the problems of applying that model in his piloting of his so-called 'reform prisons'. His ideas certainly excited many within the prison service, but were either impractical or would have taken many years to achieve. As Liz Truss told us Michael had 'good ideas' but he did not 'do details'.

For the first time in many years, there had been no criminal justice bill in the Queen's speech and Gove was the first Minister during the period covered by our research *not* to steer such a bill through Parliament. Throughout his time in office, however, there were ongoing concerns about prison safety as the number of assaults on officers and fellow prisoners as well as incidents of self-harm continued to increase. Immediately upon taking office in a debate in which the opposition challenged him to respond to the prison crisis, the court's crisis and the diminution of access to justice, he replied

> 'I'll be honest with you: although I would not use the word "crisis", there are difficult issues to be addressed in our prison estate and in our courts'.
>
> *(Hansard, HC 28.5.15)*

A month later the opposition itemised a formidable litany of criticisms: the prison violence, the understaffing, the £45 million cost of the redundancy package, the loss-leading contracts with CRCs that resulted in staff cuts in the private sector, the closure of 18 prisons since 2010, the overuse of remands in custody despite Clarke's attempt to reduce them in his Legal Aid, Sentencing and Punishment of Offenders Act (LASPOA) 2012, poor physical and mental health care and the fact that both prison governors and Prison Ministers did not stay long enough in their posts. These problems were the legacy which he inherited and Gove was able to report that £10 million had been found within the NOMS budget to mitigate the problems of violence and tackle staffing problems. A new recruitment process with 'premium pay rates' for hard to recruit areas was introduced, reversing Grayling's insistence on 'standardisation', and was beginning to turn the tide.

When Gove arrived on the scene, he told us that he could see that 'our prison system is working at and above capacity … and that as a result it's very difficult to engage in effective rehabilitation' but he had no immediate plans to find significant ways of reducing the prison population through changes to sentencing policy. Like other Ministers, both before and since, he worked on the basis that if prisoners could be prevented from reoffending then the prison population would begin to come down. On several occasions in Parliament he expressed his support for Grayling's Transforming Rehabilitation (TR) agenda when that was under attack by the Opposition. But whereas Grayling had no interest in reducing the prison population Gove wanted 'to have lots of arrows in our quiver … measures that might not reduce the prison population by much' but which would allow modest reductions in some areas. Gove certainly wanted to reduce the number of women in prison, and to move towards better community facilities in line with the recommendations of the Corston Report. He had discussions with Nick Hardwick, whom he had just appointed as Chairman of the Parole Board, with a view to expediting the release of Imprisonment for Public Protection (IPP) prisoners who remained in prisons well beyond their tariff date. Gove also asked Dominic Raab, briefly one of his Parliamentary Under-Secretaries in the MoJ, to consider ways in which those determinate prisoners who would normally be automatically released at the halfway point in their sentence and who 'demonstrated their commitment to change … could earn their release earlier'. There were also discussions underway about possible reductions in the numbers of persons remanded in custody and returned to custody on recall.

There were several other welcome moves. He arranged for governors to be able to co-commission with the NHS for better mental health facilities in the wake of the Bradley Report. He continued to encourage outside employers to provide work for offenders, both whilst in prison and on release and he commissioned Dame Sally Coates, the doyenne of Academy schools, to undertake a review of prison education (Coates, 2016) arguing that the low-level qualifications encouraged by New Labour had been unrelated to future employment and left too many prisoners with very low levels of literacy. Taken together these may give a fair indication of the trajectory which might have followed had he stayed in office for longer.

But his main concern was to revolutionise the prison system in the way that he had done the education system and he pinned his hopes on identifying and then developing six trailblazing 'reform prisons' in which governors would have control of their own budgets and the autonomy to develop innovative ways of educating and rehabilitating prisoners. Although governors already had some control over their budgets, subject to safeguarding rules, these proposals went much further. The flagship of the reform prisons was to be Wandsworth with a new governor in post who was very committed to the idea. The others were Holme House. Kirklevington Grange, Coldingley, High Down and Ranby. These were to be followed by others, and all nine of the new prisons in the building programme were to be organised on the same basis. Indeed, the Government intended to bring forward legislation to extend these freedoms much further – enabling prisons to be established as independent legal entities with the power to enter into contracts; generate and retain income; and establish their own boards with external expertise. In return for these new freedoms governors were to be made more directly accountable to Ministers, for measured outcomes within their prisons and for the post-release behaviours of prisoners. Unfortunately, some desired outcomes would be difficult or impossible to measure and some – especially post-release behaviours – would never be easily attributed to causes.

One might have wondered why Wandsworth, a large multi-function prison with a chequered history, was chosen as the flagship unless it was simply that if it could be made to work there it could probably work anywhere. It was certainly something that puzzled many of the staff in Wandsworth. The most widely accepted view was that it was chosen because it already had in post a dynamic governor open to innovation and who was up for the challenge, and, as Peter Dawson wryly commented, 'the £1m that came with the deal'. The cost of rolling things out across the prison estate would be substantial. Some of the senior managers found it very liberating. One of them was quoted as saying: 'I remember sitting in Michael Gove's office and him telling us "I want you to be on the media. I want you to do interviews with newspapers. I want you to be on TV. If it all goes a bit wrong I will come and stand beside you and put it right"' (Parmar, 2018). Several prison officers also found it exciting to be part of a 'trail blazing' establishment. Middle managers more often found it chaotic and confusing.

Michael Gove recognised that there would be difficulties about measuring outcomes. His preference was for improved performance by 'prisoners after they leave the prison gate' but he also had in mind 'time spent out of cell, time spent in productive education and so on' which had been in (and sometimes out) of the list of prison Key Performance Indicators for 20 years. He also contemplated a more robust role for the Inspectorate in assessing prison performance. In any event, David Cameron declared in his Policy Exchange speech that this would 'amount to the biggest shake-up in the way our prisons are run since Victorian times.' A White Paper and Prison Reform Bill were clearly on the cards, although Gove first wanted governors to have the opportunity to explore their new freedoms before proceeding to legislation. But it was not to be. Andrew Selous, who continued to serve as Junior Minister under Gove, told us that 'we were going to do the Prison Reform Bill ... there was a big reform programme to get underway ... but obviously we lost half of it after the Referendum'.

We discussed with Michael Gove why the programme had fallen apart. He told us that 'it ran into the sand' because 'Michael Spurr, the head of NOMS, thought that what we were trying to do was arguably naïve' and that he did not wish to take the risks involved in exercising 'the indulgence he felt was there in the reform prison idea.' Gove said that Spurr argued that 'the single most important thing involved in the management of the estate was to ensure that security came first.' Gove was at pains to stress that he had the greatest respect for Spurr as 'a very effective manager, an immensely good and moral man but with a different philosophy.' He told us that the impression he had was that after he left office, Michael Spurr was able to persuade 'the new Secretary of State and subsequent Lord Chancellors that the biggest danger and challenge was violence, in particular violence fuelled by new psychoactive substances'.

But whilst it is easy for Ministers, and sometimes for civil servants, to see problems in terms of the personalities involved, there were powerful structural reasons why such an audacious plan was unworkable. Grayling had already introduced levels of standardisation, both through benchmarking and his review of Incentives and Earned Privileges (IEPs) – both of which Gove had defended in the Commons. To have 'trailblazing' governors blazing different trails could have very far-reaching consequences in an overcrowded system where it was necessary to move prisoners from one prison to another either as part of a sentence plan or because of the need to separate gang members or prevent radicalisation, or simply to find spaces for the next intake of prisoners. It could create both confusion among staff and grievances among prisoners. In a system suffering under ever-growing rates of assaults on staff and prisoners, high levels of self-harm, and the effects of drug abuse it was never really a starter. It was very much the school academy model applied to prisons. But whereas schools were previously organised under a large number of separate local education authorities and could easily become free-standing entities prisons were interdependent parts of a large and complex national system – the surprising thing was that anyone could see how this would work. And it could not. As Peter Dawson told us the rhetoric whereby Cameron declared that 'governors would be given a budget and total discretion over how to spend it' was 'utter nonsense' because 'the government can't simply disapply its own rules or the national agreements with the POA on pay and working practices'. Peter Clarke, whom Gove had appointed as Hardwick's successor as Chief Inspector of Prisons, told us that the now discarded reform prison pilots had left 'a mantra of autonomy and devolved budgets to governors' which led to lack of clarity on the ground.

A more promising initiative of Michael Gove's was to respond to overtures from Judge John Samuels and others about reviving the concept of problem-solving courts. Gove had already visited some examples in the USA and was hugely impressed by what he saw. In December 2015 he announced that he and the Lord Chief Justice (LCJ), John Thomas, had established a working group to advise on the feasibility of possible pilot models to be taken forward in 2016/17 and some six pilot projects were proposed. This commitment was reiterated by David Cameron in his Policy Exchange speech, but in arguing that this would bring 'less severe, but much swifter and more certain punishments' that would be 'a real, meaningful deterrent', he seemingly missed the main point of them – namely to solve problems. However, there were undoubted difficulties to overcome before there could be widespread use of problem-solving courts and we were unable to discover whether any such pilots were established. In the event, Gove did not remain in office long enough to see this through but in his Longford Lecture, delivered in November 2016, he praised the commitment of his successor, Liz Truss, for 'trialling new problem-solving courts' which he hoped would 'play an increasingly important part in our justice system' (Gove, 2016). Although Liz Truss expressed enthusiasm for such courts she seems to have done little about it. When we asked Gove why the idea was not pursued, he told us that 'it was another initiative, subsequent to my departure, which wasn't taken up – whether that was because of small c conservatism, caution, or worries about cost I don't know.'

Although in his Longford Lecture he still espoused the idea of Reform Prisons becoming legal entities, there was much sense in his wanting to reorganise the prison estate so that there were fewer local or 'reception' prisons, which take prisoners on conviction from the courts. He wanted to see more training prisons offering specialist programmes for different groups of offenders, and the majority of 'resettlement' prisons situated in communities to assist prisoners to work towards release. However, making even minor changes to the configuration of the prison estate is problematic without the luxury of substantial excess capacity. He also, belatedly, became convinced of

> 'an inconvenient truth – which I swerved to an extent while in office – that we send too many people to prison … a far higher percentage of our population than similar developed nations' (and for) 'significantly longer sentences. … Rehabilitation will only be successful … if we either spend far more on our prisons or have significantly fewer offenders in them.'

This was one of the strongest statements we had found amongst our politicians on the realities of imprisonment in this country – unfortunately delivered only when out of office. In our interview he told us that 'most frontline politicians would accept the prison population is too high and there needs to be an emphasis on improved rehabilitation.'

Before Gove left office there had been a widely reported refusal by prison officers to enter Wormwood Scrubs on health and safety grounds, and there were five other such walkouts elsewhere. There were also concerns about the frequent deployment of so-called 'riot squads' to deal with incidents and disturbances, as well as abuse at Medway Youth Training Centre, and self-inflicted deaths among young prisoners. On these and other matters, as the referendum campaign got underway, it was often left to Andrew Selous, to answer questions in the House. Selous told us that he focussed on throughcare and worked hard to encourage small charities. He recognised that prisoners like everyone else needed 'somewhere to live, something to do, someone to love' and he continued his interest in rehabilitation after leaving office, including initiating a 10-minute bill to encourage public services to do more than 'pay lip-service' to employing ex-offenders. He was proud that he had managed to squeeze in the commissioning of the review by Michael Farmer (2017) on prisoner family relationships, which was carried out in association with the charity Clinks. He spoke out regularly on the issue of prisoner homelessness.

We asked Michael Gove what could be done about the lack of continuity in policy from Minister to Minister, pointing out that Wandsworth continued as a reform prison only until March 2017, when it reverted to ordinary prison status following the departure of the governor, just four months after Liz Truss published her White Paper on *Prison Safety and Reform* (Cm 9350). He responded by saying 'I don't know that I can fairly mark her homework or judge what progress has been achieved in every area.' He continued: 'my view is, well it's someone else's responsibility now. If I pay too much attention, if I'm too closely involved … I'll want to say please don't do that … You've got to move on.' In regard to Ministerial churn, he could not

> 'see an instant way out of it. It's a perennial problem in politics, but I think it's absolutely better if someone can be in those roles for longer.'

After coming out for Brexit in the referendum, then at first supporting Boris Johnson in the leadership campaign that followed Cameron's resignation, before deciding instead to stand himself, Michael Gove was removed from his office by Theresa May when she became Prime Minister. As Gove himself put it: 'Theresa May felt it would be better after all the upheaval of the referendum and the leadership election if I spent some time in the sin bin.' His time in office had enthused Martin Narey, and Richard Tilt, although by then from a distance having long ago retired, regretted that he was not in office long enough to implement some of his ideas. However, Michael Spurr said he was known as 'a disruptor' who had 'little understanding of the realities of prisons', with others suggesting he had greater regard for his SpAds than his officials. Michael Gove had been in office for just 14 turbulent months.

Liz Truss (July 2016–June 2017)

Elizabeth Truss will probably be remembered not for being the first female Lord Chancellor in its 1,400-year history but for being slow and unconvincing in honouring her constitutional oath to defend the Judiciary. The occasion was the publication on 4 November 2016 by the *Daily Mail* of photographs of Lord Chief Justice Thomas, the Master of the Rolls, Sir Terence Etherton, and Lord Justice Sales above an article by James Slack (later to become an official spokesman for Theresa May) headlined 'ENEMIES OF THE PEOPLE'. The judges had just upheld Gina Miller's contention that the consent of Parliament was necessary to trigger Article 50 to exit the European Union. The *Mail* website had also made reference to Etherton being openly gay, and to Thomas's work with the European Law Institute, as though that were an indication of 'remainer' bias. The *Telegraph* published similar front-page photos albeit their headline 'Judges versus the people' was in lower case. The *Sun* and *Daily Express* were not far behind. All effectively claimed the judgement was political. None of the three Judges concerned could speak out, because of their own constitutional obligations and neither could Lord Neuberger, President of the Supreme Court which would hear the Government's appeal. But it was more than a day after pressure from the Bar Council that Liz Truss issued her statement:

> 'The independence of the judiciary is the foundation upon which our rule of law is built and our judiciary is rightly respected the world over for its independence and impartiality'.

Her statement was widely regarded as a feeble and minimalist defence. Charlie Falconer, a former Lord Chancellor, echoed the Bar Council's complaint that the judiciary could no longer have confidence that their independence would be defended and called for her to be replaced by someone who was brave enough to stand up to the Press. In response, she said

> 'I believe in a free press, where newspapers are free to publish, within the law, their views. It is not the job of the Government or Lord Chancellor to police headlines, and it would be a dark day for democracy if that changed'.

On 24 January 2017 the Supreme Court Judgment on Article 50 was handed down which upheld the earlier High Court judgement and LCJ Thomas assured his colleagues that he would speak out as soon as the Act concerning Article 50 was passed into law. In February 2017 he took her to task when speaking to the House of Lords Constitution Select Committee. He told them that he had to ask for the police to provide protection for Gina Miller and openly criticised the Justice Secretary for not supporting the judges and for saying that she could not criticise the media. We say more about that in Chapter 6.

We interviewed Liz Truss on 13 December 2018 at the Treasury, where she was now Chief Secretary, although our interview was cut slightly short when she was called away for a meeting with Philip Hammond who had replaced George Osborne at the Exchequer. It was clear that Liz Truss believed that New Labour's transfer of prisons and probation from the Home Office to the MoJ, along with the changed role of the Lord Chancellor, had produced more problems than they had solved. She told us that while it had been necessary 'to reform the previous system' the new arrangement had 'created fragmentation at the top of the judiciary between the Lord Chief Justice, the Lord Chancellor and the Judicial Appointments Committee'. This 'tripartite structure' had made it 'very hard to achieve change'. In particular, she told us that she found it frustrating 'that the Court Service is jointly run by the MoJ and the Lord Chief Justice … but since the Judiciary had powers over things like court listings … court reform has been a very difficult thing to do.' She assured us that she thought 'it is important to have an independent judiciary and they should be in charge of the decision-making in courts, but I think they have too much say over the running of the operation.' She wanted to bring about 'a Court Service which is run by the Justice Secretary' leaving 'the Judiciary to act as independent operators within that service.'

With the Judiciary frustrating her on the one hand, because of what she called their entrenched values in a 'very old fashioned system', she also felt no less frustrated by NOMS on the other. She told us that she 'was not a fan of quangos' and thus did not like the idea of agency status because 'when there's a riot the Minister gets the blame so you might as well have the levers to deal with it.' It may be that Liz Truss spoke rather loosely in our interview, wrongly conflating Executive Agencies (EA) – of which there were five within the MoJ – including HM Courts and Tribunals Service and the NOMS – with Quasi-Autonomous Non-Governmental Organisations or Quangos. Theoretically, the former offer protection *for* the Minister when disaster strikes. But there are also other Arms-Length Bodies (ALBs) which clearly offer protection *from* Ministers. Some confusion would not be surprising given the complexity of such arrangements, but the reality is that Truss was against all such ALBs and wanted to pull as much back to the centre under ministerial control as she could. A cull had begun – the so-called *bonfire of the quangos* – with the arrival of the Coalition in 2010. A report on Public Bodies in 2016 by the Cabinet Office outlined ongoing plans to transform all such ALBs with the aim of reducing their number and increasing accountability – to be measured by reduced costs – and having closer relationships with Departments.

When Liz Truss took office events proceeded at a breathless pace, with press releases coming thick and fast. She had 'lots of discussions' with Michael Gove who 'had good ideas but none of them had actually been implemented'. She 'broadly agreed with his direction of travel, but there was no White Paper … and there was no game plan about how to do things.' She published her own White Paper, *Prison Safety and Reform* (Cm 9350) within four months of taking office and this has to be seen against the background of the Cabinet Office report on public bodies. Her proposals were designed to do away with the top-down, command and control structure in the prison service and replace it with the empowerment of prison governors, thus 'putting our prison professionals in the driving seat' and allowing them 'to determine what works best to reform offenders'. In words which echoed those of Cameron and Gove before her, the White Paper would mean 'the biggest overhaul of our prisons in a generation.' It shifted their arguments on governor autonomy to governor empowerment, but intriguingly the proposed changes to NOMS, and its reinvention as HMPPS were not in the White Paper at all and were first mentioned only in the second reading of the *Prisons and Courts Bill*. The main thing Truss wanted to tell us when we interviewed her was that 'having so-called independent bodies just complicates' structures of accountability 'which is one of the reasons I wanted to get rid of NOMS and replace it with HMPPS.' She still wanted to have 'more integration between prisons and probation' but whereas NOMS 'had its own Board. I wanted to embed it more within the Department so it was more directly accountable to Ministers' who would have the ability to monitor their performance against agreed targets

At the heart of the White Paper was the intention to set out statutory purposes for prisons against which performance might be measured. These were fourfold: protect the public; maintain safety and order; reform offenders to prevent more crimes being committed and prepare prisoners for life outside prison. Five, if you count the fact that these were prefaced by the statement that prisons exist to punish offenders for crimes committed. The idea of having a clear set of statutory purposes was well received during the reading of the Prisons and Courts Bill, although there was considerable debate about what they should entail and a clear hope expressed that they should be improved in the committee process. As Peter Clarke observed the proposals were 'very non-specific'. But they never made it to the statute book because the bill was lost when Theresa May called her snap election. However, many of the proposed changes went forward anyway, in one form or another, because only the proposed new aims of the Prison Service actually required legislation, and some had already started before the White Paper. Indeed when we spoke to Liz Truss nearly two years later she seemed decidedly vague about the need for statutory aims and more interested in the 'things that are measurable – league tables if you like' to hold newly empowered governors to account.

The White Paper listed Michael Gove's six Reform Prisons, naming the executive governors and again referring to them as 'trail blazers'. However, Liz Truss told us she didn't 'really agree with Michael … that they should be independent like academies or free schools' because 'we hadn't done the basics. We didn't know what each prison was achieving in terms of outcomes'. Instead the White Paper listed six areas in which governors would be given greater authority – choosing relevant accredited programmes; joint commissioning with the NHS for health needs; developing local commercial relationships to provide meaningful work for prisoners; designing their own staffing structure and hiring the senior leadership team; greater freedom in spending their budget to reflect local circumstances; and developing local operational policies so long as they met minimum national standards. There was a sting in the tail, however: governors would be held to account through 'a transparent process overseen by Ministers' and there would be sharper 'inspection and other scrutiny arrangements, with provision for inspection reports to trigger action to improve the system.' (Cm 9350, p 13) Discussions with the Inspectorate had been ongoing for some time and were finalised between Peter Clarke and David Lidington, who succeeded Liz Truss, about the Urgent Notification (UN) procedure that provided the trigger. Truss argued that she was giving 'governors the power to turn lives around' (Hansard, HC 1.11.16) but not surprisingly the Prison Governors' Association (PGA) expressed their concerns about the possibility that they might be asked to sign up to agreements and then held to account for matters which were beyond their control.

The White Paper also identified ten public sector prisons amongst the worst performing in terms of violence and self-harm to benefit from earmarked funding to help them improve. It was noticeable that although there was to be greater accountability for governors against whom decisive action was to be 'taken if performance is of serious concern' (para 70) there were no provisions for governors to voice their concerns publicly. Nor is there any recognition of the role of the Director of NOMS at the centre of these changes, to speak out on behalf of the agency. Indeed, the organisation chart (para 68) shows an emasculated NOMS, reduced to various management and operational tasks, and expected to intervene in cases of poor performance 'as directed by the Secretary of State'.

The final section of the White Paper proposed a major reconfiguration of the prison estate. The main factor influencing the use of the prison estate was, necessarily, the security categorisation of prisoners, but although the high security estate was functioning well there was a mismatch 'between the types of prisons we need and what is available' (para 239). In 2016 there were 10,500 more places in our local prisons than were needed for their main purpose of receiving persons remanded in custody awaiting trial or sentence. But for the remaining sentenced prisoners, there was a shortfall of over 14,000 places so that far too many prisoners were held in overcrowded and higher security conditions than they needed in the local prisons and where they had little or no access to work, education or programmes and services which they very much needed. The plan was to reconfigure the estate, along the lines proposed by Michael Gove so that there was a smaller number of reception prisons serving the courts and to use what decent accommodation that remained in the former local prisons to expand regimes for sentenced prisoners. The oldest and most inadequate local prisons would be considered for closure and sale – a solution that Grayling had thought had little economic merit – to help fund the transformation programme. It was also planned to create five small community prisons for women, although this went against the spirit of the Corston Report. There was certainly merit in the proposals to reorganise the estate – but changes on a grand scale require either large amounts of excess capacity or substantial investment or both.

Liz Truss realised her programme was ambitious and would not be easy to achieve – but she expected 'to see tangible improvements by 2020'. In introducing her White Paper to the House of Commons she said she believed the proposals would enable 'those stubborn reoffending rates to come down' and in a precipitate hostage to fortune declared 'that will be the marker of whether these reforms have been successful.' There has been some investment over the last 20 years, in education, health and offending behaviour programmes as well as providing work and opportunities for post-release employment – but there can be very little prospect that this will bring about the changes in re-offending envisaged by Liz Truss – yet another case of hope triumphing over experience. As we have argued already there is no measure of re-offending and even if there were it would be difficult to relate cause to effect.

The White Paper had re-engaged with the accountability versus responsibility debate which had simmered, mostly beneath the surface, at least since the dismissal of Derek Lewis by Michael Howard. Truss seemed to depart from the position of some of her predecessors who claimed that they were accountable, but not responsible, for operational matters which could be laid at the door of the Chief Executive of the Agency. In taking back 'overarching responsibility for the prison system and what it achieves' (para 63) Truss appeared to accept that Ministers would be both responsible and accountable. How far that would hold in future emergencies seemed an open question. Rory Stewart later declared that he would resign if conditions in the ten worst prisons did not improve significantly, but it was never put to the test because of the 2019 election. Certainly Liz Truss, by her own account, was not afraid to get involved in operational matters. We were surprised, given that she appeared to have no relevant experience when she told us

> 'I had to spend most of my time doing operational stuff to reduce the level of violence and deal with various bits of industrial action. I didn't come into politics to run a prison but you effectively spend quite a lot of time doing that kind of thing because of failings within the operation'.

Small wonder, perhaps, that she was widely regarded by those with knowledge, training and experience, as yet another ideologically motivated Minister ill-disposed to learning about the complexities of running a large and beleaguered service. One person we spoke to, who wished to remain anonymous, described her

> 'hands-on approach as frantically rushing around the system like the proverbial blue-arsed fly and to no good effect'.

No sooner had the White Paper been published than what every Home Secretary and Justice Minister since David Waddington most fears happened: on 16

December 2016 a serious riot took place in HMP Birmingham which had been contracted out to G4S from the public sector in 2011. The riot lasted for about 12 hours and, according to Liz Truss's statement to the House the following Monday, control of the prison was finally regained late that evening. In that statement, she also announced the introduction of new tests to detect dangerous psychoactive drugs, the rolling out of new technology to prevent mobile phone use and a new national intelligence unit to crack down on gang crime. Her Prisons Minister, Sam Gyimah, who had declined in somewhat peremptory fashion all three of our invitations to be interviewed, was said to be chairing 'daily task force meetings' with Michael Spurr to try to spot 'indicators for potential violence and unrest.' The Opposition wondered why Gyimah hadn't taken action on the basis of those meetings. During her watch there continued to be high levels of violence and self-harm, there was an escape from Pentonville, and several incidents of industrial action by the POA, as well as disturbances in Moorland, Bedford, Lincoln, Lewes and Swaleside.

On 8 February 2017 Liz Truss announced her intention to replace the NOMS with a new Prison and Probation Service which would come into official being in April to coincide with the granting of greater powers to prison governors to control their own budgets. Michael Spurr was to be the Chief Executive of the new Agency and for the first time there would be a Director with specific responsibility for women reporting directly to him. Crucially, whilst HMPPS would be responsible for some operational matters, the MoJ would 'take charge of commissioning services, future policy development and be accountable for setting standards and scrutinising prison and probation performance.' When HMPPS was duly launched as an Executive Agency of the MoJ, Michael Spurr had little choice but to make a public statement welcoming the fact that it was 'being backed by new investment' which he expected to 'make a real difference' as it worked relentlessly on a 'compelling agenda' intended to 'protect the public and reduce reoffending'. But the reality was to be rather different. It was certainly a very different agency from the one launched by Ken Clarke when he appointed Derek Lewis. As NOMS transitioned into HMPPS a number of its former operational responsibilities were removed and transferred to Ministry-wide unified functional teams as Truss wanted. The changes certainly took much of the command and control out of the agency and handed it back to Ministers so by the time of the 2017–18 Annual Report the technology team, finance and human resources functions had all been lost.

But if these changes were intended to improve matters the benefits were not easy to see. Anne Owers, a former Chief Inspector of Prisons, told us that without the new and statutory purposes of prisons 'you haven't got anything against which you can judge what's going on' and she complained that although HMPPS was still technically an agency 'it's not got what you would call agency status any longer.' Peter Clarke, the then Chief Inspector, recognised that 'some stuff you've got to hang onto at the centre' but thought that the changes had resulted in the lack of 'anything that looks like a strategy'. Nick Hardwick described the situation as 'wildly confusing' with 'policy functions in a prison service that dare not speak its name because they're not supposed to be doing policy'. Non-operational staff in the MoJ, supposedly in charge, were soon besieging Spurr demanding to know things like wing manning levels – until their interest waned or moved on to other matters when they would come back with new demands. As Peter Dawson put it 'people who didn't really understand prison were sucked into how we can make prisons safer'. As Spurr himself told us, he was constantly 'briefing up' instead of running the agency. At times Truss set up twice daily 'bird table meetings' designed to hold him to account as he was expected to report on events in the morning and resolve them by the evening. He had to spend 'half my time' just trying to 'get permission to be able to run the organisation'. How things had changed since the time when Joe Pilling might meet Ministers 10 or 12 times a year!

Nevertheless, a new Offender Management in Custody (OMiC) model was to be phased in predicated upon the introduction of prison officers as 'key workers' each with a case load of six prisoners, and with senior probation officers in charge of all offender management to be known as Probation Offender Managers (POMs). In truth this was a re-invention of the old personal officer scheme – dressed up in new clothing as cover for getting the money to recruit more badly needed officers – but it is none the worse for that. There were to be enhanced professional qualifications for probation officers, a new leadership programme, improved promotion opportunities including for specialist skilled officers dealing with complex issues such as counter-terrorism, suicide prevention and assessment and support for those who self-harm.

Though Truss told us that Michael Spurr was 'good at his job' and recognised 'a certain element of truth' in the argument that many of the problems of the prison service were down to benchmarking and 'money being taken out of the system' she thought 'you need a different sort of leader in a modern public service.' She found him to be 'quite command and control' and she rued the fact that it was 'quite difficult for ministers to replace civil servants who aren't performing.' Despite her belief that Ministers ultimately carry the can and that it was difficult for Ministers to replace civil servants, all the evidence points the other way.

Truss spent less of her time on the problems besetting probation and was content to defend Grayling's TR, despite concerns that licence recalls had increased by 79% over the previous year. Almost half the recalls were in respect of prisoners who had been serving sentences of less than 12 months and who previously would not have returned to prison after release unless they were convicted of a further offence. However, she told us the problems with Grayling's 'probation reforms' were because they 'were not very well implemented.' As with other Ministers it was far easier to lay blame on the implementation of policy rather than on the policy itself. Michael Gove had diplomatically fallen just short of describing the prison and probation services as being in a state of crisis but he had recognised the many problems and succeeded in getting some additional monies to start reversing some of the damage caused by benchmarking. It is to Truss's credit that she supported the bid for substantial monies to recruit more staff and for which Michael Spurr had fought tooth and nail. She told us that she wanted to see closer integration across the criminal justice system and she thought it was unfortunate that when prisons and probation were transferred from the Home Office to the MoJ those responsible for sentencing policy were left behind. As a result, the Home Office 'can keep on jacking up sentences and doesn't have to face the consequences' which are borne by the MoJ – whose 'budget is always in the red because of that.' Her vision would have been for the 'Home Office to take back responsibility for prisons and probation.' To the best of our knowledge sentencing policy *had* moved to the MoJ in 2007 and although other departments, including the Home Office, could lobby for changes in the law in areas of policy which they 'owned', those changes would have to be agreed jointly with the MoJ.

We took up her comments about the Home Office jacking up sentences with her because in a speech she gave at the Centre for Social Justice on 13 February 2017 she indicated that she was not interested in cutting the numbers in prisons. In that speech, she acknowledged that sentences had got considerably longer but, without reference to the fact that we had more people serving life sentences than the rest of western Europe put together, justified those increases as reflecting genuine changes in public attitudes: 'this is the right thing for victims and the right thing for the British public.' She noted that for several years the prison population had remained relatively stable at around 85,000 but wrongly claimed that England and Wales were around the middle of nations in its *rate* of imprisonment. She acknowledged that the prisons remained violent and overcrowded. She argued that the answer to prison overcrowding 'is not to cut prison numbers in half' but 'to make sure we have the right resources, the right workforce, the right buildings and the right regimes to reform offenders and turn their lives around.'

In our interview she told us that she found 'the whole debate about sentence length very frustrating'. She said she was a 'big supporter of using more tagging so allowing more people not to go to prison … but the real problem is the people we've got in on long sentences for sex and violent offences.' She acknowledged that 'as you rightly say sentences have gone up' and then went on to say 'but nobody really believes it. I mean if you ask the public they all think sentences are too short.' When we pointed out that this was not actually borne out by research (MoJ, 2013) she expressed her surprise: 'Isn't it?' The research was evidently not known to her and when we explained it she said 'Really, that's interesting'. We admitted that some critics questioned whether it was fair to draw conclusions from an artificial research context, but we thought it important for Ministers to challenge sometimes simplistic assumptions. She in turn admitted that 'we've got ourselves into a hole with the whole sentencing framework' and when we asked how she would remedy that she laughed and said:

'if I could wave a magic wand and politics didn't exist I would definitely do something about some sentences which are too long and I would remove mandatory minimum sentences ... and if we had a more meritocratic judiciary I would like to allow them to use more judgement to make decisions'.

We asked for her views on the role of the Sentencing Council. 'I don't agree with its existence because that's another Quango ... and when you've got a lot of guidelines ... you end up creating a ratchet effect.' Indeed that has seemed to be the effects of sentencing guidelines in other jurisdictions and most of our interviewees seemed disappointed that the Sentencing Council had not been more effective.

Liz Truss was certainly interested in problem-solving courts and she thought 'the judiciary should be more engaged in the life cycle of people coming through the system.' However, we were unable to establish whether she had actually done anything towards setting up the proposed pilot studies of such courts because our time had come to an end.

Less than three weeks after the launch of HMPPS the *Prisons and Courts Bill*, which had been announced with a fanfare on 23rd of February to implement the safety and reform agenda, was unceremoniously dropped when Theresa May won parliamentary approval for her snap election to be held on 8 June. May famously lost her small majority and had to settle for leading a minority government with the confidence-and-supply support from the Democratic Unionist Party. In the re-shuffle which followed Liz Truss was replaced by David Lidington.

David Lidington (June 2017–January 2018)

When David Lidington was a postgraduate student at Cambridge his PhD thesis was on the *Enforcement of Penal Statutes in 16th Century England*. Had it not been for the lack of legal training it might have seemed fitting that, having entered Parliament, he would one day become Justice Secretary and Lord Chancellor. His tenure, however, was one of the briefest in that role – and after just seven months at the MoJ he was moved to the Cabinet Office where he was widely seen as Theresa May's *de facto* Deputy Prime Minister. We interviewed him on 13 November 2019, in what we hoped was a quiet spot in the foyer of Hotel Sofitel St James. No sooner had we started our interview, however, than we were entertained with a recital by the resident harpist. The recital, which would have been lovely in other circumstances, was thankfully short and proved no great impediment to the work of our indefatigable transcriber.

David Lidington did have some prior experience of the field of prisons and probation when he had spent two years as special advisor to Douglas Hurd in the days when there were only about 20 or so advisors across the whole of government: when 'Margaret Thatcher had us all in Number 10 once a year there was still space around the Cabinet table.' He had also been Parliamentary Private Secretary (PPS) to Michael Howard mostly 'trying to oil the relationship between Michael and Ann Widdecombe.' The roles of SpAd and PPS are quite different, of course, but there seems little doubt that Douglas Hurd had the greater influence on Lidington's subsequent career, leaving him 'on the more liberal side of the argument because of that experience.' Although he did talk to Liz Truss, Michael Gove and Chris Grayling it was only 'over a cup of coffee, no more than that.' He agreed that one of the serious difficulties arising out of our system of government was that 'there is no process anywhere, in any department, for any sort of induction by your predecessor'. He was, however, given a clear briefing, if hardly a detailed one, by Theresa May when he was called to her office and asked to take on the role of Lord Chancellor: 'we have to rebuild the relationships with the judges.' He had regular weekly, one to one, meetings with Richard Heaton, the Permanent Secretary, with just private secretaries present to keep a record and he found these very constructive because 'we could try to talk to each other completely frankly'.

He agreed that

> 'Liz's relationship with the judges had gone downhill. John Thomas was publicly critical in a way that Lord Chief Justices very rarely are. So the relationship with the judges had to be repaired and that was urgent and a top priority'.

He looked for opportunities to 'make a supportive comment about judicial independence whenever possible. I worked that into my speech at my swearing in as Lord Chancellor'. He consulted LCJ Thomas as to the best moment for him to make a public statement re-affirming judicial independence to have maximum effect. In what may have been a veiled reference to the way things had been handled by his predecessor he told us:

> 'I would issue the statement and then we would tell No 10 I'd done it. It was very important to get that sequence right so as not to be seen as asking permission from Number 10. And it was very important to the judges that the Lord Chancellor was seen to do that'.

There is no doubt that, as one of the most relaxed and least abrasive of Ministers, he was successful in re-building bridges.

The second problem he faced 'was the ongoing crisis with prisons. I had contingency plans drawn up for executive release'. Moreover, 'the finances of the department were then, and still are, in great difficulty … and they were being expected to do things which they were simply not funded to do'. This was 'a consequence of the very drastic cuts that there'd been in the 2010 spending review.' Legal aid, which made up a quarter of the MoJ budget had borne the brunt of the cuts but there was a perpetual need to look for savings. He went on to say that 'Liz had made some real steps forward, particularly on the prison staff numbers, but there was still a morale problem … and a reluctance to innovate and test new ideas'. He had to get a grip of this in the aftermath of a general election that nobody had expected to be called. He told us that Liz Truss had been delaying bringing forward the *Prisons and Courts Bill* because 'she was still arm-wrestling with the Treasury over money for additional prison staff ... which was the absolutely key priority.'

Liz Truss had gone from arm-wrestling the Treasury to become its First Secretary under Philip Hammond and we asked whether this had helped to ease the financial situation. He explained that 'when you come into office as a Secretary of State the budget for at least the next twelve months is already spent and so you are always planning for the next financial review'. He and his colleagues spent a lot of energy 'trying to soften up the Treasury' in order to get what was

> 'needed for capital spending. Liz did understand this ... but she needed to have the evidence because of Philip Hammond's scepticism. There was a stunned silence in Cabinet when I gave a presentation showing that, on current trends, if we didn't bring on more capacity we were going to run out of prison places shortly before the next general election'.

In his experience the first instinct of most members of the public as well as MPs, in so far as they think about prisons at all, is to 'lock them all up and make life tougher, whatever that means'. However, 'when you actually take them through an argument about rehabilitation stage by stage, they get it.' Few politicians have bothered to go through that process of converting people and when they have they tend to link it to overly optimistic statements about reducing reoffending. Even fewer politicians have argued the case that if prisons are to have a chance of rehabilitating offenders, the size of the prison population and the length of prison sentences, need to be reduced. Liz Truss had told us it would take 'a brave politician to do that.' David Lidington pragmatically recognised that he had 'to search for both short- and longer-term ways in which to bring the prison population down ... and I did say publicly on more than one occasion my objective was to secure a reduction in the overall numbers.' One area where he had planned a significant reduction was in the women's estate, but in order not to fall foul of anti-discrimination laws, the planned reductions had to be packaged as a pilot scheme. There was some modest reduction in prison numbers, largely through Michael Spurr's leadership of a drive to increase the use of Home Detention Curfew (HDC). As a result Lidington was able to pass on to his successor, David Gauke, 'a couple of thousand extra slack in the system .... David was nice enough to thank me for it.'

Although the Prisons and Courts Bill had been dropped he found that much of what had actually been recommended in the Bill could be accomplished without the need for a statute and he pointed particularly to the UN procedure.

> 'That was supposed to be written into law, but we just established it as a practice ... and that's one of the things I'm most pleased I did at Justice ...

because it has made a difference. It's made life less comfortable for my successors, and designedly so.'

When we had spoken to Peter Clarke about this he said 'I'm still astonished that politicians have actually agreed to a protocol that makes them so publicly accountable … for what is essentially an operational matter. What's the long term impact going to be? We don't know yet.' According to Anne Owers, when she had been Chief Inspector of Prisons, she had been 'lucky enough to be around when a lot of resource was going into prisons' and that she didn't have problems getting governors to follow her recommendations. However, looking at the situation today, she said 'I don't think it means that Ministers … will feel themselves to be responsible' because there was a lack of clarity about the procedures. Nick Hardwick was cautiously optimistic and thought that UNs were 'a good thing' but that the jury was still out on whether they could make a difference.

We told David Lidington that many of the prison governors to whom we had spoken felt that the UN procedure made them feel nervous because so much that happened in prison was outside their direct control, and we wondered whether the distribution of responsibility and accountability was properly balanced. He told us: 'I think it's getting there. The Secretary of State and the head of the prison service will always get a battering … but it's when there's rats and rubbish everywhere …' the sentence was not finished but the unsaid implication was that this is where it was harder for governors not to be regarded as responsible. Lidington, like Liz Truss and others before him, said that 'you can talk until you are blue in the face about how HMMPS is operationally in charge, not MoJ but it's not the Director General who has to stand up at the dispatch box and answer an urgent question, or deal with the *Daily Mail*.'

It was not too many years, however, since Richard Tilt and Martin Narey did just that or at least had the freedom to speak out. Although Truss had wished to emasculate NOMS which had its own independent Board, Lidington suggested that under David Gauke there had been 'important advances … in the creation of a more independent board for HMPPS … getting non-execs in there and having somebody who is not director of the prison service as chair.' Lidington told us that he accepted Michael Spurr's view that when governors were under such pressure to manage things day to day they really don't have the capacity to deal with new initiatives which Ministers wanted to pursue. When we spoke to Michael Spurr he was also keen to tell us that it was not institutional culture that deprived governors of real possibilities to innovate. Indeed governors already had sufficient autonomy to bring forward innovative ideas which, if successful, could be rolled out across the estate, or relevant sectors of the estate. But the difficulties were substantial. Running prisons is always a matter of maintaining a delicate balance and governors were always likely to be subservient to what one innovative governor called the 'exigent day' and when a good day was when 'you had got through it without incident.' Lidington, as Secretary of State, was content to leave things to his Junior Minister, Sam Gyimah, to keep him abreast of any problems that might be coming from the frontline. Gyimah had a very hands-on approach and had a 'colour-coded chart on his wall showing the prisons in ranked order of risk of violence for the next week … so we did keep a very close watch on that.'

David Lidington had talked to Michael Spurr and called in the governors of the reform prisons to discuss what was realistically possible. Spurr convinced him that a prison 'is not like a school' and that having 'completely autonomous institutions' couldn't work, not least because of the need for short notice transfers. There clearly had to be elements of consistency across all prisons, or at least particular categories of prisons, if the system was to work at all. Although David Lidington clearly listened to and respected that advice, he was still keen on applying, where possible, 'quite a lot of the Gove approach.' Indeed the devolution of powers to governors during this period closely followed those outlined in Truss's White Paper with aspects of regimes, staffing and family ties already in place. There was still room, he thought, to give 'governors greater power over things like education, contracts for cleaning and catering and other services, and you can also group prisons together where it made perfect sense for there to be a single contract for say, the prisons in Greater Manchester.' He also established a small strategy unit to 'start encouraging' governors to have 'a greater appetite for risk' in trying new projects. Like Ken Clarke and Michael Gove before him he offered governors protection if they did so, saying,

> 'if governor autonomy is to work, it has to involve governors having both the freedom and the responsibility to experiment, and to make more mistakes. But the Secretary of State and the Prisons Minister then need to be able to say … within certain parameters … I will support them to do that'.

There was still a very long way to go. They were only halfway to recruiting the 2,500 extra staff announced by Truss – and the new recruits 'were at very early stages of their careers, some were in the pipeline and not yet on the wings, and we were continuing to lose experienced prison officers' so this reduced the net increase. 'There were disparities over pension arrangements that aggravated' the recruitment and retention of staff so it was very difficult to get to, and maintain, appropriate levels of staffing who could engage in rehabilitative activities.

The third big problem, he told us, was the need

> 'to get to grips with the contracting out of probation. In August 2017 … Richard Heaton (Permanent Secretary) came to me with Michael Spurr and Justin Russell (non-operational Director of the Prison Safety and Reform Progamme) and told me that one or two CRCs are getting into serious financial difficulties and we think there is a systemic issue here. We're going to need to put some more money in and just tweak the contracts'.

David Lidington wanted to be sure that the CRCs were 'not all going to go belly up.' So in one of his bilateral meetings with Richard Heaton, he asked 'have we got a plan? If the worst happened do we have the capacity to keep a probation service going?' Heaton came back a couple of weeks later to say 'actually we've got something but it's not good enough.' He told us that he recalled a briefing note to the effect that 'if we don't provide the extra money, contractor X would simply hand back the keys and walk away.' That was when they began to question 'whether this model is sustainable in the long term' and they put in place the structure that would allow them to take the operation in-house if they needed to, at short notice – 'maybe in particular areas or even, worst case, nationally.' However, Lidington did not think that the idea of payment by results was an invalid one: the problem had been more that it was a mistake to rush into it. He was temperamentally more disposed towards incremental rather than root and branch change, especially when trying to drive through a strategy of getting *more for less*. Whereas Ken Clarke had intended to have widespread pilots and only move ahead when there was firm evidence to put to the Treasury, Chris Grayling 'got it wrong' by deciding 'to go for the big one … and I think Chris will say himself, with hindsight, that he tried to be too ambitious too quickly'. But payment by results had been in the manifesto and Cameron wanted it done yesterday, if not sooner. Lidington also thought that *more for less* had become necessary for the MoJ. He reasoned that the Treasury was 'deeply cynical about the MoJ's ability to manage its budget … not as bad as the Ministry of Defence, but it's not too far behind' or so Philip Hammond had told him. So if you want more money from the Treasury you have to demonstrate a business case as to what this extra money will achieve. He said 'That's where I think that payment by results would have helped. There were good pilot project findings – at Peterborough prison and the social impact bond study for example.'

The Peterborough social impact bond study was one of 58 social impact projects, mostly in regard to homelessness, youth unemployment and mental health, set up initially under New Labour. It aimed at involving 'social investors' paying upfront for services commissioned from local charities aimed at reducing reoffending on release. The investors reaped a dividend only if the contracted reduction in offending actually occurred and bore the consequential losses if it did not. It was a carefully designed project, although not without problems in measuring outcomes. It involved 1,000 prisoners, in three *tranches*, with matched control groups who received no support on release. However, it was undermined because under TR *all* short term prisoners received supervision upon release thus effectively depriving the study of its control groups.

One of the consequences of handing over so much responsibility to the CRCs, and which Lidington 'found infuriating' was that 'the prison governors just pulled out of this.' Michael Spurr understood more than anyone that *Through the Gate* only worked if probation and prison governors worked hand in hand and knew that this would be more difficult under the new arrangements. David Lidington had talked to Michael Spurr about this and admitted that 'Michael was largely right'. He also thought that Spurr tried to rebuild more of that sense of shared responsibility and cooperation between prisons and probation which was central to maintaining prisoners' family ties emphasised by Lord Farmer (2017). In fact, Lidington thought that there were far more good news stories both in prisons and probation than ever came to public attention. He thought that Michael Spurr was reluctant to seek publicity on these because they would be likely to lead to 'a bad story in the *Daily Mail*' even though Lidington told him that 'I'm perfectly happy to put up with bad stories in the *Daily Mail*.' He recalled his time with Douglas Hurd all those years ago when Hurd had leaned back in his chair saying 'if the *Daily Mail* or the *Sun* hasn't called for my resignation at least once a month I must be doing something wrong.'

Lidington thought it important to shift the balance away from prisons and more towards community penalties and he contemplated the possibility of trans-ferring responsibility for 'probation and non-custodial penalties, but even pos-sibly for some prisons, to metro mayors. I think there's a case for that'. He also supposed that one 'could take the NHS model … where you have some specialist services that are funded centrally but the bulk of elective and other services in hospitals are purchased by the Central Commissioning Group. In practice that is how a lot of public services are being reconfigured.'

But he also thought there was no perfect model for prisons and that one was constrained by the physical legacy of the past, not least in the inconvenient loca-tions of prisons. Amongst the things he took credit for, *en passant*, during his time in office was that 'we did solve the prison voting issue in the end' which had rumbled on since the UK was found by the European Court to be in breach of Article 3 Protocol No 1 because we deprived *all* convicted prisoners of their right to vote (*Hirst v UK* 2005). Many statutory solutions were proposed over the years but without Parliamentary agreement. Lidington came up with an *admin-istrative* solution which *because* of its minimalism satisfied most MPs and most of the Press, and *despite* its minimalism satisfied the Court. The solution allowed 100 or so prisoners to vote if they were on ROTL but retained the universal ban on voting in prisons.

When David Lidington was asked to take on the number two role in the gov-ernment he said to Theresa May 'of course I'll accept this job … It's an honour to do it but I will be sad to move on from Justice just as I've got a grip on the personalities and issues involved.' But just as he had no briefing from Liz Truss so he gave no briefing to his successor, David Gauke, apart from another chat over a cup of coffee. He had no time to do more. He left the MoJ at 2.45 pm on 8 January and arrived at the Cabinet Office at 3 o'clock. At 5 pm the Cabinet Secretary, John Manzoni, put his head round the door saying 'we need to have a word about Carillion – it's about to collapse.'

David Gauke (January 2018–July 2019)

David Gauke had worked as a solicitor before entering Parliament in 2005. He became a Junior Minister in the coalition government and spent some seven years at the Treasury, ending up as Chief Secretary, and then six months as Secretary of State for Work and Pensions before becoming Secretary of State for Justice and Lord Chancellor on 8 January 2018. Four days earlier it had been announced that the 'Black Cab' rapist, John Worboys (later Radford), was to be released on parole after serving two years *more* than the eight-year minimum set by the judge for his IPP sentence. Had he been given a determinate sentence of 17 years, rather than the discredited sentence of IPP, he would have been released without going to the Parole Board at all. The only issue was whether he was still a risk to the public. Nick Hardwick, as Chairman of the Parole Board and with the active encouragement of three previous Justice Secretaries, had been working, where possible, to release those still in custody under IPP sentences beyond their tariffs. He had played no part in the decision to release Worboys beyond appointing a highly respected member of the Board – as it happened a former probation officer – as chair of the panel. Each panel, Hardwick told us was 'a court in its own right' – and he had not expected the decision that was made. Hardwick was acutely aware that the Parole Board was under-resourced to cope with its increased workload of some 1,500 hearings a year despite a substantial increase in membership approved by Michael Gove. He told us that Worboys was not a particularly exceptional case – since most prisoners who come before the Board 'have done something pretty horrible'. He noted that less than 1% of parolees went on to commit a further serious offence. But when some of Worboys' victims protested that they had not been informed about the release Hardwick, who had long argued for greater transparency in such matters, immediately apologised unreservedly for that oversight. It was the beginning of a test of the judgement of an inexperienced incoming Secretary of State, a test which many thought he failed.

According to Hardwick, Gauke initially 'praised' him for the way he had handled the matter when he was interviewed on the radio. But a campaign started for a judicial review of the decision to release. As Secretary of State, he was the obvious person to mount such a review if he thought the decision was wrong and had he done so the prevailing legal opinion seemed to be that the review would have had to uphold the Board's decision because it could not be shown to be irrational, given that Worboys had met the usual criteria for the reduction of risk. However, Gauke equivocated and announced an internal review of the 'case for transparency in the process for parole decisions and how victims are appropriately engaged in that process' (Hansard, HC 9.1.18). Then, under mounting media and political pressure from among others, Sadiq Khan, the Mayor of London, on the one hand, and influential supporters of one of Worboys' early victims, Carrie Symonds, by now Director of Communications for the Conservative Party, on the other, Gauke took 'legal advice to establish whether there were grounds to challenge the decision in the courts' (Hansard, HC 19.1.18). The advice he received was that there were no grounds for him to proceed to judicial review, although he encouraged 'victims to take their own legal advice' and he extended the remit of his review by asking 'whether there should be a mechanism to allow parole decisions to be reconsidered'. There had undoubtedly been poor decisions originally by the Metropolitan Police and the Crown Prosecution Service (CPS) about which of the many allegations against Worboys to investigate and prosecute. And there had also been some civil litigation in which two victims had successfully brought actions against the police and been awarded damages. The Metropolitan Police appealed unsuccessfully and the judgement against them, although reached on the 'balance of probabilities', was finally upheld by the Supreme Court. Worboys himself had by then paid compensation to a number of other victims but without admitting liability. Neither the Parole Board nor the MoJ, whose officials prepared the parole dossier and one of whom attended the hearing, believed that any of these matters could properly be addressed. Any failings attributed to Hardwick thus applied equally to the MoJ and Gauke himself.

There was no doubt that with the law as it stood the ostensibly independent parole panel was properly constituted, and in reaching its decision it had rigorously followed the Secretary of State's directions. These required IPP prisoners to demonstrate that they no longer constituted a risk. That risk had been assessed by three psychologists in the light of Worboys having successfully completed a sex offender programme, statistical evidence that spree offenders stop when caught and that in not fully admitting his guilt he was exhibiting 'shame' evidenced as 'a good protective factor' for someone with 'his strong social networks'. However, the matter finally went to judicial review on behalf of victims, who were not party to the matters for which he had actually been convicted. In that review Lord Justice Leveson held that the panel should have considered the many other allegations against Worboys, to which he had never confessed and for which he had never been charged. This was a landmark judgement: not only was it the first time a decision to release had been judicially reviewed by victims (it is usually prisoners who seek to review a decision not to release) but it created a new precedent, opening up the dubious possibility of considering hearsay evidence which had never been tested in court. Once this decision was handed down Gauke insisted that Hardwick's position was untenable and pressured him to resign. As Hardwick later gave testimony, Gauke had twice told him that he 'did not wish to get macho' with him which he 'understood to be a clear threat'.

In light of Hardwick's treatment, another IPP prisoner, Paul Wakenham, then sought leave to bring a judicial review against the MoJ. This was on grounds that he would be unable to get a fair hearing since the Board – which was a *de facto* court – was manifestly not independent of the government. Mr Justice Mostyn duly granted leave to proceed to judicial review on grounds 'that the provisions of tenure of Parole Board membership fail the test of objective independence' and went on to say that putting pressure on the chair of the Parole Board to resign breached 'the principle of judicial independence enshrined in the Act of Settlement 1701'. As Hardwick, broadly smiling, told us

> 'that does me nicely … breaches the Act of Settlement of 1701 … you couldn't get more emphatic than that'.

In an echo of the situation that Liz Truss had put herself in with the judiciary, Nick Hardwick, was surely entitled to have received the support of the Lord Chancellor. If Hardwick was culpable then Gauke was equally so. Hardwick told reporter David Wurtzel for *Law, Practice and Society*, that

> 'I wasn't told my position was untenable because the Parole Board had made a wrong decision, it was because the Parole Board had made an unpopular decision. I am absolutely clear that the Justice Secretary felt that his position would be under threat'.

Ken Clarke, whilst supporting Gauke and Leveson's decision, pointedly told the House that the Parole Board 'is often asked almost impossible questions' and that decisions had to be made 'on the basis of the best judgement they can make in the public interest. Criminal sentencing must never be simply a question of campaigning and responding to popular pressure' (Hansard, HC 28.3.18).

Gauke's first review of the law, policy and procedures relating to Parole Board decisions, in April 2018 lifted the blanket prohibition of Rule 25 on disclosure of proceedings and made summaries available to victims, the public and the media upon request. By the end of March 2019, summaries of 1,171 decisions were provided, 99% of them to victims and the remaining 1% to the media and other interested parties. A second review, following a period of public consultation on mechanisms for reconsidering parole decisions, was published in February 2019 and for the year 2019–20 the Ministry estimated that the Secretary of State may challenge between 1% and 5% of decisions to release and that prisoners might challenge between 13% and 16% of decisions not to release. Together these challenges might generate between 25 and 90 additional hearings. A further review of possible long-term changes to the Parole Board was planned with the possibility that it might be placed into the Judicial or Tribunal system, the preferred options of both Hardwick and the Justice Committee.

Hardwick told us that he thought the changes to transparency thus far 'hadn't gone far enough' and that it was important, especially in apparently counter-intuitive decisions, as in the case of Worboys, to make clear the evidence base 'otherwise the decisions won't be understood.' He was rather more concerned that the Parole Board would become even more cautious and doubted 'whether we release enough of the people who aren't dangerous.' He also questioned the fairness of a system based almost entirely upon assessments of risk that at best show moderate predictive validity and would wish to see decision-makers being allowed to give 'less weight to the risk and more weight to the behaviour' in prison. Another problem area, in his view was the 'fraudulent political statement, we'll put victims at the heart of the system' which increased victims' expectations, when victim statements could have 'nil effect on decisions' because they spoke to the past and have 'little to do with future risk.' These views were largely also shared by Peter Dawson, and both he and Hardwick expressed their scepticism about the ability to diagnose the problems of prisoners and apply a cure despite the increasing political rhetoric concerning rehabilitation. It should be added that Sonia Flynn, the new Chief Officer of the National Probation Service (NPS), told us that her 'victim liaison officers' said that the new disclosure process was welcomed. It reduced the anxiety of victims who 'want to get on quietly with their lives, but they do want to be kept informed.'

We interviewed David Gauke on 18 September 2018 at the Ministry of Justice a few weeks after the Mostyn judgment, and some way into the interview, after the ice had been broken, we asked what his thoughts were in the light of that judgement. Understandably he said

> 'I don't want to dwell very much on that particular issue. Nick Hardwick resigned but we did have a very frank and candid conversation after which he resigned. I think there's not much more I want to say about that'.

Although, the Worboys case was undoubtedly an inauspicious beginning to his career as Secretary of State and Lord Chancellor, David Gauke thereafter doggedly pursued a process of trying to persuade the Press, the Public and fellow politicians about the folly of short sentences of imprisonment on which he was able to present a strong united front with his Junior Minister Rory Stewart. He also continued with what David Lidington had started in strengthening the position of the Inspectorate of Prisons via the UN procedure as well as taking back control from the CRCs and handing many of their responsibilities over to the NPS. It is also important to note that although Lord Woolf strongly disapproved of Gauke's treatment of Hardwick, he gave Gauke his full support on *these* matters.

We had started our interview on safer ground when he told us that having been at the Treasury when Liz Truss was Minister of Justice he had been pleased to provide 'some additional spending to increase the recruitment of prison officers … one of the wisest things I did as Chief Secretary'. It also meant that he had come into office 'with his eyes open … knowing something of the challenges and financial constraints … something I wanted to get my teeth into.' At the time of our interview he claimed that 'we've got three and a half thousand more prison officers than we had in October 2016.' Hardwick was concerned that the damage of staff cuts had already been done:

> 'one of the consequences of the staff reductions, particularly the loss of experienced staff, which you see in places like Birmingham, means that

it's created a real vacuum, into which has moved organised crime. Staff are frightened to come out of the office … and it's basically being run for the management by the prisoners themselves or by their bosses'.

This was more of a problem in the large prisons, where prisoners did not know each other so well, and those who didn't pay their debts were punished severely, altering 'the prisoner economy … A long term shift in the culture that may not be possible to reverse.' Peter Clarke told us that the drugs problem was exacerbated by 'more and more restricted regimes' and after four years of such restrictions

> 'people get angry and bitter, they turn to drugs and you end up with people emerging from jail possibly more angry, more criminally capable, more full of drugs, more embittered than when they went in. Where's the public interest in that?'

Obviously David Gauke was well aware of these problems: 'not all of the new officers stick it out … and when you recruit a lot of people all at the same time you're left with a lot of inexperienced officers.' This meant that the Prison Service had a continuing problem which would take time to resolve:

> 'part of this is about training, part about leadership and part about experi-ence … but we have probably turned a corner in a lot of prisons … Are the levels of violence still too high? Yes they are. If you look at the statistics they are still increasing. Is the level of drug use in prison still too high? Yes it is. There's something quite dangerous going on in some of our prisons where a lot of bad behaviour is being manipulated – so there is dealing with the directly bad behaviour – those assaulting prison officers – but there's also understanding who is pulling the strings and finding ways of dealing with them'.

He had spent some time talking to his predecessors, Ken Clarke, Michael Gove, Liz Truss and David Lidington and, to a lesser extent, to Chris Grayling – about the issues in both prisons and probation. He picked out some threads of conti-nuity: trying to reduce the prison population or at least stopping it from rising, and a commitment to rehabilitation. On 6 March 2018 he had given a speech to the RSA in which he had repeated the tired and implausible argument that 'it was only by prioritising rehabilitation that we can reduce reoffending and in turn the numbers of future victims of crime' so that rehabilitation sat alongside protection of the public and punishment as the main purposes of prison (Gauke, 2018). But he also insisted that prisons must 'get the basics right – secure, safe and decent' to which end he proposed to continue with the UN process and the staff recruitment programme for 'key workers' to engage in one-to-one work with prisoners. Much of the talk was devoted to dealing with the ingenious ways in which drugs were now delivered to prisons by drones to cell windows, and through fake letters from lawyers and children's paintings which had been soaked with liquid psychoactive substances. One strategy for dealing with this involved re-thinking the categorisation of prisoners to include not only security risk in terms of escape but also behaviour in prisons. A similar policy had been advocated by one of us (King and Elliott, 1977) but was officially rejected by the Home Office. The talk also embraced the importance of proper incentives to good behaviour including extra visits to help maintain links with prisoners' families, the development of education and work opportunities in prison, and the need for cross-government links to help prisoners on discharge.

Gauke told us that 'A lot of work that David Lidington did I have taken forward and brought to fruition – and which David would have done had he stayed in place'. Five months after our interview, on 18 February 2019, he set out his vision for 'a smart justice system' which would involve a new conversation instead of the polarisation of 'soft versus hard justice'. Unlike Liz Truss, he rightly noted that we imprisoned at one of the highest rates in Europe, and that whilst part of this was down to hardening attitudes towards sexual and violent crimes we were also imposing longer sentences for lesser non-violent offences and 'taking a more punitive approach than at any point during Mrs Thatcher's premiership.' He didn't want to reverse the tougher sentencing approach for serious offences but he was strongly critical of the routine use of short sentences of imprisonment for lesser offences, which were expensive, ineffective and counterproductive. He had already announced a new programme of GPS tagging and looked forward to increasing the number of community sentences with a renewed focus on mental health, drug and alcohol treatment requirements which were being tested in courts in five areas. He wanted to switch resources 'away from ineffective prison sentences and into probation' and planned to 'return to the subject of probation in much greater depth later this year.' On 18 July 2019, he delivered another speech in which he was able to use some internal research to point to the potential for community sentences to deliver fewer reoffences than custodial sentences for comparable offenders and with considerable savings in costs. He told us that he was 'determined to have a probation service that defends the public ... and would deliver tough community sentences ... with less reliance on ineffective short prison terms.' However, when pressed, he insisted he was against setting artificial targets preferring 'to get the measures in place first'. It was a familiar refrain: 'improve the non-custodial options and then let's try to discourage the use of shorter sentences. Let's focus on rehabilitation to reduce reoffending because the purpose of the system is to reduce crime'. Although he had acknowledged that we had ever-increasing lengths of prison sentences he clearly felt unable to begin to address that problem.

Meanwhile, Gauke had to sort out the chaotic situation that surrounded the CRCs. Despite mounting criticism from the Justice Committee (2018, HC 482), the Public Accounts Committee (2016, HC 484), and the National Audit Office (2016, HC 951) Gauke continued to defend TR. He had already bailed out the CRCs to the tune of £342 million (Hansard, HC 10.7.18) but in the light of Glenys

Stacey's increasingly devastating Inspectorate reports in which she now declared that 'none of government's stated aspirations for Transforming Rehabilitation have been met in any meaningful way' (HMIP, 2017, p 12) it was clear that more had to be done. On 27 July 2018, he announced that the eight companies that ran 21 CRCs would have their contracts ended two years early in 2020, but at that time he planned 'to work with the market to design new and improved contracts.' The areas covered by the CRCs and the NPS were to be re-aligned to improve joint working with key partners in the third sector, local authorities and Police and Crime Commissioners, and an additional £22 million was to be invested to improve *through the gate* services. The Opposition had commissioned Lord Ramsbotham to report on returning probation to the public sector but at the time of our interviews with Ramsbotham and Richard Burgon, Shadow Minister of Justice, that report had not yet been delivered. At the start of 2019 two CRC providers, Working Links and Interserve, called in the administrators.

In May 2019 Gauke announced a reunification model whereby all offender supervision would be returned to the NPS, albeit without Probation Trusts (MoJ, 2019). Improved IT systems were planned to reduce the amount of time probation staff spent sitting at their computers, and a new inspection model providing clear standards, as well as the promise of 'professional registration for probation officers' returning them to their pre-Howard professional status, although now not as social workers but as risk assessors, law enforcers and public protectors. These developments were welcomed by Sonia Flynn. There had already been some shifting of budgets and responsibilities to local bodies through the 'Justice Devolution Memorandum of Understanding (MoU) with London Councils and the Mayor's Office for Policing and Crime (MOPAC)' and it was hoped in future 'to foster a whole-system approach to offender management …, early intervention and prevention' with the possibility of 'budget devolution for certain groups of offenders in custody' (Hansard, HC 26.3.19). With cross-party support, it was planned to draw in other departments and providers to assist probation, through 'a regional outcome fund to attract matched funding from other departments or commissioning bodies' (Hansard, HC 16.5.19).

At the time of writing reunification is in place in Wales, with England to follow in the Summer of 2021 across 11 probation divisions, with regional directors to maintain local partnerships, and a new probation structure in place at the top of HMPPS. Private and voluntary sector involvement, would continue through the delivery of unpaid work and accredited programmes.

Throughout his time in office Gauke had become increasingly concerned about the Brexit negotiations – which had dominated Parliament during our field work – and by the summer of 2019 things were heading towards a climax. On 4 July 2019, he had given his second speech – about the problems caused by populist politicians – to the annual judges' dinner in the City. With a touch of gallows humour he noted that like Michael Gove before him he had been in office long enough to make two such speeches to the same audience. But whereas Michael Gove survived for one more day before Theresa May dispensed with his services, Gauke expected to last another three weeks. An impassioned opponent of a 'no-deal Brexit', on 23 July 2019 he fulfilled his pledge to resign if Boris Johnson won the Tory leadership election. By then, after an inauspicious start, he had earned the appreciation by, among others, Peter Dawson of the Prison Reform Trust that he had been establishing 'a reputation as a thoughtful, balanced policy thinker, driven by evidence, not preconception'.

When we interviewed Gauke's Junior Minister, Rory Stewart, in Portcullis House, on 23 January 2019, we suggested that together they had recognised, and were prepared to speak about, the crisis in prisons and probation more than many of their predecessors – and we asked him for his view of the current problems and how they might be solved. 'Well firstly, when I came in to office in January 2018 prisons were a complete disgrace,' he told us.

> 'Some of our prisons continue to be a complete disgrace and fundamentally HMPPS had not gripped this problem. There was no sense of urgency, there was no sense of guilt. Now part of this was down to resources but it isn't all to do with resources. There is no reason why in Bedford prison – in a modern wing – prisoners should be sleeping on mattresses on the floor and eating rats. I turn up in Liverpool prison – every single window is broken'.

He then discovered that after nearly 18 months into 'Special Measures, the Inspectors went into Bedford again and found

> 'they are still sleeping on mattresses on the floor and they are still eating rats. Why does nobody do anything? And why has nobody been to Liverpool? At some level these conditions are not humane and they are not decent'.

When he asked himself how could this be, he had concluded

> 'yes they don't have enough resources but fundamentally there was a challenge of priorities and there had been an inability to acknowledge that the world had changed since 2010. We have 10,000 fewer prison officers. If you are going to cut, design the cuts in such a way that you are going to keep your most experienced staff. … If you <u>have</u> lost your senior staff … you need a much more serious training course because you're no longer going to be able to learn on the job – 85% of the people on the wings are new. What they did was to take the cuts and then try to run the prisons in the way in which they did in 2010 but with 10,000 fewer officers [and they] had completely de-prioritised basic operational efficiency'.

This was a pretty damning indictment. We knew that all successive directors of prisons held very much to the decency agenda. In Bedford that commitment had clearly not got across to the overwhelming numbers of inexperienced staff.

The broken windows in Liverpool may have been a consequence of outsourcing minor works which Richard Tilt told us was 'a serious blunder'. We can understand Stewart's frustration, but we can also understand how past and present leaders of the service saw Stewart's approach as confrontational rather than supportive, and why they thought he had very little understanding of the realities of running prisons. Martin Narey saw him as 'brilliant on his personal PR but motivated massively by personal ambition'. He told us that Stewart 'made life intolerable for Michael Spurr and that the gulf between what he thought he understood about operational issues and what he really understood was very wide indeed'. Nowhere was this more clear than in regard to searching. Stewart complained that 'when I tried to suggest that Bedford or Leeds would benefit from searching staff and visitors I was told there was no evidence that had any impact on the amount of drugs going into prisons.' He told us that the service was allergic to the idea of putting airport-style security into Cat B locals and had been very slow to use body scanners. But Phil Wheatley pointed out that Stewart had no idea of the cost implications of such proposals and that to be effective

> 'entry searching has to operate for as long as the prison is in an unlocked state – about 14 hours a day, requires multiple scanners to cope with peak movements, and up to three members staff per scanning line'.

He estimated the cost at about £25m a year just in addition staff costs alone. In essence, Stewart saw the problem as the development of a new senior management culture which embraced the belief 'that the answer to our drug problems and violence is better relationships with prisoners … and talking nonsense about empowerment' at the expense of 'greater security, cell checks' and so on which were 'culturally troubling for them.' Any talk about governor empowerment may well have had something to do with the policies fervently espoused by Cameron, Gove and Truss but in any case it had been deeply ingrained in the prison service since the 1980s that security depended on three elements, physical (fences, CCTV, etc.), procedural (searching and counting), and dynamic (intelligence through relationships with prisoners).

It was clear that, whilst Stewart recognised the many excellent qualities of Michael Spurr, and knew that he was held in the highest esteem by pretty much everyone who worked for him, they did not see eye to eye and that he would prefer to have had someone at the head of HMPPS who 'shared the same ideas'. He seemed to have little appreciation of how difficult it must be for an operational manager, with knowledge and long experience, to 'share the same ideas' with so many Ministers in such a short space of time, especially when their ideas were so different from each other and pulled both the prisons and probation service this way and that against a background of deep cuts. When pressed he agreed that 'yes they do care deeply about the decency agenda but what they actually do is issue hundreds of complicated instructions … and they are incapable of indicating what a priority is.' He therefore felt that he really had no alternative but to intervene. He completely disagreed with the idea that it was not the Minister's job to get involved in operational details: 'I came into this system. I disagreed with what's happening, I don't think these places are properly run. What am I supposed to do?' What he did do, amid much publicity, was to put his job on the line. In August 2018 he had announced that he would resign in a year if he hadn't managed to bring about a substantial reduction in the numbers of assaults and the use of drugs in the ten worst prisons. At the same time, he announced a £10 million programme to improve security and conditions, and that military-style training was to be introduced for prison governors. Richard Burgon taunted him by noting that only three of those prisons were in the bottom categories of all four performance areas and that there were 15 other prisons which did fall within that remit. But he also assured us that it was Richard Heaton, the Permanent Secretary, and not he, who had decided that Michael Spurr should go at the end of April, although he was unlikely to have done so without consultation with Ministers. And he was not totally unrealistic when he told us that the Government's own position was sufficiently fragile that Michael Spurr might well outlast him.

Peter Clarke, Chief Inspector of Prison, shared Stewart's frustration at the failure of the Prison Service to act on his recommendations. In addition to the UN procedure, Clarke introduced three other measures to help improve 'the impact' of his reports, including 'careful targeting' of the media and new 'independent reviews of progress', with a focus on prison leadership. He insisted these were 'fundamentally different' to follow up inspections in that they looked at 'progress not outcomes ... asking whether action plans are realistic, are they targeted, are they resourced, and are there accountabilities?'. He hoped these would 'get round the Liverpool problem where clearly one end of the prison service didn't know what the other end was doing ... It's not a long chain of command is it? ... it shouldn't be that hard'. But it is important to note that Peter Dawson regarded this as an unwarrantable extension of the essential role of the Inspectorate from reporting on observed outcomes and into the realms of speculation about the quality of leadership – something he considered was beyond the Inspectorate's area of expertise. Clarke's third change involved the reintroduction into the prison service's own performance framework of 'achievement of inspectorate safety recommendations' which had been 'taken out by the prison service'. On the basis of these changes and increasing prison staff numbers Clarke described himself as 'very, very guardedly, cautiously optimistic' as he believed, like Stewart, if you can get the simple things right, the rest will follow. He did add a note of reservation that with the 'conveyor belt of Ministers ... it's a bit difficult to hold people to account when they're not there any longer'.

Stewart argued that the high turnover of Ministers was not unique to the Ministry of Justice but a regular feature of British political life and it affected all departments of state.

'In the Ministry of Defence Ministers come, they go, they all have different views, they all know nothing about the army, they're all only there for a year. Do you think the Chief of General Staff cares? ... Take DfID for example Ministers come and go and they make no impact ... the civil servants decided in 1997 what DfID did – and they simply ignore what the Minister says'.

What was different was the response of civil servants – for some reason, which he attributed to a loss of confidence in what the prison and probation service was actually about – there was simply less 'push back' in the face of Ministerial demands. Why didn't they say to Clarke and Grayling 'if you make those cuts you will find that violence in prisons will increase five-fold over the five years, drug rates will triple, weapons will triple' which is what Ministry of Defence or DfID officials would have said if faced with a similar situation. We asked if he was saying that the NOMS or HMPPS civil servants had not made that argument. He replied 'Well, they certainly didn't articulate it and win the argument.' We pointed out that there was no equivalent operational organisation of staff and clients in DfID and that quite different arguments were available to Generals at the MoD, and as far as we were aware there had not been successive Ministers pulling in significantly different directions in such short order. It was at this point where he admitted that he had been

> 'partly playing devil's advocate. Obviously most of the blame rests with the Ministers, I accept that. But I'm getting a little fed up with the argument that the civil servants were purely innocent and had no potential to argue back. This ministerial thing is a distraction – there is no other department of government where they spend all their time saying the problem is that Ministers keep changing. The whole civil service is set up to deal with changes of Ministers'.

We agreed to differ about whether HMPPS's position within MoJ was or was not like other departments of government.

We had a lengthy discussion, which at times became a robust argument, with Rory Stewart on sentencing policy in light of his recent advocacy of eliminating or at least curtailing the use of short sentences of imprisonment. This had brought down some flak from the *Daily Mail* and we began by asking how he saw the proposals developing. He explained:

> 'Well the fact is that the Government is immensely fragile – we don't have a majority in Parliament and we could collapse at any moment. But the sequence would be for us to publish a Green Paper in May and then we wouldn't be in a position to introduce legislation until next year. If I were still in power and if I had succeeded in winning the argument in the Green Paper and if it had not been torpedoed by the media, or by No 10, my dream would be to remove the 46% of the people who come into prison

each year. The number of beds they occupy at any one time, of course, is very much smaller about 6%. But my dream would be to prohibit all sentences of under three months, prohibit sentences of under six months but with some carve outs for violence and sex offences, and have a presumption against sentences of under 12 months'.

He rehearsed a well-considered set of arguments for converting fellow Parliamentarians, the Press and the Public pointing out that those on community sentences have lower rates of reoffending than those on short sentences, and that short sentences of imprisonment were long enough to be damaging but not long enough to effect improvement in behaviour. Whilst we supported those measures we said that they did not address what many regard as the real problem which concerns the incredible increase in the length of prison sentences. His response to this was:

'It depends what you mean by the real problem, It's the real problem in terms of crowding and it's the real problem in terms of costs. But it's not the real problem in my prisons. If you're interested in violence, cleanliness, decency of conditions, I think it is the short sentence prisoners who are the most destabilising factor. From the point of view of prison management, I get relatively few problems from my long term prisoners'.

When we suggested that the judges we spoke to complained about how they had to calibrate sentences according to mandatory terms increasingly laid down in legislation, he said:

'I disagree with that. I cannot see the point of putting a shoplifter in gaol. I can see the point in putting a murderer in jail. And I can't see why a judge should feel it is better to put a murderer in for 10 years rather than 14 which is the kind of difference we are talking about. I am very, very confident that the public feel that sentences are too short'.

We pointed out that this was somewhat different from the case he had put before the Justice Committee when he said that he was in favour of reducing long sentences but there was not the political will to do so. He agreed that we were

'right to pull me up on that. If I thought I could win the argument on long sentences I'd probably do that too. The honest answer is I lose more sleep at night over short sentence prisoners than I do over the issue of long sentences'.

We noted that he didn't use as an argument, as many of his predecessors did, that legislating for reduced sentences would interfere with the independence of the Judiciary. Something which did not bother politicians so much when they increased sentences or imposed mandatory minimum terms. He agreed. 'I do need to be honest about that. Parliament broadly speaking does ultimately control sentences so I don't buy into the argument about the independence of the judiciary. I think we should take responsibility for that.' He continued: 'I think there is a very strong sense among the public that we don't take crime seriously enough. As a constituency MP I am pretty deferential to public opinion. I feel that I can win the argument with the public on short sentences and I can't win it on long sentences'.

We asked whether he would nevertheless accept that reducing sentence lengths would have a much greater impact on the size of the population and make it easier to manage and without exposing the public to greater risk. He retorted that for 15 years the Ministry had been crippled by what he called

> 'the fantastic illusion that they are going to be able to reduce long sentences. Ken Clarke accepted a colossal reduction in budget believing he was going to reduce the number of prisoners … It is completely mad. I need another 20,000 prison places to accommodate my prisoners. I don't want to be stuck in a world where I am artificially crowding my prisons because people somehow believe that will force a change of policy'.

We suggested that the prison population was kept artificially high because of assumptions which politicians make about the public demand for stiffer penalties. At this point, he interrupted us to say 'what the public demand and what society expects – and that is my judgement as a working politician.' We briefly rehearsed the evidence that when asked the general question are sentences too lenient the answer is yes, but if you ask a specific question about what sentence should be passed in relation to an actual case they mostly underestimate the sentence actually given. Rory Stewart replied: 'I am aware of that research. If you wish to argue with me because you disagree with me that's fine. But if you're interested in my views …' It seemed the right moment to change the subject and we turned to the situation regarding probation.

We asked whether he thought it appropriate for Grayling to have introduced post-release supervision to all offenders regardless of their length of sentence. He told us that 'I don't think I have come to a view on that but my instinct is that we may not have to do that for all offenders.' So what then would be the role of the probation service in future?

> 'On probation my basic view is a variation of my view on prisons, which is that we have to stop talking about the grand objectives about reducing reoffending and we need to get back to basic questions. Are you meeting your offenders? Are you seeing them regularly? Have you done a decent assessment? Have you come up with a proper plan? I am trying to boil it down to the basic expectations to be placed on a busy staff. What is your caseload? What are you actually doing? There are a lot of things you have to do in probation which are not about reducing reoffending. I'd apply that to prisons too. There are a lot of things you have to do in prisons which are not about reoffending'.

Many within the prisons and probation service would agree with those sentiments: it is more often Ministers, including David Gauke, who prioritise rehabilitation over process.

We were left in no doubt that Rory Stewart was extremely passionate about his role and his commitment and ownership of responsibility as evidenced by his frequent references to 'my prisons' and 'my prisoners'. We were also left, however, with a slight feeling that there was some irreconcilable ambivalence in Rory Stewart's approach. On the one hand, he was fond of contrasting the chaotic state of the MoJ to the smooth running bureaucratic machines of the Ministry of Defence and DfID – where the civil servants, by his account, ruled the roost. On the other hand, he clearly enjoyed getting his teeth into the problems of HMPPS no matter how frustrating that was and would perhaps not relish the quiet life in another department where he might have little to do. Ironically, as events turned out he had no need to honour his promise to resign because three months after our interview and one day after Michael Spurr left office, he was promoted to Secretary of State at DfID in the reshuffle consequent upon the sacking of Gavin Williamson. Three months after that he resigned from the government and the Tory Party, when Boris Johnson became Prime Minister, and he sat as an independent MP until the General Election. He was replaced by Robert Buckland, who, after announcing in his first speech as Prisons Minister that he was going 'to do it my way', went on to replace David Gauke as Secretary of State and Lord Chancellor. Intriguingly both Spurr and Stewart, after leaving office took up honorary professorships – Spurr at LSE and Stewart at Yale.

Part two: The Directors of Prisons and Probation

Michael Spurr

Michael Spurr had survived nearly five of the most turbulent years ever experienced by the prison and probation services under the coalition during which there had been both massive cuts and major organisational changes. He now faced four years of ministerial churn at its most extreme: Michael Gove, Liz Truss, David Lidington and David Gauke followed one and other in quick succession, although Lidington put the brakes on change for change sake. But Justice Ministers still seemed quite unable to grasp the complexities of running large operational organisations or to appreciate the difficulties created by the ideological interventions and failures of their predecessors. Moreover, behind closed doors blame games were directed at civil servants. 'You end up' Spurr told us 'having to work through a whole load of stuff time and again that, eventually, often gets you back to the same place you were before'.

After the Conservatives won the election in 2015 Michael Gove was appointed Justice Secretary, and according to Spurr 'suddenly we had more cuts' expected of us, 'an immediate £300 million saving' to be made. Without the modest restraints of the Coalition, Gove, 'a friend of Osborne' at the Treasury, was keen to go 'even harder on austerity'. Gove believed that 'department civil servants are inefficient' and whilst at the Department of Education had brought in his own team and cut administration costs by 50%. He believed the same was possible in Justice, despite the 37% cuts which Spurr had already made in that area and notwithstanding the fact that, unlike at Education, Spurr's admin team were also managing operational matters. With the agreement of his 'Director of Finance' and the 'hugely helpful' cover of Nick Hardwick's powerful final Annual Report as Chief Inspector of Prisons, Spurr 'refused to take any more cuts after 2015'. As a result it was the wider Justice Department rather than prisons or probation that took most of the hit, despite the fact that they were already running at a deficit. In retrospect, Spurr wished he had gone further and asked for more money at this time. He didn't believe that he would have won the argument but 'would have felt better' for trying. Instead the only new Treasury money was for capital investment, '£1.3 billion … for new prisons' which had the potential to be 'transformative' if old prisons were closed. However, this never 'really materialised' and there remained 'nothing for day-to-day running' and the issue of reducing prison numbers was untouchable given that the Prime Minister was against it and Gove 'was grateful to David Cameron for appointing him'.

Spurr believed that when Gove was first appointed he was unable to do anything about probation because that had already been tackled by Grayling – 'which is why he threw everything into prisons.' In Spurr's view, Gove's attitude was that anyone who was associated with a policy he didn't agree with 'shouldn't really be around'. Gove, and later Rory Stewart, seemed always to be saying 'how did you allow all this to happen?' as if the Prime Minister and a previous Secretary of State hadn't been involved in the matter. He accepted that Gove was genuinely 'horrified about the conditions in prisons' but that was 'a good day' from Spurr's perspective because it might help to bring more resources to put things right. However, Gove's credentials as a 'disruptor' meant that he always wanted to do things differently, and was simply not interested in 'where we'd got to' with the decency agenda. Gove's plan was to transplant ideas from his independent academies to create 'autonomous reform prisons.' Spurr described this plan as 'complete nonsense' when you have an 'integrated' national system of well over 100 prisons with significant daily movement of prisoners between them. The logistical implications were huge and a major shift away from Grayling's standardised approach to prison regimes. When this was explained to Gove he simply took the view that the agency was 'too entrenched'.

Theoretically, Spurr's role was set out in a framework document, a legacy from the original agency model, which set out an agreement between the Chief Executive of the Agency, the Chief Secretary of the Treasury and the Secretary of State for Justice. Although Spurr did not agree with successive wordings that he should deliver a 'world class' system, the framework should have been the main point of reference. However, in his experience it was 'not seen as that important by the Department or Ministers'. Ministers seemed to be able to make changes at will because it was not set out in 'primary legislation'. It was supremely ironic that Gove wanted increased autonomy for governors whilst reducing the autonomy for the agency itself: things that Spurr 'used to have control over … were increasingly … pulled into a shared model' across the MoJ. Spurr certainly wanted 'greater flexibility', but at 'agency level', a return to 'a next steps agency with a proper line of governance where the Chief Executive is accountable to the Non-Executive Chair.' However, this was not acceptable to Gove. Gove 'got rid of people' who challenged his perspective or who 'weren't radical enough', including the board non-executives. The board was left without a non-executive chair for a year when Gove's latest choice, who was recruited 'the day before he was sacked,' was rejected by Liz Truss. It was becoming increasingly the case that senior officials were less able to 'stand up' to Ministers and give 'robust advice', and Gove in particular favoured the 'American system' whereby those 'around him should believe in' what Gove believed in. This sometimes left Spurr in a minority of one: 'the voice consistently saying this is going too far'. Gove, however was an early supporter of the UN process, to give the Inspectorate 'greater teeth … in statute' to hold the Secretary of State to account, who would be required to respond publicly in 28 days.

Gove's ideas had little time to take root because after the referendum the new Prime Minister, Theresa May, in effect, told Gove's successor, Liz Truss, that she didn't 'want individual autonomous prisons. I want a system'. And, according to Spurr, just as those in charge of Grayling's payment by results were shunned, under Gove those in charge of his 'five reform prisons' became 'persona non grata' under Truss. She wasn't interested in learning much about how prisons were run and 'didn't have much general policy' but she did understand 'about safety' and the need for resources to maintain it. However, agency status no longer guaranteed a direct line to the Treasury, and the MoJ

> 'had no clue about why we believed that if we had more prison officers that would make a difference to prison violence'.

Truss has generally been given the credit for gaining more resources so that something could be done to recruit staff but in fact it was Spurr who had to fight tooth and nail to get the money. He told us

> 'At one point I was removed by the Department from engaging with the Treasury and the Cabinet Office because they thought I was being too forceful in my arguing.'

However, 'the Cabinet Secretary, Jeremy Heywood, had got the point'. In December 2016 he got the money for '2,500 staff' but by then they actually needed to recruit 4,500 because they were now operating 2,000 below bench-marking numbers. The whole case for change was based on the 'offender man-agement in custody' (OMiC) model, 'effectively, bringing back the personal officer scheme', which was certainly something the service could readily buy into. By this time Spurr had long since rejected the offender manager in the community model and believed that bringing probation officers *back* into prison was vital. Under OMiC there would be 'a senior probation officer responsible for offender management' in every prison and all told some '300 plus probation officers' working alongside prison staff to 'manage' what in old fashioned terms was called 'sentence plan progression'. It would also enable probation officers to take back work that had been 'switched over to psychology' and oversee both multi-disciplinary work in prisons and the transition to aftercare in the commu-nity. It should provide consistency between how risk management and desistance is seen across both environments.

Although Liz Truss 'quickly … decided she did know about organisation structures,' Spurr described her as not having 'any clue whatsoever about how to run an organisation'. Gyimah, her Junior Minister, was capable but his personal ambition meant that he didn't want anything 'to touch him'. Liz Truss had told us when we interviewed her that she wanted to bring things more under direct ministerial control and in this she was assisted by Richard Heaton, the new Permanent Secretary. Heaton had come to the MoJ from the Cabinet Office but Spurr told us that he had 'previously worked in the Department of Work and Pensions when they had brought all their agencies, including Job Centre Plus, back into the main Department'. The MoJ Director of Finance, Mike Driver, had also worked in DWP and both were supporters of the single Departmental approach. This was something that was happening across most, if not all, government departments. Truss appointed Justin Russell as the MoJ Policy Director General for Prisons and Probation thereby creating a split at the top and functions which had been within the Agency – commis-sioning services in education and for intervention programmes, for example – were transferred to Russell's Directorate. Crucially Russell also took respon-sibility for the Performance Framework to 'hold us to account' and to prevent us from 'marking our own homework'. The performance management arm, established under NOMS in 2008, was at first queried by Ken Clarke but he then accepted that the model worked well and that 'we were honestly report-ing on our own performance targets'. The risk of taking this away from the agency was to put it with people who didn't understand what they were meas-uring, and in Truss's time the system became 'less good than it was before'. This restructuring, from Spurr's point of view just created 'more distraction, fragmentation and duplication'. Russell had been a special adviser to John Reid and Jack Straw before joining the civil service, and although Spurr regarded him as a 'capable and decent man' the new arrangements 'inevitably created some tensions'.

Spurr told us that the loss of functions left him spending 'half my time' just trying to 'get permission to be able to run the organisation'. This was 'encouraged by Truss' with a focus on 'driving down costs'. However, Spurr had 'red lines' which he sought to defend, including keeping control of his Human Resources, which was enshrined in the framework document and which he regarded as essential in a 'people organisation' managing difficult 'trade unions'. He also wanted to keep his commercial, procurement, finance and IT expertise, but these were eventually all lost to 'the centre'. The Permanent Secretary was under constant threat from Truss who wanted to maintain her 'grip' and this meant he in turn was always wanting 'to know what was going on in prisons … he tries to be all over it but can't be'. As a result Spurr was put in an impossible position, where he was constantly 'briefing up' rather than getting on with the job of running the agency, no longer in charge of his own operational team.

In Autumn 2016 Spurr came close to quitting as Truss set up twice daily 'bird table meetings' designed to hold him 'to account' for the series of disturbances that culminated in the Birmingham riot. Here he was expected 'to report on events in the morning and resolve them by the evening', and on a couple of occasions Ministers checked with governors to see whether 'what I was saying was right or wrong' which risked totally 'undermining how we ran the whole operation'. However, he felt he couldn't leave because there were no others ready to step in at this point.

'David Lidington' followed Truss but 'wasn't there long enough' to effect change, although Spurr recognised his potential as someone who 'understood … because … he … was … a historian … he'd worked in the Home Office … and he'd been a lot to his local prison at Aylesbury'. He had some interesting ideas, closer to the early years of New Labour, planning a 'broader, cross-government group, or board, that was looking at how you would tackle the wider issues of reoffending'. He also took a keen interest in the Homelessness Reduction Act 2017, recognising that prisons and probation can't do it all. However, Lidington opposed some of Spurr's plans for the women's estate. When Truss's White Paper had talked of creating five new community prisons, interest groups expressed reservations about their financing and location, and whether they might lead to an expansion of the estate. Michael Spurr did not wish to expand women's prisons: he had closed Holloway and planned a second closure but his intention was to continue the practice of placing the new '60 bed units' outside the gates of existing prisons. He reflected that one of the aims of TR was to reconfigure the estate so 'that people could move prisoners closer to home', but this had 'been much more problematic than we'd anticipated. You end up always having to make compromises.'

Truss's *Prison and Courts Bill* was lost but Lidington continued with the implementation of the UN process, although the first was not issued until Gauke's time in office. Spurr thought that the UN procedure had 'a lot of merit' although he had warned Truss that 'it was going to be very painful' without the 'money to respond'.

> 'Liz Truss said to me … don't be silly, Michael. That gives us the ammunition … to get money out of the Treasury. I said well, I'm not sure it'll work quite like that, and … you need to recognise that there will be a significant amount of political flak if we're getting negative reports about things that we're unable to do anything about. And, of course, that's precisely what's happened'.

However, despite the Secretary of State being accountable and required to respond to a UN within 28 days, the responsibility, and therefore the blame, remains with the agency not the Minister or the Department, despite Michael Spurr's much reduced autonomy. He was now only able to speak out 'in front of a parliamentary committee' but it was important that they asked the right questions: 'if they asked the right questions, they'd get the right answers'. Neither Gove, nor Truss had to live with the painful consequences of the UN procedure and Spurr had said 'to David Gauke that he should go back to Liz Truss, because she's now Chief Secretary of the Treasury' to remind her of what she had said by way of the appropriate 'response to urgent notifications'. Because ultimately all you can do in response to a UN is put more resource in, 'experienced staff' or 'capital expenditure to improve conditions' or 'reduce the prison population', all of which Spurr would be trying to do if these were within his control.

When David Gauke replaced Lidington he walked straight into the Worboy's parole case. Spurr told us

> 'I was surprised by the decision to release Worboys and had some sympathy for David Gauke's situation but was uncomfortable with the process which followed and feel it has created unrealistic expectations for victims. I profoundly disagreed with the decision to remove Nick Hardwick'.

However, once that was out of the way Gauke 'wanted to be a socially reforming Secretary of State,' focusing on reducing 'short sentences'. Gauke was ready to look at probation and address the problems produced by TR, although he remained 'keen to defend the market'. Spurr agreed with Glenys Stacey, that the TR model was wrong and they shouldn't have split offender management in the way that they had, but he did not believe that it was 'irredeemably flawed'. He recognised that 'the private sector providers' were 'never funded' to deliver 'to the same level as the National Probation Service.' They were 'undone by the volume change in cases and the outcomes of payment by results which were nothing to do with them.' He had, in fact, always predicted this would be a problem. The only charge you could fairly lay at the door of the CRCs, he thought, was whether they were delivering 'value for money' in 'providing greater support' to facilitate desistance from crime. This had been the basic argument for extending supervision to all short sentence prisoners, and here he thought they could have 'done better'. However, Gauke's reason for returning probation to the public sector was 'that he was persuaded' that this would 'significantly enhance' the confidence of magistrates sufficiently for him to pursue his focus on 'reducing short term prison sentences and improving community sentence provision'. Spurr was 'in favour' of that approach but also believed that magistrates still needed the ultimate sanction of imprisonment, and that anyway the short-term population was now 'below 7,000'. He agreed that there was scope for further reductions but told us that the only way to address the problem of our inflated prison population 'is to address the length of sentences'.

Rory Stewart was undoubtedly trying to address conditions in prisons through his high profile 'ten million pound', 'ten prisons project' wherein he presented himself as 'the saviour of the prison service'. This involved a move away from the concern of Liz Truss about prison culture towards concerns over 'perimeter security' and the need for military-style 'leadership'. Spurr was not against Stewart's focus on technology but, like his governors, he believed that money for scanners could be better spent on staffing. Rory Stewart's views were 'very, very quickly … determined' in response to governors' non-standardised approaches on his early prison visits. Spurr argued that 'there are things you do standardise, but, actually, how a person leads is not one I would standardise'. Stewart did recognise the limitations of Truss's performance measures but simply sought to replace them with his own, offering no greater clarity of direction to establishments. Spurr's job was somehow to align the changes into a coherent whole. Much of the policy was 'not wrong' individually, but it showed little continuity with what had gone before.

Stewart actively undermined Spurr's leadership position with his troops, by blaming him for the current state of prisons. This happened increasingly in a 'public arena' with staff hearing political rhetoric from the Minister which didn't match the reality as seen either from the top or from the ground within the service. Stewart's criticisms of staff training and the line management structure was 'ridiculously simplistic' according to Spurr. It did not recognise either the cost of training or the context of the 'fair and sustainable' changes, that in 2012 had introduced a lower pay rate for new staff, and removed costly line-manager duties for senior officers. According to Spurr, Stewart was 'naïve' about trade unions and financial matters, having never worked in a 'department where staff didn't do what you asked them' or where there was 'a problem with money'. He was angry that Stewart argued he should have fought harder against the cuts, given that the Department continued to demand that he should 'take more money out of the organisation' whilst Stewart was in office. Spurr deliberately overspent his budget 'by £120 million … for the first time' in his final year of service, to avoid the alternative of 'reducing prison officers'. Spurr believed that Gauke recognised the money problems having had experience as Chief Secretary to the Treasury. Stewart did not.

Ultimately, the UN process led to Michael Spurr's departure although it had been clear that Stewart, with the support of the Permanent Secretary, wanted him gone. Peter Clarke's UN focus on leadership, as well as that of the Justice Committee, left Gauke unable to resist. Spurr believed that the 28-day turnaround for UNs drove unrealistic expectations that 'deep-seated problems' can be solved 'in relatively short order'. He claimed that Peter Clarke's focus on 'using the Press as a lever to get traction' affected his choice of where to issue a UN, and that this demoralised staff at prisons where they were working hard to make a difference. He cited the example of HMP Nottingham which received a UN despite having been found to be improving in many areas and being told by the inspection team, of which Clarke was not a member, that 'they would not be recommending an urgent notification'. So that when the UN came it knocked everyone back, and that was compounded when they were further criticised for not turning everything around in 28 days. The effect of a UN, and indeed Stewart's 10 prison project, is that if you put all your resources and effort into a few prisons your plates start to spin slower elsewhere. Spurr was also concerned that Clarke's recent focus on 'leadership' sometimes left him blinkered to other issues such as resources. Nevertheless, Spurr hoped that in the long term the UN procedure will make a positive difference, 'if it exposes the under resourcing, and can tackle crowding'. But the collateral damage in the short term, which included that to himself, has the potential to make the service untenable if the blame game goes on and staff continue to leave.

When it was announced that Spurr would leave at the end of April 2019 a flood of commentators came to his defence arguing that most of the problems that bedevilled prisons and probation were the result of conflicting ministerial decisions and in no way down to his leadership. The former New Labour Lord Chancellor, Charlie Falconer, wrote:

> 'Michael Spurr is a terrifically impressive, decent public servant who has given his working life to prison and probation, and has been dealt as shitty a hand by the government as it is possible to deal'.
>
> *(The Guardian, 20.9.18)*

But before he left Spurr was nevertheless asked to try to provide a more coherent restructuring of the Agency. On the assumption that his successor would be unlikely to have an operational background he argued for separate Directors General for Prisons, Probation and Youth custody each working to a single CEO with overall responsibility for the system as a whole. He also argued for the return of operational policy, commissioning and interventions to the Agency. This model was accepted and in due course Phil Copple (Prisons). Amy Rees (Probation) and Helga Swidenbank (Youth Custody) were so appointed as well as Ian Blakeman as Director of Performance (including commissioning and interventions) – all working to Jo Farrar as the new CEO. This reduced the responsibilities that fell to Justin Russell.

Roger Hill

By the time we interviewed Roger Hill in his office at Sodexo he had had plenty of time to reflect upon what had happened to prisons and, especially, probation from his position of working both in the public and private sectors. Under Grayling's strategy of TR, Sodexo had become the largest private-sector provider running six of the 21 CRCs contracted to provide supervision and intervention services to medium and low-risk offenders on a payment by results basis. The NPS retained control of offender management for high-risk offenders and court services. This artificial split of probation services on the basis of risk had stifled communication and progress in his view. He had previously told us that this had left CRCs 'unable to form relationships with the courts', which would be integral if you wished to encourage them to use CRC interventions. He would have wanted CRCs to be able to go to courts and explain the innovations they had to offer and which constituted alternatives to custody. By way of elaboration, he told us that it would have been far better if the introduction of private involvement in the probation service mirrored the competition process adopted in prisons. That would have meant taking 'a free-standing piece of the probation service, which could only have been geographical … and put it to the market. And everything that probation area does you contract with a company to deliver it' or a public sector bidder. Perhaps it would also have been necessary to create a separate 'public sector court report writing service'. But that opportunity was lost in a completely bodged process. Regrettably, such a possibility was precluded in the planned return to the public sector of all offender management in 2021, leaving the private sector to manage community payback and to compete for intervention programmes (MoJ, 2019).

Roger Hill had also come to the conclusion that organisational changes really had to stop. He told us that 'my biggest regret is that no credence was given to the idea of fine tuning what you already have'. If the contracts for services had been longer it would have been possible to learn from mistakes to improve the delivery of the service. But successive Ministers seemed averse to a sustained approach of gradual improvement and were much given to short term and sudden changes of direction.

> 'The solution always seems to be to discard what existed and replace it with something utterly different. The cost of that type of approach to re-structuring is huge and never properly recognised. Every time government re-structures it takes two years to dismantle what's in place and a further two years to build the new arrangement, and in the meantime performance dips and delivery stagnates'.

He thought we needed to 'accept that there is no perfect structure' and that instead, we should 'build on the strengths that are emerging'. He went on to say that 'if working in the private sector has taught me anything it is that subtle changes and fine tuning what you have, even if it's not ideal, is the way to move forward and improve delivery'. If only Governments would learn this simple lesson and 'accept that there is no perfect structure' and that turning both offenders and organisations around is 'a very lengthy process'. He still saw probation as the most vulnerable of the criminal justice services because the emphasis on enforcement, public protection and reducing reoffending, still leaves them in the spotlight. They are not only more liable to take the blame for offenders reoffending but also have less of a voice to defend themselves. He therefore feared that the pattern of 'sheer destructiveness' could be repeated. Why did he think so?

> 'Because … if you see the criminal justice system comprising by and large four groups, one being law and legal, one being police, one being prisons and one being probation, three of those four groups are devilishly difficult to change, and one isn't.

Although he now preferred gradual consolidation to reorganisation, if he was pushed his ideal would be a return to local arrangements for probation, with close but well defined, working relations with the courts and the police. He would like funding to be managed locally so that local authorities had a stake in who they sent to prison and who they dealt with in their communities. Let prisons do imprisonment, let community sentences do punishment and helping separate from one another. He thought punishment should be an important part of *all* community sentences and social work type interventions used in addition for those offenders who also had problems they were unable to solve by themselves. He wanted life-experienced qualified probation staff to be active in the community not stuck behind computer screens on their desks, and probation to be held to account to National Standards that nevertheless left room for innovation, and to be held responsible only for what is within their power and not for the failings of the system as a whole.

Phil Wheatley

Although Phil Wheatley had retired as Chief Executive of NOMS and Director General of the Prison Service in June 2010 he had kept a close and critical eye on what happened during both the Coalition years and the Conservative Government elected in 2015 and he took what opportunities he could to draw attention to the failings of government policy. In December 2016, for example, he wrote a newspaper article under the headline 'It took years of Tory cuts and wild policy swings to create this prison crisis' (*The Guardian*, 12.12.16). He pointed out that when he left the service it was 'performing strongly' with 'suicides, escapes and serious incidents of disorder … at an all-time low … and … more than 10% improvement in reoffending since 2000.' This had been achieved despite the 'organisational upheavals' initiated by Ministers as they 'created and then reformed the National Offender Management Service.' When Wheatley had refused any longer to comply with Ministers' 'unwillingness to fund the increases in the prison population that were driven by their obsession with populist law and order policies' or their failure to accept advice about the attendant risks of dangerous levels of overcrowding, he was obliged to resign.

After cataloguing the consequences of the cavalier twists and turns of policy under Clarke, Grayling and Gove, Wheatley turned his critical gaze on Liz Truss. On the plus side he noted that her proposed league tables, greater budgetary freedom for governors, and accountability for hitting performance targets represented some kind of return to the system operated prior to 2010. But he was aghast at her transfer of the control of human resources, finance and procurement – all of which were 'integral to the management effort to resolve the problems faced'– from HMPPS to the MoJ. Not only did this undermine those management efforts but it meant that those services would be managed by staff 'who have no experience of the operational challenges faced by prisons.' In our interview, Wheatley reiterated the critical analysis that he had already made publicly, arguing that Michael Spurr was no longer 'responsible for … his own personnel department, his own finance'. The MoJ was now responsible for operational as well as policy matters, which was a very far cry from the original conception of an independent Agency. He extended his criticisms to the then current monitors on prisons – HM Chief Inspector of Prisons, Peter Clarke, and the then (Acting) Prison Ombudsman, Elizabeth Moody, both of whom he regarded as essentially political appointments. He described the Chief Inspector, as 'Gove's man' and someone who had 'no understanding of the link between resources and performance' in prisons. Although Clarke presented 'an accurate perception of prisons' he blamed governors for not following up on his recommendations despite the fact that they were 'running 20% light on staff' – and he failed to understand why 'not enough staff had been recruited.' It should not have been too difficult to understand, given that 'the rates they're paying are not even comparable to the rates that they pay in *Top Shop*'. The Inspector, in his view, was 'letting Ministers off the hook nicely'. Elisabeth Moody had spent much of her career as a civil servant within the Home Office and then the MoJ, so that most of her experience was about 'getting on with Ministers'. She returned to her former role as Deputy Ombudsman when Sue McAllister, an ex-governor was appointed as Ombudsman. The current system allowed Ministers to 'pick people who are not likely to be problematical to them' whereas the whole point of Reports and Inspections is that they should be 'fair … independent and expert' and should make you feel 'not at all comfortable.' Indeed, now that so many operational matters are in the Ministry as well as policy, there is an argument that Ministers must be more than held to account by the Inspectorate, they must take a fair share of the responsibility, the blame.

Wheatley recognised that there were many ways in which the performance of prisons and probation could be improved, and he told us that 'you've always got to keep on working at a prison service. You never think you've got it right and stand back, because if you stand back it'll just fall back on you'. But he could also look back upon a time when politicians took responsibility for the failings of the system, realised change was long term and listened to the voices of experienced administrators and researchers, and when, for a time at least, Directors were given greater freedom to speak out. However, research on outcomes could not be done quickly and was too complicated to fit into the political cycle. The implementation of reforms needed careful planning and time to bed in, if they were to be successful, and that extended way beyond the span of individual Ministers. The system was thus forced into 'quick fixes' in an attempt to deal with deep-seated problems. He sometimes thought it would be necessary to precipitate some kind of 'political disaster', say by taking some accommodation out of the system on safety grounds, using the Health and Safety at Work Act 1974, thus forcing the Minister to find alternatives. This would be a high-risk strategy but ultimately 'you've got to make them understand' that this is their responsibility and they have to solve it.

With the benefit of hindsight he thought benchmarking had been a step too far which oversimplified the complexity of prison life and prison officer work, leaving the system on a knife-edge. The many versions of NOMS did not help although they highlighted the lack of efficiency in probation and the lack of measures of effectiveness. Gradual changes were successfully applied to both prisons and probation but the effects of austerity were devastating and what had once been a reasonably efficient system was simply unable to absorb the enormous cuts laid at the door of his successor Michael Spurr. Despite this, Ministers have continued to play the game of upping sentences for political gain – sentence lengths had 'more than doubled' since Wheatley had first become involved with prisons. And there appeared to be no end to this process as 'the ability to appeal lots of sentences' was now 'enshrined in legislation.'

In considering where we go from here if we are to deal with the continuing crisis, Wheatley said 'there are only two ways out of this. Put more money in, or have fewer prisoners'. The current focus by Ministers on short sentence prisoners is nothing like enough. There were 'about 6,000 prisoners serving sentences under 12 months. So, if you make a 20% reduction in that group, it's worth having, but it's pretty marginal'. The focus, which Ken Clarke was the last Minister to recognise, needed to be on 'sentence inflation'. We should stop focusing on the smaller targets of women and children and focus on the big one. Politicians need to be willing and able to say 'we're locking people up for much longer than makes any sort of sense. We can't afford it, and therefore we're going to reduce sentence lengths'. Alternatively, if they 'say we really have to lock them up for this long, then they have to fund it.' If politicians were prepared to take the lead in trying 'to get some sort of grip on our desire for revenge' and provide the necessary 'political cover,' Wheatley believed, the Judiciary would be able to begin reversing the recent trends without jeopardising respect for the law. The Sentencing Council could be required to return to 'paying attention to the effect they have on the prison population' and become 'the engine for making changes.'

As Liz Truss had reminded us, although many politicians were honest enough to recognise the need for this in private, it would take a 'brave politician' to argue the case in public.

References

Coates, Dame S. (2016) *Unlocking Potential. A Review of Prison Education*, Ministry of Justice, May 2016.

Farmer, Lord M. (2017) *The Importance of Strengthening Prisoners' Family Ties to Prevent Reoffending and Reduce Intergenerational Crime*, Ministry of Justice.

Gauke, D. (2018) *Prison Reform*, Speech given at the RSA 6th March.

Gove, M. (2016) *What's Really Criminal About Our Justice System*, Longford Lecture, 1st November.

HMIP (2016) *An Inspection of Through the Gate Resettlement Services for Short-Term Prisoners*. Criminal Justice Joint Inspection.

HMIP (2017) *Her Majesty's Inspectorate of Probation*, Annual Report, 2017.

Justice Committee (2018) *Transforming Rehabilitation. Ninth Report of Session 2017-18 (HC 482)*.

King, R. D. and Elliott, K. (1977) *Albany: Birth of a Prison – End of an Era*, London: Routledge and Kegan Paul.

Public Accounts Committee (2016) *Transforming Rehabilitation. Seventeenth Report of Session 2016-17 (HC484)*.

Ministry of Justice (2019) *Strengthening Probation, Building Confidence. Response to Consultation. (CP93)*.

Ministry of Justice (2013) *Attitudes to Sentencing and Trust in Justice: Exploring Trends from the Crime Survey for England and Wales*.

National Audit Office (2016) *Transforming Rehabilitation. Session 2015-16 (HC 951)*.

Parmar, K. (2018) *HMP Wandsworth and the Reform Journey*, MSt Dissertation, Cambridge.

6

VIEWS FROM THE LORD CHIEF JUSTICES

Introduction

All four of the most recently retired Lord Chief Justices responded to our request for an interview with enthusiasm and without delay. Although we had a range of topics we wanted to cover, time permitting, we wished first and foremost to listen to what the Chief Justices had to say. Only occasionally did we offer prompts once the discussion had started. On the topics we did cover there was substantial agreement between them.

Lord Woolf

We interviewed Lord Harry Woolf in his rooms just a short walk from the House of Lords on 19 November 2018. He had been Lord Chief Justice from 2000 until 2005 when Derry Irvine had been Lord Chancellor and Jack Straw, David Blunkett and Charles Clarke had been Home Secretary. He was, of course, the principal author of the report on Strangeways and his conclusions and recommendations were largely couched in terms of requiring closer cooperation between different parts of the criminal justice system and matters concerning the procedures and internal organisation for the prison service to take on board. Apart from recommendations 6, calling for a system of accredited standards which he wished to see eventually as a statutory requirement, and 7, that no prison should be allowed to hold more prisoners than its stated certified normal accommodation, (neither of which was ever accepted by any government), and recommendation 8, that Ministers should commit to a timetable to end slopping out (which was actually done even more quickly than Woolf requested), the report steered clear of direct criticism of government policy.

DOI: 10.4324/9781003201748-7

After his retirement, Woolf became a tireless campaigner in furtherance of his ambition 'to achieve a prison system imbued with justice and fairness'. That this had not been achieved in the quarter of a century since Strangeways he attributed unequivocally to 'inflation in sentencing, which increases the likelihood of overcrowding without producing any corresponding benefit.' In his speech, 'Strangeways 25 Years On', delivered at the Inner Temple, Woolf (2015) wanted political parties to 'include an undertaking to advance the cause of achieving a just system without engaging in a political contest. Let's take politics out of prisons.' When we spoke to him, almost five more years had passed and the situation had only got worse. He told us:

> 'Unfortunately they have never been able to resist the temptation to be tough on crime without being tough on the causes of crime …. I always tried to warn them when they are bringing in new offences – which they love doing – or raising the punishments for existing offences – that there is no counterbalance for keeping people who commit less serious offences out of prison, or to reduce other sentences. Sentence inflation has been the most serious problem and the Sentencing Council has no sensitivity to the importance of it acting as a brake against this, which I hoped it would. The Sentencing Council is failing to realise that if you raise the sentence in one part of the system, you're going to have to raise it across the board'.

Woolf explained that he had 'huge respect for David Blunkett.' In July 2002 Woolf, Blunkett and Derry Irvine, the Lord Chancellor, had issued a joint statement urging sentencers to consider carefully whether custody is the most effective option, and this led to a tentative agreement that the then Sentencing Guidelines Council would take account of the availability and cost of prison places in an attempt to prevent the prison population exceeding 80,000. But Blunkett's Criminal Justice Act (CJA) 2003, with its sentences of Imprisonment for Public Protection (IPP) as well as mandatory life sentences with statutory minimum terms, was a major contributor to the growth of the prison population. At the time Woolf (*The Guardian* 28.11.03) had criticised mandatory sentencing as 'a politician's knee-jerk reaction to a particularly serious incident'. In our interview, he told us that Blunkett had got things 'very sadly wrong' and he was critical of his motives for imposing mandatory minimum terms: 'It was to stop, as he thought, the European Court from impinging upon his rights as Home Secretary.' When we asked whether the judiciary and himself, as Lord Chief Justice, had been consulted about the provisions, he told us:

> 'The Chief Justice can exert a certain influence. They don't like ignoring you completely, but I know from experience that the ability to really dampen them down from doing really stupid things is very limited. In those conversations you're very much the junior partner'.

He had, however, 'got Blunkett to go and see the problem-solving courts in the USA.' Woolf had earlier visited Red Hook in New York and had been impressed. Blunkett was similarly impressed 'and he introduced it here and it was doing well, I gather, but unfortunately, he then moved on and since then it has not been enthusiastically received. The Home Office were never attracted by it.'

Unsurprisingly, Lord Woolf was aghast at the way politicians had 'demoralised the probation services to a terrible extent' and created 'huge problems within the prisons, from the point of view of keeping control of the population … even though they are already suffering from being starved of resources, they are still imposing cuts.' He thought it was absurd that they had cut resources so much that the prison service no longer had sufficient experienced staff and that 'they're now having to try and attract the people they got rid of back …. a most uneconomic way of doing things'.

Lord Woolf told us that 'Gauke really disappointed me with regard to the dismissal of the Chairman of the Parole Board.' He thought 'it was a really bad case of shifting the blame. It took me back to the times when Howard got rid of Derek Lewis.' However, since that poor start, he now thought that David Gauke and Rory Stewart had 'recognised that there is a crisis' and were saying 'encouraging things.' When we explained that part of our concern was with the 'politics of churn', as Ministers came and then quickly went, he agreed that we 'were quite right to focus on the turnover of Home Secretaries and now Secretaries of State for Justice.' He evidently was in touch with David Gauke from time to time because he told us of a conversation in which he had 'said to Gauke the other day that I hope he's there long enough to do some of these positive things.' But the real issue in the current crisis was the 'lack of resources'. Indeed, he hoped

> 'that the lack of resources may be the key to them giving up on some of the policies, which I think are so mistaken, that they will realise that the situation will continue to deteriorate'.

He had been very concerned, for example, about the proposals to build Titan prisons, which were 'not where the answer lies. We want to be closing prisons rather than opening more and more.' He also thought we could learn things from Scotland, where they had 'really turned their faces against short sentences of imprisonment' and he hoped that the Sentencing Council could use that as a precedent in England and Wales because 'If you reduce sentences, you might find that it actually reduces crime'. There were also lessons to be had, he thought, from Glasgow in relation to knife crime. Although sentences for knife crime had risen substantially, the Glasgow police had realised that more stop and search, more prosecutions, convictions and tougher sentences would never eliminate it. Substantial reductions in the number of deaths as a result of the use of knives by gang members had been achieved by the adoption of a more public health approach giving attention to the needs of gang members including support for families over rehousing.

However, it would be fair to say that Lord Woolf was no longer hopeful about taking the politics out of prisons – 'I'm afraid the omens aren't auspicious' he told us. 'There just seems to be an unwillingness to see what's staring them in the face. That's what makes me really pessimistic.' But he did take some small comfort from the situation over Brexit at the time, where he thought the frenetic political activity had served to take prisons, probation and criminal justice generally out of the front line. Moreover, Brexit divisions and alliances were crossing party lines, so it was possible that there could be cooperation on other issues once Brexit was resolved. And he urged us not to be 'dissuaded by the difficulty of the task from trying, because once you've got the facts that will be more persuasive than aspirations.'

Lord Phillips

Lord Phillips was interviewed at his home on 28 January 2019. His period in office from 2005 until 2008 saw the transition from the Home Office to the Ministry of Justice, during which time Charlie Falconer – the last of the old-style Lord Chancellors – was succeeded by the first of the new, Jack Straw.

Lord Phillips has been a prominent critic of government criminal justice policies and we can here refer to just a few examples from his many speeches. In 2017, he opened his speech during a debate on prison overcrowding in uncompromising fashion:

> 'My Lords, we are dealing with a problem that successive Governments have failed to solve for over half a century. The cause of that problem is that we send far too many people to prison for far too long; far longer than is necessary for rehabilitation and far longer than is needed for an effective deterrent'.
>
> *(Hansard, HL 7.9.17)*

He regarded this, somewhat generously, as the product of '40 years of "sentence creep", brought about largely by well-intentioned but misguided legislative intervention.' Lord Philips went on to argue that what was needed was a change in public attitudes which called for

> 'leadership and courage on the part of Government. The aim should be, for a start, to halve the number of those in prison. IPP prisoners should be released. Old men who no longer pose any threat should not be held in expensive custody. Most importantly legislation should reverse the trend of requiring ever longer sentences'.

The previous year, in a debate on prison reform, he asked the Minister to tell us 'how the Government will break the vicious circle' of 'improving rehabilitation without reducing prison numbers?' (Hansard, HL 15.3.16) Three months later, he had argued that Ministers should not hide behind 'the usual response that sentence lengths are a matter for judges' because 'the overall scale of sentencing is determined by legislative action that ratchets up minimum sentences …. they are much longer than is necessary to achieve the objects of deterrence, punishment and rehabilitation' (Hansard, HL 14.6.16). On that occasion, he told us ruefully, that he was addressing a far-from-crowded House late on a Thursday afternoon and that 'the House of Lords isn't the ideal loudspeaker for getting views across to the populace'. But he said, there would be little point in writing something for the *Daily Mail* 'even if they were prepared to publish it' because they would probably 'have somebody the next day saying exactly the opposite only in much bigger type.' In any case he wondered,

> 'to what extent did that matter? If you talk to individual members of the public you will find that they are not baying for blood and longer sentences at all … ultimately, it's the politicians who need persuading and when you occasionally get a good Lord Chancellor, then you are preaching to the converted'.

He had in mind here a Lord Chancellor such as Ken Clarke, whom he described as 'an extremely enlightened man and if he had been in charge for five years you would actually get somewhere.' But he told us that so much also depends upon who is Prime Minister. He and Clarke were not Lord Chief Justice and Lord Chancellor at the same time, and Clarke had told us that he had only been offered two years back in the Cabinet and that Cameron effectively pulled the rug from under his plans to reduce the prison population.

Lord Phillips and Lord Woolf had gone to see Tony Blair and succeeded in resisting the idea of merging the prison service with the Lord Chancellor's Department, although something rather like that eventually 'came to pass' and without proper, or indeed any, consultation. Like all the judges we have spoken to, he regretted the passing of the old-style Lord Chancellor who was better able to defend the independence of the Judiciary. Traditionally, these were distinguished lawyers at the end of their careers, but 'now you get a Lord Chancellor who is in charge' for whom

> 'this is a step up or a step down in a political career, normally a step up rather than dumping some second-rate person on the way down. Either way they don't stay there very long because it's not rated as a top job in government so you're looking to move on'.

In our interview, Lord Phillips described the current situation in regard to attitudes to punishment and rehabilitation as

> 'absolutely horrific. Politicians react to any criminal situation by increasing sentence length notwithstanding that it's quite plain that sentence length

is not really critical in deterring crime. Basically people commit crimes because they think they are not going to get caught'.

He was 'perfectly happy for fraudsters and others, who weigh up the odds and act cold-bloodedly in terms of self-interest to be sent to prison for reasonable lengths of time.' But, echoing the findings of the Bradley Report, he noted that large numbers of prisoners had mental health problems and ought not to be in prisons at all, indeed 'a vast range of people in prison are inadequate in one way or another' including many young people who suffered 'horrific social deprivation'. He thought that the kneejerk response to knife crime was particularly pointless:

> 'Youths who stab people; they don't control their emotions and so they do something horrific. But there is no point in locking them up for 10 years or 20 years for a two-minute loss of temper'.

He certainly thought it obvious that 'you've got to have punishment in society in order to stop society taking punishment into their own hands' but he was completely opposed to the introduction of statutory minimum sentences. He believed that the knock-on consequences, whereby the Sentencing Council felt obliged to go into greater and greater detail about aggravating and mitigating circumstances that judges had to take into account, were unhelpful. He was equally opposed to Blunkett's introduction of sentences of IPP on the basis of judgements about future risks rather than the gravity of the current offence.

> 'It's never been our justice system that you keep someone permanently in prison who has committed perhaps a comparatively minor offence if you decide he's a risk to society. It's grossly unjust that these people have ended up in prison indefinitely. Let's face it almost anyone who's in prison is a risk. Give them a chance to re-offend and then lock them up for their reoffending, or give them a chance not to reoffend and let them be free'.

In the past, the government and the judiciary agreed that some ideas might not match public expectations but were necessary for the smooth running of justice, such as time off for an early guilty plea. 'The public might not think that was a good idea, but this is what government is all about'. Such pragmatism was given short shrift when Ken Clarke tried to extend the idea in the Legal Aid, Sentencing and Punishment of Offender (LASPO) Bill. Now, the situation has changed.

> 'They don't trust judges to be severe enough to satisfy what they see as the public appetite, and so they react to a particular crime by saying "Right, we must have a minimum sentence of five years for this or that" with the additional 'tick' list of the Sentencing Council instead of trusting 'judges to apply their own common sense'.

Although Lord Phillips believed that 'we ought to be .... properly rehabilitating those who are in prison, tending for those who come out of prisons so they don't re-offend', he thought that the best way of getting the 'resources to do what we ought to be doing' was by cutting back on 'the number of people in prison.' He was acutely aware of the huge costs of imprisonment – at around £40k the same average cost per annum as a year's tuition in private education – it was extremely poor value for money. And when the sentence is 25 years, that is £1million that could be better spent. He regarded it, in fact, as 'complete nonsense' and whilst he did think that prisons should do their best to rehabilitate prisoners he also recognised that 'prison is not the best place to rehabilitate offenders'. But our beleaguered prison system has to spend what funds it has 'fire-fighting, finding places for evermore people who are being banged up.' It follows that Lord Phillips was a great supporter of effective community sentencing which had a far greater chance of rehabilitating offenders by giving them responsibilities rather than taking them away, and giving them dignity and encouraging self-respect. He went further than our other judges and officials to ask 'what's wrong with being soft if it's actually doing the job?' He believed community sentencing options were rejected as judges lacked confidence in the resource to carry them through. He also saw the potential of problem-solving courts as another opportunity to show offenders that someone cares, 'hands-on involvement with the people you are sentencing, so they actually feel that there's somebody that cares about how they're doing.' He famously donned a high viz jacket and spent a day incognito doing community service whilst still Lord Chief Justice. However, he regretted that he had allowed his Press office to give the exclusive story to *The Observer* which resulted in all the other papers calling it

> 'a publicity stunt. It would have been much better if I had had a press conference for everyone and said 'I just wanted to get across that community service is a good thing and I can tell you because I've just done that'.

Maybe some of our politicians interested in criminal justice might give it a try and, by way of contrast, perhaps spend a night or two in prison. One of us once took a party of Yale students on a field trip to a Connecticut prison then used for training prison staff where we all spent a few days and nights locked up – an eye-opening experience for us all.

Lord Judge

Our interview with Lord Judge, whose term of office lasted from 2008 until 2013, took place on 11 February 2019 in the House of Lords. He had overlapped with Jack Straw, Ken Clarke and Chris Grayling as Lord Chancellors and Secretaries of State for Justice.

In his public statements, Igor Judge tended to concentrate more on the process of law making and the extraordinary amount of detailed criminal justice legislation that had been generated, much of it without adequate scrutiny by Parliament, than on the outcomes. But he did speak out loud and clear. Thus, at the Lord Mayor of London's dinner for judges in 2009, he made a plea: 'Can we possibly have less legislation, particularly in the field of criminal justice?' In 2003, there had been six statutes affecting criminal justice matters, 'the great Daddy of them all' being David Blunkett's CJA 2003 with no fewer than 1,169 paragraphs (*BBC News*, 15.7.09). In his Annual Bingham Lecture on 3 May 2017, he noted that 'during the last few years something like 3,000 typed pages of primary legislation have been produced annually, and in addition laws are made by some 12,000 -13,000 pages of delegated legislation' (Judge, 2017). How much of this, he wondered, 'has been read, just read, let alone scrutinised, by how many of us in Parliament in advance of the enactment coming into force?' He thought it was 'bad practice' whereby the government introduced a so-called 'Christmas tree' Bill apparently focussed on the title of the Bill but then festooned it with 'multiple miscellaneous, potentially controversial provisions, with no apparent connection to the title of the Bill. Included in a bundle like this they can escape scrutiny in the Commons.' He was particularly scathing about Henry VIII powers which had become 'commonplace. In the last session no less than 14 Bills included no fewer than 41 of them.' These empowered a Minister to use regulations 'to amend, repeal, revoke or otherwise modify' a statute to which they applied. In theory, such Statutory Instruments are considered by the Delegated Legislation Committee (DLC) but the average length of DLC debates in 2013–14 was just 26 minutes and the shortest 22 seconds. He made it clear that he was stressing that the 'sovereignty of Parliament' required more scrutiny of legislation if it was not to be the 'sovereignty of the Executive or the Government'. But he was obviously concerned about the diminishing voice of the 'other' branches of the State, the Judiciary and Parliament, in legislation. When we asked directly about his input into legislation, he replied 'of course there are conversations between the Lord Chancellor and the Lord Chief Justice ... but in the end the only thing that matters is what's in the legislation'.

In a radio interview (*Law in Action*, 27 October 2009) he made one of his rare public statements about sentencing policy. In it he criticised the growth of out of court disposals through the use of fixed penalty notices, on the spot fines and conditional cautions. He also defended the right of judges to impose short sentences. To some extent, he differed from his fellow Chief Justices in that, he went on: 'I do not think that we can organise sentencing policy on the basis that it is our role to reduce the prison population.' But when we taxed him on that position he gave a carefully measured response, in part playing the devil's advocate, asking us,

> 'what is the impelling reason why it has to be reduced? Are we saying that our penal arrangements are too high, by some objectively ascertainable assessment? Or are we saying they're too high because the result is that prison conditions are awful? You could justify it, I'm not seeking to, but you could perfectly well justify that we have the right number of people in prisons, what we do not have is the right number of prisons for them'.

However, he did recall that as a judge, long before he became Lord Chief or the existence of a Sentencing Guidelines Council,

> 'when conditions in prison are disgusting you have to allow for that when you're passing sentence because the time in prison is going to be significantly more awful than it would be if the situation was less crowded. So if you're thinking nine months reconsider whether it should be six. These are ordinary sentencing considerations; how severe is the punishment'.

That pragmatic approach was probably widely shared at the start of our period but has largely disappeared from the political debate over the last 30 years.

He had always had reservations about sentencing guidelines, which he thought had the effect of ratcheting sentences up as they sought to maintain proportionality with other offences in line with legislative changes. They had become too mathematical and left too little room for discretion, effectively tying the hands of the Judiciary. Among the sentences which had gone up and which he thought fully justified, either by real changes in the gravity of the offence or understandable and overdue changes in public attitudes, were some of the more horrific cases of rape and cases of causing death by dangerous driving. And he reminded us that on occasion sentences could be reduced as they had been in relation to theft – although that change went back to the days when Douglas Hurd was Home Secretary. Though he conceded that there was little point in keeping large numbers of elderly men in prison for historic sex offences, when they probably now needed social care, he nevertheless defended the lengthy sentences handed down in such cases because 'to me the victim issue is really important in any discussion about sentencing.' When we suggested that perhaps successive government policies of putting victims at the centre of the criminal justice system had gone too far, he agreed with our statement, echoing what Lord Phillips had said, that 'the reason we have a court system was to prevent vigilantism, vengeance and private justice.' But he told us that

> 'we've got this difficult balance to strike, so that the court is not exercising private revenge. I think you have to be slightly careful; there is an under-sentencing problem, which is that the victim feels as though what she has gone through isn't really worth very much'.

Lord Judge was very clear that 'minimum sentences are just wrong in principle …. and dangerous because they're usually political responses to show we're tough' but he regretted 'that they are so established within our sentencing system that you're a voice crying in the wilderness' if you try to oppose them. We told him how Ken Clarke had explained to us that David Cameron had insisted he put in a tough sounding minimum sentence clause into the LASPO Bill 2011, behind which more liberal reforms could be hidden. Clarke did so but set criteria for its application that nobody would qualify who was not already doomed to get at least the mandatory term. He told us that he had run the measures past Lord Judge, who he said 'was quite laid back about them so long as they had the usual safeguards' – namely that unless it would be unjust to do so in all the circumstances (Clarke, 2016, p 454). Lord Judge's recollection was slightly different: 'I told him that I thought the legislation was quite unnecessary, because ... the judge's starting point would be ... a life sentence ... and then to work out whether that is appropriate'. But the real problem of minimum sentences, he thought, had set in 'when David Blunkett was Home Secretary' since when the safety clauses which Clarke talked about had become necessary and 'on the whole they work well.' However, he went on to express concern about how now it was possible for the Attorney General to have a look at any sentence – 'there is no point in putting someone on probation if you know the Attorney General will appeal and the Court of Appeal will then say two years.'

Two weeks before our interview, Lord Judge had addressed students about 'Tomorrow's Constitution'. Afterwards, there was a lively question and answer session in which he was asked 'why don't we have better people becoming politicians?' Turning the question back he asked them: 'Is anyone in this room thinking of going into politics?' No hands were raised. 'I said: "There is your answer."' All these bright people and they're just not interested in it', which brought us in our interview to broaching the subject of relations between the Judiciary and the Executive. Lord Judge was incensed that the first that Harry Woolf had heard about the proposal to abolish the Lord Chancellor's Department and make him the Head of the Judiciary was from the lunchtime news on the radio. He learned later, from the account by Jonathan Powell, who had been Tony Blair's Chief of Staff, that avoiding consultation with the judiciary had been quite deliberate (Powell, 2010, p 153). According to Powell's memoir, he and Blair had long wanted to dismember the Home Office to create a MoJ. Blunkett had got wind of one early attempt and 'saw it off in the press'. On a second occasion, they proposed to move the courts into the Home Office and the Lord Chief Justice exercised the nuclear option by demanding to see the Prime Minister. A deputation comprising Lord Woolf, Lord Bingham, Lord Phillips and Lord Judge were, in Powell's words, 'adamantly opposed and insisted that it would compromise their independence.' Hence the decision, in effect, to act first and answer questions later, but it did nothing to inspire confidence in good relations between the Executive and the Judiciary. There was similarly little or no consultation when John Reid managed to off-load prisons and probation from the Home Office.

In terms of the under-use of community sentences he suggested, unlike Lord Phillips, that one of the problems 'is the extent to which judges are confident that a community-based penalty has the elements of punishment that the crime deserves, and also has the element, of course, of rehabilitation'. However, he recalled a time when 'the probation officer who produced the report was an officer of the court'. It was possible for the judge and the probation officer to develop real trust in each other's judgement. It was possible that 'a judge would take what would seem to be an extraordinarily lenient view of a sentence, and put somebody on probation because, for example in the case of a sex offender … he thought that actually there was a prospect that this young man, with some treatment, some advice and some help would grow up and not commit a rape next time'.

We asked for his views on problem-solving courts but his only experience, which had been positive, was of the Lambeth drugs court so beyond that he felt unable to pass judgement. But he recalled a time when the judge could ask for regular reports of progress made by the defendant in the course of his sentence, and he regretted that there was no longer the money in the system for this ongoing interest on the part of the judge. And he also told us that 'the ability of a sentencing court to know what has happened to the man or woman who has had sentence passed on them, is pretty elementary'.

Lord Judge had deep misgivings about the position of the Judiciary now coming under the MoJ which also accommodated prisons partly because of budgetary issues. The Ministry had a budget for all its activities but by far the largest demands would always come from the prisons potentially leaving less for the court service and legal aid. There was also anxiety that the Lord Chancellor, who was under oath to protect the independence of the Judiciary, had been reduced to a middle-ranking position in the Government and the post holder wasn't even required to be a lawyer. Like everyone else we spoke to, he had been concerned about the poor response of Liz Truss when the Judiciary was under attack in the Press. He would like to see a restoration of a separate Lord Chancellor's Department, where there was 'somebody who hasn't got another department to worry about, and who is of such a standing that sacking your Lord Chancellor's rather serious', somebody 'around the table in the Cabinet' to point out 'Constitutional problems'. The way in which the position was removed, reflected the way the Judiciary were viewed by the Executive at the time. 'If you take the view that the Judiciary is an important arm of the State, it is rather setting it at nought when you just say, "This is going to be it, and this will be the legislation."'

Lord Thomas

We spoke to Lord John Thomas at his home on 21 January 2019. He was LCJ from 2013 until 2017 and thus had dealings with Christopher Grayling, Michael Gove, Liz Truss and David Lidington at the Ministry of Justice.

In his speeches and writings since his retirement Lord Thomas has, with good reason, been very much focussed upon the position of the Judiciary within the State in the years following the Constitutional Reform Act 2005. In his two-part lecture series (Thomas, 2017a, b), he gave a very careful analysis of the relationship between the three separate and independent branches of the State – the Executive, Parliament and the Judiciary. He drew attention to the fact that, though separate and independent, for the constitution to work effectively it was necessary for them to work together, with the understanding of each other's roles and with mutual support and respect but without interference in the proper functioning of the other branches. To the extent that a free press was also an important foundation underpinning democracy, it was implicit that some of that understanding, support and respect should also apply to the fourth estate. Given the divisive propensity of Brexit, such clarity of exposition was sorely needed. It was inevitable that some reference be made to the publication which described judges as 'Enemies of the People' and which should have evoked, but did not in fact evoke, an immediate response from a Lord Chancellor who was bound by constitutional oath to uphold the independence of the Judiciary. The Judiciary were equally bound by constitutional requirements to remain silent. The points were made firmly but without the naming of names.

In our interview, Lord Thomas explained that obviously he could say nothing at the time, nor could Lord Neuberger who would be hearing the appeal, but he had given an undertaking to colleagues that he would make his views public as soon as the bill bringing Article 50 into effect had been passed. The first opportunity had been an invitation to give evidence to the Select Committee of the House of Lords shortly before the second of his lectures, by which time it was not necessary to name names because he could simply give references to the evidence to the Select Committee. He told us that

> 'so long as you choose your words reasonably carefully, if a Minister does not do something they were obliged to do, then you have to say so .... you will have to wait thirty years to find out who told Liz Truss to behave as she did'.

We asked how was it that the role of the Lord Chancellor seemed not to be well understood within the MoJ or the Government generally. In reply, Thomas told us that he had the greatest respect for the governmental legal service who were doing excellent work in relation to Brexit. But 'lawyers do not play the role in government that they do in other countries so they do not have much influence.' In fairness to the civil service, he pointed out that 'the cuts of the last eight or nine years have put immense strain on them and they do not have the time to think and reflect and be as educated as they once were.' Over the years since the Constitutional Reform Act 2005, the MoJ has 'been run by non-lawyers apart from Richard Heaton' and 'the Lord Chancellor's Department has not had a chief advisor'. The problem had been exacerbated by the turnover of Justice Ministers. He was pleased to see that 'David Gauke has now been there for a year, but ... one does not know for how much longer' [it turned out to be another nine months]. He had regular meetings with each of the Secretaries of State and Lord Chancellor every four to six weeks to discuss a whole range of issues and although relations deteriorated after he had criticised Liz Truss, that had happened 'very shortly before she was moved so that did not make any practical difference.' In any case, he did not think that 'relationships have ever been as bad as they were between Blunkett and the Judiciary'.

We asked how the changes in Ministers affected the development of sentencing policy and how he thought that had impacted on the prison population. He told us that, in some circles, there had been 'speculation that had Ken Clarke continued in office the Legal Aid, Sentencing and Punishment of Offenders Act 2012 would have been different and had Grayling come in earlier we would still have IPPs' but he indicated that he had 'never discussed' those matters. He described a significant period of consultation between Clarke's team and the Judiciary on the technicalities of the LASPO Act whereas 'In the 2003 Act, there was virtually no discussion between the Home Office and the Judiciary'. He added 'it ought to be easier now to discuss penal policy than it was when the Home Secretary was the penal person and it was the Lord Chancellor who had the relationship with the Judiciary'. However, he said that

> 'during Grayling's period it was clear that there was no desire for lessening of, or changing, sentencing policy. With Gove I think he saw that there was a problem and something had to be done, but he was gone before he had a chance. And then with Truss … this was not top of her list of concerns, and with David Lidington, I think things were looking more promising but he was only there very briefly. Gauke, as far as I understand, is able to do something about the problems. Certainly his Prisons Minister, Rory Stewart wants to do something'.

Both David Gauke and Rory Stewart were keen to try to reduce the prison population through action in regard to short sentences. Lord Thomas thought that 'Rory Stewart's policy of reducing short sentences is probably sensible' but was 'not quite clear whether he was wanting the Scottish model of a presumption against (imprisonment) or to stop them altogether.' Like Igor Judge, however, he was also concerned about what the courts should do with the 'persistent trouble maker when you have tried everything else.' He told us that reducing the use of short sentences 'would address a bit of the problem but not very much of it'. It would thus be

> 'foolish to think of it as an isolated step …. the real problem with the prison system is the great length of sentences and we have pointed this out and pointed this out and pointed this out …. that is a far more serious problem than this transient population'.

Most of the problems with the long-term prison population stemmed from David Blunkett's CJA 2003 which under Schedule 21 introduced 'starting points' for fixing the minimum term in mandatory life sentences. For example, for murder committed with a knife, the starting point was 15 years for an adult or 12 years if committed by a young offender. This was amended in 2010 to 25 years for an adult and 15 years for a young person. In Judge Thomas's view, and it was a view expressed 'consistently by the Judiciary for a number of years, you cannot design a sentencing structure without taking that into account – it obviously affects attempted murder, and it affects GBH' because of the need to keep sentences proportionate to the gravity of offence and one to the other. Lord Thomas told us that, in general, minimum sentences as such are not that much of a problem because they usually leave the judge some discretion because of

> 'exceptional circumstances. What is really having an effect, of course, is the application of the sentencing guidelines. In most criminal appeals now you go straight to the guidelines and you work out whether the sentence was within the guidelines, but the guidelines themselves are driven by the statutory maxima and the overall approach to sentencing'.

In his view, the constitutional way in which a sentencing policy should be set by Parliament would quite properly be through setting maximum sentences – which would give a clear steer as to Parliament's view of the relative gravity of offence – but the problem is, he thought, 'that the sentencing maxima are too high'. Indeed, it seemed that there was now an impasse whereby 'politicians are unwilling to reduce maximum sentences' or 'to deal with the IPP problem by revisiting the issue through statute' on the ostensible claim that it would interfere with the independence of the judiciary – a claim which Lord Thomas dismissed as 'absolute nonsense'. Meanwhile, 'the judges take the view that it is for Parliament to do so' and so this was now 'a constitutional issue.' He believed, like Clarke, that it was necessary for the Government to 'make changes in the burden of proof for the Parole Board'. It was up to 'the Judiciary, the Sentencing Council and the Government to get together' and 'resolve things, and it does seem to me that it has got to be solved. We simply cannot afford the prison population that we have got.' In fact, he went further later in the interview and argued that 'mandatory sentencing is completely pointless' and that we should get as much criminal procedure off the statute book as possible because if it's 'in a primary act of parliament you have to do it'. This, he believed, would give the Sentencing Council greater room for manoeuvre.

The only way to bring the prison population down, he thought, would be for a courageous government

> 'to reduce maxima and be quite prepared to say this is our policy. We intend to introduce it and we should set about bringing the sentence level down. My own view is that the prison population ought to come down first to sixty thousand and I hope … back to forty thousand. We should not have a problem'.

At the time of our interview, Lord Thomas was a year into the task of chairing the Commission on Justice in Wales which had been established by the Welsh

Government in December 2017. In the course of that they had reviewed policies in a number of countries which had 'brought the prison population down and been successful at keeping it low. The crime rate had not gone up.' He recognised that in the UK we would have a problem in keeping the prison population down because of our policies of using imprisonment as a sanction for failing on community sentences and for breaching licence conditions on parole. He noted that 'the recall population had gone up very substantially' which contrasted sharply with elsewhere in the world and that 'the business of recalling to prisons is again something that we never properly thought through.' He also confessed to a feeling of 'regret' that he had supported a 12-month supervision for all in the community through the Offender Rehabilitation Act 2014 without entirely appreciating the

> 'seriousness of the fact that someone is at risk during that period. If you are to take the probation or community sentencing route, the only way to give it teeth without sending people to prison is to have a tough viable alternative. This means properly organising the probation service and getting rid of this nonsense of privatisation, [which he thought had been] a disaster … there is no other word for it'.

Probation, he thought, needed to be remade into 'a proper career and training people to be tough but kind' and 'judges have to be involved in a dialogue with the local probation service so they provide something that people have confidence in'. He wished for a return to the formal relationship between the Judiciary and probation whereby judges had been members of Probation Boards and then Trusts but this arrangement had been lost in the Transforming Rehabilitation initiative. In terms of the organisation of the prison system, he reflected that 'running everything from Whitehall, it never works', particularly given that 'no Minister is interested in delivery', instead he looked forward to a more devolved approach.

Lord Thomas was not happy that the prison service had been transferred from the Home Office to the much smaller MoJ. This was partly for budgetary reasons: unlike virtually all other government departments or services, including the military, the system seems to be led solely by demand-side considerations rather than supply-side costs. 'In the Health Service' he pointed out

> 'it is possible for NICE to say we cannot afford this drug but where is this facility in the justice system? Over the last ten years the justice budget has been cut in real terms by about 30 or 40%'.

As a result,

> 'the prison problem is destroying the Ministry of Justice. There is no way you can cut the prisons budget more than it has been cut and therefore

it eats into everything else from legal aid to the courts. There has been a failure to have a grown-up conversation about this. The difficulty the government faces is the two main newspapers – *The Daily Mail* and *The Sun* basically jump on anyone who suggest a lower population'.

Lord Thomas's Commission on Justice in Wales reported in October 2019 and recommended, *inter alia*, the establishment of a new Wales Criminal Justice Board to establish an overall criminal justice strategy, the development of problem-solving courts, the application of the basic principles set out in the 2018 Report of the Chief Inspector of Probation to the new integrated National Probation Service of Wales, the rapid establishment and sustained development of comprehensive services and centres as alternatives to custody for women, the development of intensive alternatives to custody with judicial oversight, and the raising of the age of criminal responsibility to at least 12 years as well as the development of family, drug and alcohol courts. When we discussed problem-solving courts with him, he observed in relation to the Liverpool court, 'I'm never certain that it was properly evaluated'. He also noted that 'it requires a change, I think, in attitude and policy as to whether you are going to make the primary accountability to the judge rather than the probation officer' or at the very least shared responsibility and accountability post sentencing.

References

Woolf, Lord (2015) *Strangeways 25 Years on: Achieving Fairness and Justice in Prison*, Lecture delivered at Inner Temple, April.

Clarke, K. (2016) *A Kind of Blue; A Political Memoir,*London, Macmillan.

Judge, Lord (2017) *A Judge's View on the Rule of Law*, Annual Bingham Lecture, 3rd May 2017.

Powell, J. (2010) *The New Machiavelli; How to Wield Power in the Modern World*, London, Bodley Head, 2010.

Thomas, Lord (2017a) *The Judiciary within the State – Governance and Cohesion of the Judiciary*, Hebrew University, Jerusalem,15th May 2017.

Thomas, Lord (2017b) *The Judiciary within the State – the Relationship between the Branches of the State*, Michael Ryle Memorial Lecture, Westminster 15th June 2017

7
CONCLUSIONS: AN AGENDA FOR ACTION

Introduction

Just over ten years ago, Stephen Shaw (2010), formerly a researcher for NACRO, then Director of the Prison Reform Trust (PRT), before becoming the Prisons and Probation Ombudsman, looked back at the changes since 1980 and then forward, with resigned pessimism, to what things might look like in 2030. Indeed, things did get markedly worse during the next ten years. Similarly, some of our respondents, when we voiced our concerns about various developments that we have documented here, told us that this or that ship had already sailed. That was undoubtedly true, albeit without a working compass they were heading ever closer to the rocks. They have reached the point when it makes more sense to jump ship, or at least to return to port for some badly needed repairs or, better still, a complete refit. We think that time has now come, not just for prisons and probation, but for the sentencing policies which provide their clients, and for aspects of our political system which gives birth to those policies. In truth, at the end of our study, we are much surer about what should *not* be done, and what things *need* to be done to repair the damage, than we are about the exact mechanics of how to bring those things about or what the detailed framework for the future should look like. We are first and foremost researchers with a prisons background rather than political scientists and we have no expertise whatever in the law. But there will surely be others perfectly capable of taking things forward if our analysis has any resonance. What politicians have done, honest politicians can undo.

DOI: 10.4324/9781003201748-8

Diagnosing the problem

British democracy and the separation of powers

Winston Churchill was but one among many since Plato to have taken up the theme that 'democracy is the worst form of Government except for all those other forms that have been tried from time to time.' However, there are many possible forms of democracy and it is difficult seriously to argue that the current British version is fit for purpose. We have an electoral system in which the vast majority of votes are actually wasted and have no effect whatever on the outcome of elections. And we have a system whereby, whichever party is in power can plan public investments in such a way that they benefit those constituencies which will help maintain any advantages they may have gained. But it is unsurprising that politicians, who have been elected under the existing system, should defend it 'warts and all' rather than give serious consideration to the alternatives. And they are too often prepared to blame their political opponents, their civil servants, operational managers or the Judiciary – of whom only their political opponents have a real right or opportunity to reply – for whatever has gone wrong. Our current version of parliamentary democracy is unnecessarily confrontational with politicians shouting at one another from opposite sides of the House of Commons instead of negotiating around a table to agree exactly what is in the *public* interest rather than the interest of *political parties*. By contrast, our House of Lords – shamefully unrepresentative as it is – has become a forum for serious and civilised debate.

The foundations of democratic states are to be found in the doctrine of the *separation of powers* between the Executive, Parliament and the Judiciary. To these, it has become normal to add a free press – often known as the fourth estate. We hold no brief for a written constitution but for British Democracy to work effectively, each of these pillars of the state needs both to respect the independence of the others' domains and to acknowledge appropriate limits to their scope, and yet to find ways to work in harmony. In the period we have researched, mutual respect has sometimes been severely strained. We have seen the Executive, effectively by-passing Parliament through the publication of criminal justice bills of such length and complexity, and sometimes involving the so-called Henry VIII powers, that they could not possibly receive the scrutiny required. We have also seen Ministers introducing legislation expressly designed to limit judicial discretion by the imposition of minimum starting points for sentencing different categories of offender, and sentences designed to prevent future (and unknowable) risks instead of proven past behaviours. Whilst the Judiciary accept that it is for Parliament to legislate and their own role is to interpret and apply the law, they are aghast at the folly of such legislation. At times, under both Labour and Conservative governments, there has been an unholy alliance between Downing Street and what used to be called Fleet Street. When our most senior judges were described as 'enemies of the people' by sections of the Press, our new style Lord Chancellor failed to uphold their independence until prompted to do so.

Ironically, it was New Labour's intention to *strengthen* the separation of powers when they rightly claimed that the old-style Lord Chancellor bridged all three pillars of state. But their solution was badly botched and done without consultation. We have ended up with a token Lord Chancellor role combined with that of the Secretary of State for Justice and the post holder isn't even required to be a lawyer. The situation surely needs revisiting.

Moreover, during the writing of this book, there has been a willingness to break international legal agreements as a negotiating tactic over Brexit, and there are yet further plans afoot to limit the scope of judicial review. Whether or not these are to be regarded as steps towards an elective dictatorship they are certainly matters for great concern. But it is what can happen when an electoral system with so many wasted votes can deliver governments with unassailable majorities.

Ministerial and civil service churn

The lifetime of our parliaments – normally four or five years – promotes a short-termism because, we were told by some of our politicians, 'one Government cannot bind the hands of its successors'. This is quite simply a fiction – for in what ways are decisions to build the Channel Tunnel, nuclear power stations or High Speed (HS)2 (or scores of other examples) *not* binding? Our four- or five-year parliaments may rightly produce changes of governments which may make long-term planning more difficult. But any sensible government, about to embark on a policy that it seriously wishes to succeed in the longer term, would surely be wise to seek agreement with potential successors, especially when it comes to matters regarding essential public services. But changes of government, at least as between one party and another, have *not* been the main problem in criminal justice matters. In 1990, the starting point of our research, the Conservative Government had been in power for 11 of its 17 years of continuous rule; New Labour governed for 13 years after winning three elections; and the Conservatives, aided and abetted by Liberal Democrats for nearly half the time, have ruled, so far for 11 years with the prospect of another three years before needing to go to the country. Yet despite those long periods in office, the kind of continuous development of policies, based on evidence and agreement as to where the public interest and the interests of justice actually lie, has never happened. Occasionally, there have been very hesitant steps towards that end but they were not followed through. So, it is not the change *between* governments of different party political persuasions that accounts for this lack of development – although successive governments have managed to make much the same mistakes.

Somewhat superficially, an obvious reason why that did not happen was because of the extraordinary process of ministerial churn – by which Home Secretaries and Justice Secretaries spent an average of only 22 months in office. The problems associated with ministerial churn could have been alleviated by an induction process whereby the outgoing Minister and the incoming Minister – even if they were from different parties after a change of government – got together with their civil servants and their 'political advisers' in a series of meetings sufficient to ensure continuity. A rare example of something like this actually happening was when New Labour's Jack Straw, aware of 'the looming crisis', allowed his Tory shadow, Dominic Grieve, full access to civil service briefings during the run up to the 2010 election (*The Guardian*, 6.4.21). But Grieve, in the event, became Attorney General, not Justice Secretary, after the election. Andrew Selous suggested there was 'probably a role for the Cabinet Office' to collate changes in policy, strategic decisions and so on as the basis on which briefings could take place. *None* of our ministers had anything more than a brief chat over dinner or sometimes just a coffee, with their predecessor or their successors, although Rory Stewart, when in office, set up 'round table' discussions with previous ministers. Most of the politicians we spoke to thought this situation was a regrettable, but inevitable, feature of political life. Is it possible to imagine running a business like this? We think not. Yet it is apparently unquestioned that this is appropriate for managing one of what used to be called the 'Great Offices of State'. Strange as it may seem, many Ministers thought they *were* actually running prisons and probation as though they were businesses with an output at the end that could be seen as a kind of profit.

Sadly, the process of churn among Ministers seems to have been matched by a similar process of churn among departmental civil servants which is, if anything, even more worrying. It is important to note, however, that the situation is rather blurred when it comes to prisons and probation. At the beginning of our study, there was a clear distinction between civil servants in the Prison and Probation Department at the Home Office who were essentially administrators advising ministers on policy on the one hand, and issuing directives to those delivering the services on the other. They had no operational experience. It was widely acknowledged that there was a lack of mutual confidence between headquarters and the field. There were, however, several examples of productive informal relationships, for example between David Faulkner and Anthony Langdon as career civil servants on the one hand and Ian Dunbar and Arthur de Frisching, experienced prison governors on the other. By analogy, much the same could be said for probation. But from time to time during the period of this study, operational managers have been brought closer to the administrative centre, perhaps especially as a result of Agency status. Martin Narey, for example, was also at one time a Permanent Secretary in the Home Office, and a member of the Sentencing Guidelines Council and certainly had some input into policy decisions as well as being an operational leader. We understand that Jo Farrah, Michael Spurr's successor as Chief Executive of Her Majesty's Prison and Probation Service (HMPPS) has also at the time of writing (April 2021) just been made a Second Permanent Secretary in the Ministry of Justice (MoJ). When we speak of departmental or career civil servants, we are restricting that usage to administrators without operational experience.

But career civil servants, who could always be moved from department to department in the course of a career, now seem to move much more quickly so that they never acquire that repository of essential knowledge. As we discussed our findings with colleagues, we heard reports of civil servants who were ignorant of the literature in fields that they ought to know about, and who had their eyes firmly fixed on the next job. This left ministers, with their own forceful ideas, feeling much more at home with their special advisers (SpAds) who shared those ideas, than with their civil servants. In some cases, ministers have managed to implant their advisers into civil service roles at very senior levels. Moreover, supposedly 'difficult' Permanent Secretaries who proffer the 'wrong' advice have been moved to other departments. The result has been that senior civil servants have felt less able to speak truth to power and there has been a diminution in the understanding of departmental history. After his retirement, the late David Faulkner, one of the wisest of civil servants at the Home Office, whose crowning achievement was the crafting of much of the Criminal Justice Act (CJA) 1991, felt bound to plead with his successors to 'have the courage to speak out about what is happening'. Unless the churn which now prevails within the civil service is reversed and something like the traditional relationship between departmental Permanent Secretaries and Ministers is restored then it is hard to see how even the induction and briefing advocated above could overcome the problems of ministerial churn. Corporate memory is still to be found but it is more likely to be within the operational leadership of prisons and probation. Both Martin Narey and Phil Wheatley spent about seven years at the top of prisons or National Offender Management Service (NOMS) and Michael Spurr even longer. Both Spurr and Wheatley had also occupied senior roles for many years before that. They knew what they were doing and were willing and able to speak their minds. We were therefore surprised when Rory Stewart complained that he did not get enough '*push back*' from those in charge of operations.

It is certainly true that ministerial churn is not new. In the 32 years from 1957 to 1989, before the period covered by our review began, there had been a procession of a dozen Home Secretaries, though they spent somewhat more time in office – on average about 32 months. But the speed of churn is not the real issue – it must be obvious from our account that some of the longest serving ministers wrought some of the most damaging outcomes not just for prisons and probation and for whilst they were in charge, but for criminal justice generally and for long after they left office. And the obverse of that was that some of the shortest-serving ministers were the ones who advocated an evidence-based approach but sadly left no trace. There is no need to name names: readers can judge that well enough for themselves. Our point here is that the real difference between the two contrasting periods was not so much the degree of churn as the dramatic change in the way ministers saw their role and the tone in which debates were conducted.

During that earlier period there was a remarkable degree of stability around the politics of criminal justice. Criminal Justice Acts were few and far between. One such was Roy Jenkins' CJA 1967, which among other things introduced the parole system. From then, until 1992 all determinate sentenced prisoners serving more than 18 months were eligible to be considered by the Parole Board after one-third of their sentence had been served. If they did not get parole, they would be entitled, as they always had been, to remission of sentence and released at the two-thirds point (provided they had not been awarded added days for offences against good order and discipline). The decision to release prisoners serving life sentences remained with the Secretary of State. It was a simple system and elegantly maintained the proportionality of time served as between sentences of different lengths for offences of different gravity. Some 15 years or so later, there was a move by Leon Brittan to push back the stage at which prisoners became eligible for consideration, but experienced civil servants were able to persuade him that introducing new rules for prisoners serving *more* than four years rather than his proposed *four years and over*, would be more manageable for a prison system already under some pressure and sound just as tough.

The transitions both within and between governments passed, relatively speaking, uneventfully: from Rab Butler, to Henry Brooke and on to Labour's Frank Soskice, Roy Jenkins and Jim Callaghan; then back to Tories Reggie Maudling and Robert Carr; then Labour's Roy Jenkins again followed by Merlyn Rees; before returning to Tories Willie Whitelaw, Leon Brittan and Douglas Hurd. There were few, if any, of the major twists and turns in either policy or organisational arrangements that we have seen in the last 30 years, this despite the fact that arguably those years were extremely difficult for the prison service, albeit the probation service had a much lower profile at that time. The escapes of the Great Train Robbers, and the spy George Blake in the 1960s, the serious prison riots in dispersal prisons in the 1970s and 80s, and the continuing she-nanigans of the Prison Officers Association (POA) throughout, who at one point engaged in more incidents of industrial action than prisoners did in disturbances, all hit the headlines. But they never really became party political issues and there was remarkably little attempt by Ministers to involve themselves in operational matters. Indeed, even at the start of our research, there were those who remembered an even-handed approach. Peter Dawson recalled a core of civil servants and operational managers 'who had thought through the fundamentals of the criminal justice system, or the future for prisons, in a very profound way'. Phil Wheatley described a time of 'openness' when politicians listened to their civil servants if they 'said something wasn't a good idea'. David Waddington agreed that our prisons were 'an expensive way of making bad people worse'. The Woolf Report came at a time when *all* were listening to the need for the 'right balance' of purpose in prisons between 'security, control and justice' (para 1.148). How that was to change as we have recorded in the chapters of this book.

The changing tone of the debate and ministerial roles

During the period we have reviewed in this book, the tone of the debate changed so that law and order became far more politicised. As the political parties vied with each other to show who could be the toughest on crime, extraordinary changes were made to sentencing policy dressed up as protecting the public and placing victims at the heart of the system. One or another of our judges found most of those changes as wrong in principle. As ministers came and went each seemed determined to do things, like Frank Sinatra, 'my way'. As we made clear in our Prologue, we are categorically *not* impeaching the honesty of any of the politicians we interviewed. We give them all the benefit of any doubt and believe that each of them *genuinely* thought, according to their lights, that what they were doing was in some sense *right*. This might be in terms of their *political ideology*, or what their *constituents wanted*, or even what the *country needed*, or just that it was *necessary* in the light of the economic situation – although that too, of course, would be viewed through a political lens. The politicians to whom we spoke were refreshingly candid in their interviews with us and we owe them a big debt of gratitude. But having convinced themselves that what they were doing was right, their self-belief had too often morphed into *hubris*. However, on several occasions, when we discussed with them alternative approaches that might have been adopted, they showed a marked reluctance to tackle issues that would require them to be *honest with the public*. As Liz Truss, for example, put it to us 'it would take a brave politician to do that'. And Michael Gove in a public lecture confessed that whilst in office he had 'swerved' addressing the way in which longer prison sentences had inflated the prison population way beyond those in comparable countries across Europe.

Between them they made sweeping changes to the organisation of both the prison and probation services, and in the case of the latter to its professional aims and status. There were far too many changes to recapitulate here. Suffice it to say that ministers came to see their role as two-fold. On the one hand, they looked for the holy grail of solutions to the crime problem but were unfortunately looking in the wrong places. On the other hand, they relentlessly pursued organisational change when neither prisons nor probation could deliver their unrealistic expectations and were blamed for their supposed failure. Sometimes those changes were based upon the findings from duly commissioned reports, sometimes on the basis of experience, appropriate or not, they had acquired in other government departments and sometimes on political or economic dogma. Their interventions were often 'justified' on the grounds that ultimately it was the minister who would be held responsible for failures, though the record shows quite otherwise with many more examples of officials being sacked or not having their contracts renewed than ministers losing their jobs. Gone were the days when ministers sensibly sought to manage the expectations of the public whilst proffering appropriate support for their officials and doing their best to ensure that they were adequately resourced for their task. There were honourable exceptions, of course, as we have recorded at points throughout this book – but they *were* exceptions.

Several of the politicians we interviewed were prepared to say that there was cross-party agreement about the ends of criminal justice policy but real disagreements about the means to achieve them. Unfortunately, some of those agreed ends have been badly misconceived and unachievable and politicians have yet to face up to that. The biggest misconception, shared by most, if not quite all, of the politicians to whom we spoke, is the belief that there is a solution to the crime problem through criminal justice policies. However, the aim of criminal justice policy, we believe, is, or should be, about achieving an impartial, fair and proportionate system of punishment and retribution without the need for victims to resort to feud and vigilantism. The ultimate guardians of that fairness and proportionality are, of course, the members of the Judiciary. The solution to the crime problem, to the considerable extent that there is one, lies mainly in *social* not *criminal justice* policies. More than a century ago, the great French sociologist Emile Durkheim (1895), taught us that societies get the criminals they deserve. He argued that it is impossible to conceive of a society in which crime had been eradicated. He invited us to imagine 'a society of saints, a perfect cloister of exemplary individuals', and argued that even in such a society there would be transgressors of the rules who would need to be corrected. Societies need rules and where there are rules there will be rule breakers. Of course, in a society of saints, 'crimes' will be rare but that is because, by definition, all members are bound by their faith and committed to the rules. The more diverse the society, the more divided it is between haves and have nots, the more unequal it is in terms of opportunities – the less commitment there will be to the rules and the more crime society will have.

It is no accident that, in every society, the minority groups are over-represented both in the crime statistics and the prison population, and that prisons by and large contain the least advantaged or well-educated members of society who have but a tenuous connection to what life has to offer. New Labour, initially at least, with its slogan of tough on crime and tough on the causes of crime promulgated programmes designed to bring about inclusivity but went on to exclude yet more through its anti-social behaviour orders. Charles Clarke talked about a long-term programme to tackle some of the issues but was not there long enough to see anything through. Most politicians are perfectly aware, at least deep down, that these are the root causes of the crime problem. Yet most still persist in the belief that deterring, treating or rehabilitating criminals so that they do not reoffend will provide the answer. Indeed, as we have shown, many actually believe that cutting the reoffending rate of those released from custody is the *only* way in which we will be able to bring the prison population down. That is absurd. What politicians put up politicians can take down. Their belief seems to be predicated on the notion that there is a finite number of potential offenders. The merest glance at the statistics should suffice to show that this is highly unlikely. The Crime Survey for England and Wales indicates a volume of victimisations vastly greater than what used to be called the 'official statistics' of crimes reported to the police. But it is only those who appear in the police statistics who might become subject to efforts to reform them. Of course, those who get into the police statistics could account for many of those other victimisations

– the so-called hard core of persistent offenders – but certainly not all. And for every offender who is reformed, there is another who could be brought in by the police from what used to be called the 'dark figure of crime' and duly prosecuted to take his or her place.

Despite what our politicians told us, there is no need for disagreement about the means to try to achieve the inappropriate ends they have set for themselves – they are perfectly capable of being evaluated in terms of the evidence as to their costs and their effectiveness. Whilst some of our politicians were reasonably attentive to the evidence either from research or the experience of professionals in the field, others were either blissfully unaware of the former or content to disregard the latter – sometimes both.

A major problem with our professional politicians is that they are actually complete *amateurs* when it comes to the domains over which they have been given temporary custody. There is, of course, a great deal to be said for the person in charge being an amateur without a vested interest but able to assess and balance the arguments and the evidence. A good Minister should listen to the advice of their career civil servants as well as the people responsible for operational activities, be attentive to the evidence from research and where that is lacking, ensure that the research is commissioned, and to weigh all that up *before* making decisions. But the route to the top in politics depends not so much on good management of a department and ensuring it is properly financed for the responsibilities placed upon it, as it does on carrying out the wishes of the Prime Minister and launching dramatic, eye catching initiatives, which get a good Press. Some of our Ministers were known to have ambitions to become Prime Minister themselves and may have been out to put on a show at the Home Office or Ministry of Justice.

Of course, we are aware that ultimately 'Ministers are there to decide things' and that politically they may sometimes lean 'in different directions'. But if from time to time it may be necessary to tilt the direction of travel slightly, it should be carefully planned, fully resourced and implemented over a realistic time period. As Fulton (1968) observed, 'new policy ... springs from practical experience in its operation'. Instead, Ministers have too often over-reacted to high-profile crimes and allowed themselves to be led on by the Press. They have listened to their political advisers, whose main focus is on public relations and what is politically expedient. Some Ministers have been in too much of a hurry, anxious to make their mark before being moved on – and since they were bound to be moved on, it was today's headlines rather than tomorrow's consequences that were likely to be uppermost in their minds. As a result, 'White Papers are rarely preceded by Green Papers .... not thought through, nor costed'. Ideas are not stress-tested, pilots have been announced and then seemingly disappear without apparent trace, evaluations either not built-in or the results simply ignored. We should be careful not to tar all Ministers with the same brush. Some Ministers, were prepared to listen to advice and to try to work through policy concerns in the light of that – Ken Clarke, for example, and Jack Straw when at the Home Office. But some – no names no pack drill – 'simply put their fingers in their ears' when faced with the 'practicalities of running something' and when that happened, they could not reasonably hold the services responsible for the results.

It is also important to note, that from time to time, carefully constructed and widely lauded reports have been commissioned. But sensible reforms advocated by Baroness Corston (2007) on women prisoners and Lord Bradley (2009) on the mentally disordered, for example, have sometimes been submerged as responsibility for implementation passed from minister to minister. On the other hand, the first of two reports by Lord Carter (2003, 2007), which gave birth to the NOMS was produced at speed but poorly implemented with far-reaching consequences. NOMS became a classic victim of churn. The NOMS that Martin Narey signed up to with David Blunkett, and the blessing of Tony Blair and Gordon Brown, was undercut by Charles Clarke's refusal to support plans to cap the prison population. NOMS became in Martin Narey's terms little more than a 'crude amalgamation' of the prison and probation services. Pat Carter told us it was based on a 'principled approach' and with insufficient regard to the 'practicalities'. As Agency status passed back and forth between the prison service, NOMS and later HMPPS there were tugs of war over who controlled what. Over the last few years more has been taken back into the MoJ leaving Heads of the Agency without the means for effective control of operations and lacking the voice to speak out. This has been a process affecting most government departments – but we believe it to be seriously dysfunctional when it comes to the MoJ with such large operational services to be delivered.

Our Ministers now require HMPPS, alongside private and third sector providers, to keep the public, their staff and offenders safe at a fraction of the cost of 10 years ago. Implausibly large numbers have been added to the case loads of probation officers. *All* of the Directors and Inspectors of prisons and probation, as well as the four former Lord Chief Justices, we interviewed agreed that it cannot be done. In prisons, Nick Hardwick told us that 'the decline in the prison service was not due to poor performance by anyone, Michael Spurr included, but was due to political decisions about the resources available' and Peter Clarke said 'common sense tells you that if you take 30% of staff out of a people hungry business … there's going to be an effect'. In probation Stacey agreed: you need 'a strong, supportive but challenging enduring relationship between the individualised provision and the probation worker, and you don't get that if you're swapping every five minutes, or if you're tragically under-resourced'.

Our proposals for change

We hope that our honest politicians will read our account of the last 30 years, stand back and reflect. Being too close to the centre of things can make it hard to see the bigger and longer-term picture – but there has to be a better way. It will require not only a Secretary of State for Justice prepared to be honest with the public and prepared to admit to past mistakes. He or she would need to be supported by a strong and honest Prime Minister, who was prepared to stand up to the Press and to lead public opinion, rather than blindly follow calls for new legislation that only makes matters worse. They would also need a supportive Chancellor of the Exchequer wise enough to know that 'world class' public services are not to be got on the cheap.

It would be unlikely that any government already in power would be willing and able to devote the time and resource to plan and begin implementing the kind of programme we suggest here – but they could commit to not making things worse. It is, however, in the nature of our current politics that opposition parties have time to plan so that they are ready to go if and when they take office. Ultimately, it would be necessary for Government and Opposition to reach an agreement and perhaps the most immediate starting place would be the Justice Select Committee with its cross-party membership. We are aware that the Justice Committee has an ongoing project on the work of the Lord Chancellor as well as on the Future of the Probation Service, a new model for which will go live before this book is published. Given our view that the solution to crime problems lies in social policy it would be desirable for the Home Affairs Select Committee to consider the implications.

Whilst some parts of our agenda could be initiated quickly other proposals would involve careful long-term planning and implementation over at least ten years. We do not pretend that our proposals are the only way, or necessarily the best way, of achieving the ends we seek. Other minds need to be, and obviously will be, brought to bear from a range of perspectives and expertise far greater than ours. But one has to start somewhere. We start with sentencing policy.

Sentencing policy

We start with sentencing policy because that is where the root of our problems lies. The ratcheting up of sentence lengths has had no demonstrable effect on the risks of people becoming victims of serious crime. It is extraordinary that politicians believe that the one risk we must eliminate from our lives is the rather low risk that one may become a victim of serious crime. There are other and greater risks which are largely ignored. Indeterminate sentences intended to protect against future, but unknowable, risks have never been part of the criminal justice system and need to be repealed. The arguments against deterrent sentencing are as valid today as they were when Douglas Hurd sought to eliminate them in what was to become the CJA 1991. Most criminals do not weigh up the costs and benefits of their criminal activity. As LCJ Phillips noted in relation to knife crime there was 'no point in locking them up for 10 years or 20 years for a two-minute loss of temper'. Even retributive sentences, which have a legitimate place in criminal justice, he told us are far too long and could be slashed. LCJ Woolf deplored the 'inflation in sentencing, which increases the likelihood of overcrowding without producing any corresponding benefit.' Lord Carter, Jack Straw, Ken Clarke and Andrew Selous among others wanted to see a rational debate about sentencing policy that took account of the fact that resources are finite. LCJ Thomas looked forward to honest politicians in the Executive to provide political cover for a change of direction so we 'could set about bringing the sentence level down'. This will only be possible through the three arms of the State working together rather than at odds.

So here are our proposals.

The sentencing framework should have as its main aim to achieve clarity, consistency and simplicity in sentencing and allow the Judges reasonable discretion so that they can take account of circumstances which are impossible to prescribe in advance.

The recommendations below would help move things in that direction.

The Sentencing Act 2020 has consolidated previous legislation which, if one could possibly take the time to scrutinise it, would make the disastrous mistakes of our politicians all too transparent. We have not had time to give these full consideration but as a first step on the way to reform we propose the immediate repeal of the provisions in Schedule 21 of the CJA 2003 which brought in 'starting points' for fixing the minimum term in mandatory life sentences. At the same time the mandatory minima, now enshrined in s.311–320 of the Sentencing Act 2020, should also be repealed. These relate, for example, to matters brought forward from Sections 110 (2) (drugs) and 111(2) (residential burglary) of the Powers of Criminal Courts (Sentencing) Act 2000; Section 51A(2) Firearms Act 1968 and Section 29 Violent Crime Reduction Act 2006. There are many other candidates for repeal. We have yet to see *any* demonstrable evidence that such measures have reduced crime or better protected the public. What they have done is to produce a measurable increase in sentence lengths and thus the size of the prison population. They should go. Their repeal would, we believe, have strong support from the Judiciary. It would save money. At least one of our judges took the view that where maxima were indicated for offences, these were too high and had the effect of ratcheting up sentences elsewhere to maintain proportionality. There is a case for their abolition or at least their reduction.

There should be an absolute bar on sentences intended to protect the public from (unknowable) future risks.

Sentencing offenders for what they might do rather than what they have done, or in addition to what they have done, offends principles of justice and has 'never been part of our justice system' as LCJ Phillips reminded us. 'Let's face it almost anyone who's in prison is a risk. Give them a chance to re-offend and then lock them up for their reoffending, or give them a chance not to reoffend and let them be free.' Although David Blunkett's Imprisonment for Public Protection (IPP) has been repealed, this repeal was never made retrospective and there are still many IPP prisoners serving well beyond their tariff. Michael Gove encouraged Nick Hardwick, then Chair of the Parole Board, to speed up releases wherever possible, but Hardwick was constructively dismissed when a decision, taken by a properly constituted panel, and in complete conformity with the stringent rules for release, resulted in a popular outcry. The repeal should now be made retrospective, and prisoners beyond their tariff date paroled albeit some may need restrictive conditions attached to their licence.

Short sentences of imprisonment are not the problem.

There now seems to be a building of political consensus around limiting the use of short sentences of imprisonment. It is important to say that opinions among our judges were divided. Lord Woolf welcomed the efforts of politicians on short sentences, and noted that the recent changes in Scotland had not resulted in an 'overwhelming surge in crime'. But LCJ Judge saw short sentences as necessary for 'the individual who keeps on committing minor assaults … eventually the time comes when he's got to understand that the law's got to be enforced'. But whilst short-sentence prisoners create many difficulties for prison managers the reduction in their numbers would make little difference to the size of the prison population. It is not so much the number of people who come into prison that accounts for the growth of the prison population but rather the length of time that they are required to stay there.

There should be a significant move away from prison sentences to those which can be served in the community.

Part of the argument here is simply that wherever possible crimes committed in the community should be dealt with in the community, and where there may be problems that require solutions. Community sentences would include a return to the use of unit fines, which Ken Clarke (2016) at least in his memoirs, somewhat frivolously dismissed, but which have proved successful in other jurisdictions. Politicians have repeatedly sought to make community sentences tougher for fear they are regarded as a soft option. Our judges were divided in their views. Lord Judge argued that they should have 'the elements of punishment that the crime deserves'. Lord Phillips tried both to show that community payback sentences were tough, and in any case argued 'what's wrong with being soft if it's actually doing the job' and gives offenders the 'self-respect they need?' He thought the main reason the courts were reluctant to impose community sentences was because they were not confident that the resources would be there for them to be effectively implemented. That lack of confidence has probably been exacerbated by the changing relationship between the courts and the probation service which has become more closely incorporated within the MoJ.

There is a need for changes to release and recall procedures.

The Parole system introduced by Roy Jenkins under the CJA 1967 survived pretty much intact until 1992. Since then, there have been frequent major changes to the system. Some have been for the better – what was once, in effect an executive or administrative procedure has become, under the influence of human rights legislation and court decisions, much more of a judicial body. But despite its quasi-judicial status it has little real discretion because the criteria for release are still based upon the former Secretary of State's Directions, now adopted as the Board's own, which are heavily geared towards assessed risks despite the fact that fewer than 1% of those paroled commit a further serious offence. Other changes have made the system evermore complex. Jenkins' arrangement whereby one-third of the sentence was spent in custody, one-third potentially on parole and the final third remitted for good behaviour (as it had been for a great many years previously), no longer applies. Instead, there are now different arrangements for different categories of offenders, all dramatically increasing the proportion of the sentence to be spent in custody and thereby driving up the size of the prison population. Such measures could also account for some of the increase in prison violence and use of drugs as prisoners have fewer incentives for good behaviour.

It has to be acknowledged that some of the changes were introduced as part of the drive for *honesty in sentencing*, as ministers capitulated before a Press campaign about the public lack of understanding as to why prisoners were 'being let out early' and not serving the full sentence imposed by the courts. It may be that Ministers didn't understand it either. But it is a reasonable assumption that, after a quarter of a century of operation, everyone else involved in criminal justice did understand it, including the judges who had adjusted their sentences to ensure that offenders spent the amount of time in custody required for the gravity of the offence. There was no rational debate and no honest Ministers prepared to educate the public, although judges are now required to explain all the elements involved in the sentence at the time of disposal (although all those elements had been decided by politicians themselves).

We believe that a return to something more akin to the original idea, with shorter periods in custody, and longer periods on parole or on remission of sentence, would not involve any serious lessening of the protection for the public, and would give prisoners a greater sense of hope and an incentive for better behaviour in prison. It would also significantly reduce costs.

Given that less than 1% of offenders released on parole commit further serious offences, greater consideration should be given to other factors in release decisions besides the moderate predictive validity of assessments of risks. If there were a return to shorter periods in custody and longer periods on parole, it would provide the opportunity for research to evaluate the real risks to the public of imposing shorter rather than longer sentences.

But this brings us to the knotty problem of what to do if parolees, and the greatly increased number of short-sentence prisoners now under compulsory after care, and all those people serving community sentences, misbehave during the remainder of their sentence. If they commit a further serious offence then there is no real problem about custody being an appropriate sanction. But at times the Parole Board has been so overwhelmed by recalls, often for minor breaches of conditions, that one person panels had to be convened to consider them. The adoption of 28-day fixed periods of recall in some cases has eased the situation to some degree, but this should be extended to all but the most serious cases. It would be helpful if the Parole Board only imposed conditions that were strictly necessary and, bearing in mind the experience of problem-solving courts, supervising officers could be encouraged to use discretion and only recall where there is a known and serious risk of further offending. LCJ Thomas pointed out that the recall situation in this country 'contrasts quite sharply with other countries' and needs to be 'properly thought through'. In the process of *thinking this through*, questions about consent to probation and the possibility of voluntary supervision should be revisited.

The role of the Sentencing Council

Our understanding is that in other countries which introduced sentencing guidelines, the initial hopes that they would produce greater consistency in sentencing, which in turn might lead to a reduction in the use of imprisonment, were not really fulfilled. Indeed, with the rise of penal populism they have more often served to ratchet up sentence lengths. In this country we were latecomers to the adoption of sentencing guidelines, and although we have avoided the worst effects of some grid systems, our judges have complained of the same effect. When Ministers have selected particular categories of offence, and enacted statutory maxima or minima, judges have had to strive to make other sentences proportionate. There is also widespread concern, it seems, that judges have to take too many factors into account when sentencing and would prefer things left to their own common sense.

Most of our interviewees expressed varying degrees of disappointment at the work of the Sentencing Council and its predecessor, the Sentencing Guidelines Council, at least in so far as influencing the size of the prison population was concerned. Essentially, what had been hoped for by David Blunkett and Lord Woolf, then Chair of the Council, with the support of both Blair and Brown, was that the guidelines would be tweaked whenever the prison population was in danger of exceeding 80,000 so that the population would be reduced. Lord Carter twice recommended that the council should link resource to the sentencing guidelines, although this was twice denied either by the Executive or Parliament. Although Martin Narey, then directly involved in both the Guidelines Council and NOMS, had seen that this could work in a shadow trial and was initially optimistic, the scheme foundered when Charles Clarke withdrew his support. Some dozen or so years earlier, Lord Woolf (1991) had proposed a new Prison Rule that no prison should be allowed to hold more prisoners than were allowed for in its certified normal accommodation. No such rule has ever been established.

Like prisons and probation, the National Health Service (NHS) is a demand-led service. In the former case, the demand comes from the courts and in the latter, directly from the public. Whilst the Health Service cannot control demand it has several devices through which it can be managed. National Institute for Health and Care Excellence (NICE), for example, manages the supply of expensive drugs. Prescription charges, albeit with many exemptions, may be expected to inhibit demand to some degree as well as offset some of the costs. But the main mechanism for managing demand is the waiting list already stretched before COVID-19, but now doubly so. In effect, cases are triaged between emergencies dealt with at A and E Departments, urgent cases, most commonly suspected cancers, referred by GPs to hospital consultants within two weeks, and other cases including elective surgeries via the waiting list. If this is possible for the NHS, where the consequences of waiting can be profoundly consequential, we fail to see why such an approach is not adopted for prisons where the consequences of keeping some offenders from entering or letting others out early are likely to be much smaller.

If the changes to sentencing policy outlined above are enacted the prison population would come down quite quickly anyway. If they are not, it is essential that our honest politicians implement Lord Woolf's original plan or some other plan. It is certainly not rocket science.

Problem-solving courts and judicial monitoring of sentences

Problem-solving courts were introduced to this country by New Labour and they have taken a number of forms. Specialist Domestic Violence Courts were first established in 2005 and there are now many of them around the country. Drug Courts were established in 2009, first in Cardiff and followed by pilots in Bristol, Leeds and West London. A somewhat different model, based on the community Court at Red Hook in New York, which had enthused both David Blunkett and Lord Woolf, and many others who visited it, was established in 2005 as the North Liverpool Community Justice Centre but which was unfortunately closed under Christopher Grayling. There are also other types. Actual evidence about the effectiveness of the courts is patchy and varies from one type of court to another. Some studies seem to have gone no further than 'process evaluations' without going on to assess 'impact'. In any case, we are not at all sure what would be appropriate measures to use. The Courts have received criticism on grounds of both 'cherry picking' and 'net widening' and in the case of drugs, for keeping public health matters within the criminal justice sphere.

As we noted in Chapter 5, Michael Gove re-discovered the idea in 2015. He established a working group which included, among others, Judge Fletcher who had presided over the North Liverpool Court and Judge John Samuels a long-standing supporter of judicial monitoring, to help take things forward. Five pilot studies were announced, but fell victim to ministerial churn, when Gove was moved on after the Brexit referendum. Although Liz Truss was praised by Gove for supporting the idea, she too was moved on. As we write, Robert Buckland who succeeded David Gauke as Justice Secretary has expressed his support for the idea of judicial monitoring and proposed five pilots – possibly the original ones called for by Gove. The advocates of problem-solving courts, and of judicial monitoring of sentence compliance – praise them for the powerful impact of having a judge taking a close interest in the progress of offenders who appear before them. As part of this research, one of us was able to visit the problem-solving court presided over by Sheriff Wood in Glasgow and came away profoundly impressed by the mutual respect shown between the offenders and the judge. It was clear that the Sheriff, working closely with a team of probation officers, knew those who appeared before him well including their family and other circumstances. We were also able to talk to John Samuels and correspond with David Fletcher.

Judge Fletcher told us that one of the most important lessons from the Liverpool problem-solving court over which he presided was that 'the interest of the sentencer in the compliance with the sentence could be pivotal in ensuring sentence completion'. Importantly, he has subsequently been able to use the provisions in what is now section 293 of the Sentencing Act 2020 to review almost all of the suspended sentences which he passes, even in the more traditional setting of a Crown Court. On the basis of short reports from local probation officers he conducts periodic reviews, the first after about five weeks. He spoke of his satisfaction when people have performed well and started to turn their lives around. In order to maximise the possibilities of success it is vital to be able to provide continuity, as between judge and offender. Sheriff Wood had spoken in much the same terms, whilst recognising that you couldn't win them all.

We suppose the currently proposed pilot studies may be delayed because of COVID-19 restrictions. There will undoubtedly be concerns about costs, and difficulties in recruiting suitably qualified and motivated judges, as well as problems in listings. But there is a straightforward argument in their favour – that they could give the process of doing justice a human face. They could also provide a welcome opportunity to reintegrate probation more closely with the courts, and share accountability for offender management between probation and the courts. We regard judicial monitoring as an important and exciting way forward for criminal justice in this country.

Judicial independence and the role of the Lord Chancellor

At several points in our account of developments over the last 30 years we have had to refer to the often strained relations between the Executive and the Judiciary. Although there are several other examples, nowhere was this more clear than in the deliberate exclusion of the Judiciary and the existing Lord Chancellor from consultation over the proposed intention, first to abolish, and then to change, the Lord Chancellor's role. Left to themselves, the politicians demonstrated their ignorance of constitutional matters and made very heavy weather of the run up to what became the Constitutional Reform Act 2005, as we discussed in Chapter 3.

Whilst there was a tacit acceptance among some of our interviewees, that the changes were a *fait accompli*, it was also a matter of regret that the role of the Lord Chancellor had been diminished by its merging with that of Secretary of State for Justice. Lord Phillips had seen the Lord Chancellor as someone that sat across all official branches of the State, with an independent voice, the authority to stand up to the Prime Minister, the ability to advise on legislative and constitutional matters, and a representative of the Judiciary in Cabinet – in short 'the most important member of the cabinet after the Prime Minister'. Lord Judge told us 'I would like it restored … somebody who hasn't got another department to worry about, and who is of such a standing that sacking your Lord Chancellor is rather serious'. At least one former Lord Chancellor, Charlie Falconer concurred. In our view the two roles do not sit well together and create a potentially serious conflict of interest, as was exposed during the tenure of Liz Truss. This is especially problematic when the holder is not even required to be a lawyer, or indeed, to be familiar with the constitution.

Having criticised our politicians of ignorance we need to remind our readers that we also lack both legal and constitutional expertise. However, as we have already noted, what politicians have, with hindsight, mistakenly done in the past, can be undone in the light of experience. We put forward these suggestions for others to explore whether these might be workable, or not. As on so many other matters they probably can't be worse than what we have now. In that spirit we propose that the quite different positions and responsibilities of the Secretary of State and the Lord Chancellor be separated from one another, with the latter having a genuinely independent role. We do not think that role should, or could, be filled by a politician – indeed he or she should be politically neutral or above politics, albeit with privileged access to the cabinet whenever constitutional matters, or things affecting the justice system, including criminal justice, are proposed. The Lord Chancellor would also have the right to address Parliament on such matters. The terms of that access would be enshrined in legislation. Candidates for the role should be drawn from the ranks of distinguished lawyers, and should be appointed as a politically neutral custodian of the Constitution and judicial independence by a group comprising the Prime Minister, and the leaders of opposition parties as advised by the Lord Chief Justice. The appointment could be for a guaranteed fixed period during which the appointee could not be dismissed. Alternatively, it might be considered appropriate for there to be a natural succession, whereby a retiring Lord Chief Justice would go on to become Lord Chancellor. If the Lord Chancellor were to resume the role of Head of the Judiciary, as we think should happen, then the temptation of (need for?) Lord Chief Justices to enter the political arena would be removed.

It seems to us that such a role would avoid the previous problems concerning the separation of powers, and instead become the upholder of the harmonious and respectful operation of the three pillars of the State. The fate of Lord Leveson's proposals, following his Inquiry into phone hacking, indicates the difficulties of achieving a respectful, but still free Press. Those difficulties will have only become more complex with the rise of social media. Nevertheless, we suggest that the role of a politically neutral Lord Chancellor should have powers to reprimand the Press in situations where the Press overstep the boundaries of their domain, and to impose simple sanctions.

The prisons and probation inspectorates

In general, we applaud the work of the Inspectorates and believe they have mostly operated independently exposing the extent of the crisis facing both prisons and probations whether these derived from operational failings or misguided policies. The probation Inspectorate may still have work to do in finding appropriate methodologies to assess some areas of probation work, and we have some anxieties as to the way in which the Urgent Notification (UN) procedure may be used in prisons and even more about recent plans to extend its remit from measurable outputs against standards to value judgements about leadership. But we have no recommendations for changes.

The status of prisons and probation services

In the preceding chapters, we have attempted to chart the vicissitudes which have been visited upon the prison and probation services. This has been the beginning and will now be the end of our endeavours. Both services have suffered greatly at the hands of at least some, though not quite all, ministers. There is no point in recapitulating here the many changes, of policy and organisation they have undergone, but it is important to stress that not everything has been bad. The brutality in prisons that led to the death of Barry Prosser in Winson Green, and which Martin Narey was determined to eradicate, has indeed been eliminated – although there is always a danger that it could return. The decency agenda survives if only there were enough resources to sustain it. It also has to be said that Michael Spurr, Phil Wheatley and Martin Narey, in their sometimes different ways, have made prodigious efforts to make the merger of prisons and probation work, and to provide a more joined up system of managing offenders. As befits a conclusion we must start from where we are and look to the future. But we do need to pause for an update on probation before we can proceed.

We are all too aware that the present Government's new future for the probation service, which involved periods of consultation, and several re-thinks, goes live in June 2021. David Gauke had initially intended to strengthen and re-build confidence in probation through the establishment of a professional register, and revised training, and the recruitment of 1,000 new officers, whilst retaining significant private involvement in relation to unpaid work and accredited programmes, albeit with more rigorous contracts. The National Probation Service (NPS) was to be realigned with Community Rehabilitation Company (CRC) areas. But this plan was quickly jettisoned following Glenys Stacey's final report and CRCs were abandoned and their staff are to become part of the NPS which would deal with offenders of all risk levels – similar to the arrangement already adopted in Wales following the review chaired by Lord Thomas at the time we interviewed him. A year later, Gauke's successor, Robert Buckland, announced that he was cancelling the competition for unpaid work and accredited programmes thus reversing most of the aberrations of Grayling's Transforming Rehabilitation (TR). The new service is to be organised in 12 areas each with its own Regional Probation Director, accountable for commissioning of services. At the time of writing there are many issues yet to be resolved in the new arrangements.

In his Report, Woolf (1991) had wisely argued that the last thing the prison service needed was more organisational change and that Waddington's recently implemented proposals should be allowed to bed down. Like Woolf, we would prefer a gradualist approach to get from where we are to where we would like to be. Nevertheless, we have to say that we hold to the view that both prisons and probation would be better off separately rather than joined together.

In our view whilst prisons should continue as a *centralised* organisation probation should be firmly linked to *local* communities because that is where its main business lies and where the social, economic and cultural solutions to criminality need to be sought. We recognise that it is possible to think of a *regionalised* prison system with each region having a range of appropriate services, with a centralised high security estate to which the regions might send their most difficult offenders. It might be possible to devise prison regions which match the proposed probation regions but a major stumbling block is the geographical locations of the prison estate. There are some bits of our history with which we just have to live.

Our preference for probation would be for a return to a highly localised service firmly linked once more to the courts from which it sprung. Local Chief Officers would be better able than either regional or central bodies to provide a range of services relevant to the courts they serve, and to draw upon the services of other local bodies which are appropriate for the area. They should also be able to speak out on behalf of probation in ways in which centralised civil servants never could. Above all, we would like to see a return to a situation where the local courts had a significant role, including a financial interest, in the management of probation. The courts are the *real* commissioners of probation services – for timely, but thorough, pre-sentence reports, for immediate supervision of community sentences and deferred supervision on release from custodial sentences. Nowhere in the current proposals does this seem to be fully recognised. Accountability seems to run upwards to the centralised Ministry rather than outwards to the local communities. It remains to be seen how far probation services have a real connection to the local communities under the current plans, and how far Regional Probation Directors will have the voice to speak out in ways that will be needed if the service is to regain legitimacy in the eyes of the bench. We are rather doubtful as to how far the new structure will meet those needs. Perhaps it will be possible, as the system beds down, to devolve matters from the 12 regions to court areas and give courts and local councils, a greater say and financial interest, in the management of probation in their areas. Nor are we sure what will be involved in the revised training but we would want to see a move backwards from the law enforcement mode favoured by politicians and a return to something like a social work mode, with a professional University-based training as well as less compulsion and more voluntary agreement in the relationship between the probation officer and offender.

With the above in mind, here is our provisional suggestion for a framework that would allow those things to happen without undue ministerial interference in operational matters, whilst still giving them the possibility for a light touch on the rudder.

The status of the prison and probation services should be enshrined in a short Act of Parliament. Legislation wouldn't offer complete guarantees but it would take time and effort to undo and would put a brake on Ministers who may not know how long they are there. This would provide for either a single Agency – the current HMPPS with an overarching Chief Executive and separate Directors of Prisons and Probation – or two separate Agencies, HM Prison Service and HM Probation Service, each with their own Chief Officer. For simplicity we write here as for a single Agency, but if two Agencies were contemplated the same general rules and principles would apply to both.

The Agency would be genuinely at 'arms-length' following the successful model operating in Sweden, under which the Minister is expressly excluded from interference in operational matters once the general direction of policy travel has been set for the lifetime of a parliament. If any change in the direction of travel were proposed following a change of Government, the new Minister would be required to follow a full process of consultation with the Chief Executive and Directors of the two Services as well as the Lord Chancellor (in their new role above), the Lord Chief Justice and the Treasury to ensure that any changes would be fully funded.

All of the necessary functions to carry out the operations of the Agency – administration, finances, estates, human resources, commissioning of services and so on would be returned to the Agency from the MoJ (some already had been returned in the package that Michael Spurr secured for his successors). This will go against the tide of current policy across government departments where control of such matters has been clawed back to the centre. But we cannot emphasise enough that one size doesn't fit all. Prisons and probation are very large-scale *operational* concerns with an extremely large number of staff and very difficult clients. Operational directors need control of such functions, and cannot reasonably be held responsible and accountable if they do not.

A Framework Document would set out a code of standards, including the expectations placed upon the Agency and its Chief Executive. These would include well-defined inputs and reasonable outputs – which is to say that unrealistic outputs in terms of so-called reoffending or reconviction rates would be expressly excluded and vacuous slogans such as the current delivering a 'world class' service avoided. Ministers should understand that hoping for rehabilitation by putting offenders in a situation expressly designed to de-habilitate them – as in prisons – is not a reasonable expectation. However, it would be right that reasonable inputs should be expected to facilitate the return of prisoners to the community and would include the provision of educational and work opportunities, health and welfare facilities, high-quality visits and telephone facilities to help maintain family relationships. Reasonable outputs would be measured in terms of escapes, incidents involving disturbances, assaults and self-injury and the control of drugs, cleanliness and time out of cells for prisons. The code would also include a provision, underwritten by the Treasury such as the one proposed by Lord Woolf 30 years ago, to ensure that the prison population would not be allowed to exceed its certified normal accommodation (CNA).

For probation, Ministers need to understand that, turning the lives around of people who have led disorganised lives, never enjoyed supportive families, or the luxury of a good education and a secure place in society takes time and heavy-duty inputs rather than yet more controls. Inputs would be measured by type and frequency of contacts with supervisees, provision of services such as drug or other programmes and attempts to solve related problems. Outputs would include getting suitable housing, getting and keeping employment and managing finances and relationships.

The Chief Executive, and Directors of Prisons and Probation, should be held both responsible and accountable for all those matters directly under their control to a new Prisons and Probation Board, under a distinguished Chairman. The Board would comprise experienced and knowledgeable figures from across the criminal justice field – the courts, the police – and former Directors of Prisons and Probation. The Chief Executive would answer questions before Parliament and the Justice Committee, but as the operational head the Chief Executive would also have the duty to speak publicly on behalf of the Agency, as would the Directors of Prisons and Probation on behalf of their respective services.

A final word

We can only hope now that Honest Politicians will come forward in common cause and work together, regardless of political party, on an agreed future plan for prisons and probation within a sensible framework of sentencing policy. They should have the courage always to speak truthfully about what is realistically possible, whether they are in power or not, and resist the temptation to raise public expectations in knee-jerk reactions to rare events. Having read this book we hope that they will be cautious about what they wish for in criminal justice, reflect upon the dangers of hubris and be aware of the potential consequences of their enactments and their supposed organisational reforms.

References

Bradley, Lord (2009) *Review of People with Mental Health Problems or Learning Difficulties in the Criminal Justice System*, April.

Carter, Lord (2003) *Managing Offenders – Reducing Crime*, The Strategy Unit.

Carter, Lord (2007) *Securing the Future. Proposals for the Efficient and Sustainable Use of Custody in England and Wales*, House of Lords.

Corston, Baroness (2007) *A Report by Baroness Jean Corston of a Review of Women with Particular Vulnerabilities in the Criminal Justice System*.

Clarke, K. (2016) *Kind of Blue: A Political Memoir*, London: Macmillan.

Durkheim, Emile (1895, English translation 1982) *The Rules of Sociological Method*, New York: Free Press.

Fulton Report (1968) *The Civil Service*, Report of the Committee 1966–68, Volume 1 (Cmnd 3638) London: HMSO.

Shaw, S. (2010) *Fifty Year Stretch: Prisons and Imprisonment 1980–2030*, Hook, Waterside Press.

Woolf, Lord (1991) (The Woolf Report) *Prison Disturbances April 1990*, Report of an Inquiry by the Rt. Hon. Lord Justice Woolf (Parts I and II) and His Honour Judge Stephen Tumim (Part II) Cm. 1456. Feb.1991, London: HMSO.

EPILOGUE

Half a century ago Norval Morris and Gordon Hawkins, in their book *The Honest Politician's Guide to Crime Control*, placed the fear of crime ahead of the fear of epidemics in the national consciousness of Americans. We need hardly say that, with the worldwide devastation to lives and livelihoods wrought by COVID-19 and its variants, all that has changed. Headlines about crime and punishment have largely given way to matters such as the failures of 'test and trace', the miseries of lockdowns, and latterly to the progress of vaccinations. But this hasn't stopped politicians from continuing to produce legislation in much the same vein as before.

We planned to end our research with the general election of 2019. But in this brief epilogue we reflect on what has happened since then. First, we comment on continuities in sentencing policy and further changes within the Ministry of Justice (MoJ) which affect the structure and organisation of Her Majesty's Prison and Probation Service (HMPPS), before proceeding to consider some of the experiences of COVID-19 in our prisons and probation, as well as the ongoing effects of staff shortages and probation unification, and finally to consider some possible lessons from the experience of handling the pandemic.

Sentencing matters

The Conservative manifesto for the 2019 election promised to establish a Royal Commission on the Criminal Justice System, but by November 2020, although a budget had been allocated, no decisions had been taken on the terms of reference or its composition. Royal Commissions do not have a good record in the criminal justice field and so the expectation of a report by the summer of 2022 was rather optimistic. Given the onset of COVID-19, apparently the time was not right for hasty decisions. This had not stopped the crafting of a Smarter

DOI: 10.4324/9781003201748-9

Approach to Sentencing White Paper 2020. Whereas David Gauke's use of the phrase 'smarter sentencing' was intended to end talk of being tough or soft on crime, under his successor, Robert Buckland, it now captured the manifesto promise of toughness but with added 'nuance'. Nor did it prevent the progress of the subsequent Police, Crime, Sentencing and Courts Bill 2021 designed to improve the efficiency and effectiveness of criminal justice – described as 'an end to end Bill' (Hansard, HC 15.3.21).

We cannot review these developments in any detail here. Suffice it to say that between them they do not speak to our sentencing recommendations but instead continue in the same sad way of upping sentencing lengths, introducing new mandatory sentences, new minimum starting points for life sentences, new inde-terminate sentences and new whole life sentences (including for young adults under the age of 21), in a broad range of areas which will likely ratchet up other sentences. Sexual offenders have again been singled out to serve a greater part of their sentence in custody and have stricter requirements on release, despite evidence of their low rate of reoffending under existing arrangements. Community orders are to be made yet more robust with the possibility of extending curfews to a maximum of 20 hours a day. The highly publicised new powers of the police to curtail the right to protest and criminalise aspects of the lives of travellers, gypsies and Roma (all things that are rightly being challenged) have limited debate on other aspects of the Bill that will inevitably increase numbers in prisons, on probation and coming before the Parole Board.

Where have we heard all this before? And how many times? When will they ever learn? What is very worrying is that there was either cross-party agreement on these things, or Opposition calls to be even tougher, during the second, curtailed, reading of the Bill. Two welcome developments concern the renewed commitment to judicial monitoring and problem-solving courts, and long-promised changes regarding the rules on spent convictions. However, the determination to resist further changes to prisoner voting does not speak to the promotion of reintegration of prisoners into society. It would surely have made more sense to await a more carefully considered approach given the promise of a Royal Commission rather than to tie its hands.

Although prison sentences continue to be served immediately during the pandemic, with no formal expansion of community sentences, the Court of Appeal has provided advice to the courts that they may take account of the conditions in which prisoners were being held in fixing sentences. In *R v Manning* [2020] EWCA Crim 592 the Appeal Court decided *not* to increase the sentence despite the reference by the Attorney General on grounds of undue leniency. Following this, in *R v Jones* [2020] EWCA Crim 764, the Court of Appeal held that it was appropriate to take account of the custodial conditions under which an offender was to be held when considering an appeal against sentence. In that case, the sentence was *reduced* from eight months to six. It is impossible to know how many people, who would 'normally' have received a given custodial sentence, actually received a shorter one or a community sentence instead because of the pandemic.

But given the impact of COVID-19 on the already beleaguered police service and the courts there would be fewer new cases passing through the system.

Changes at the Ministry of Justice

During the year since our project ended Antonia Romeo, once the responsible owner of Transforming Rehabilitation (TR), returned to the MoJ as Permanent Secretary. And more recently, the CEO of Her Majesty's Probation and Prison Service (HMPPS), Jo Farrar, has been made a second Permanent Secretary within the Department. This seems, at first sight, to be a return to the situation which applied during the first iteration of NOMS when Martin Narey was at the helm. Under that arrangement, Narey was able to have some degree of direct contact with the Prime Minister, and the Treasury, and was also a member of the then Sentencing Guidelines Council. He had a real voice in policy matters affecting prisons and probation, particularly in regard to the supply of, and demand for, prison places. It was a full-time job firmly rooted in prisons and probation. However, we understand that the new post covers not only the HMPPS Agency, but also the Legal Aid Agency, which has a budget of £2 billion, as well as the Office for the Public Guardian, and Criminal Injuries Compensation, among possibly others. This appears to be in line with what has been happening across government generally with a number of other departments appointing second Permanent Secretaries responsible for 'delivery' – part of a centralising of power arrangement now preferred by Ministers.

It seems to us that it would be quite impossible for anyone to perform that role of extended departmental responsibilities without becoming more removed from day-to-day operational matters – a detachment which would make the expanded role of advice to Ministers less well informed or useful. It would also mean that the Chief Executive of HMPPS would not be able to provide the downwards operational focus, and dedicated leadership, that such a large and complex organisation so badly needs if it is to remain as a single integrated agency. Viewed from below the CEO would inevitably be seen as remote: someone overseeing/administering the services on behalf of the Department rather than leading and managing the services on a day-to-day basis. Essentially that responsibility will now fall squarely on the shoulders of the Director General of Prisons, Phil Copple, and the Director General of Probation, Amy Rees. But if that is going to be the model then, in our view, the logical outcome should be to replace the combined HMPPS Agency with two separate Agencies for Prisons and Probation – each with a Director General (or Chief Executive) as Head of Service and Accounting Officer with a designated budget. They could each report to the Second Permanent Secretary, but would be able to provide more visible leadership to their Services and be available to advise Ministers as the Professional Head of Service and give evidence to Parliamentary Committees on that basis. We believe such an arrangement would be very positive for probation and address the 'Cinderella service' tag which still lingers. It would also make a move back to a local delivery model sometime in the future much more straightforward to achieve.

Prisons, staffing and COVID-19

The effects of COVID-19 on prisons and the people who work in them, as well as prisoners for whom a small cell is their home, have been huge. On 24 March 2020, the prison service had moved into an exceptional state of lockdown with very large numbers of prisoners confined to their cells for more than 22 hours every day, with non-essential visits and employment suspended, and education severely reduced. Given the poor state of physical and mental health of many prisoners such levels of sustained deprivation can barely be imagined. In April 2020, Public Health England, unnecessarily one might have thought, advised that the best way of restricting the spread of the virus in prisons was to house prisoners in single cells. But it was also argued that the benefits of prolonged infection control needed to be weighed against the negative consequences for mental health.

The Government responded by announcing that since many prisoners were currently sharing cells they would start to release *up to* 4,000 low-risk prisoners who were close to the end of their sentences under an End of Custody Temporary Release (ECTR) scheme. The Secretary of State had also advised that prisoners could apply for Release on Temporary Licence (ROTL) by way of Special Purpose Licence (SPL), whereby release would be for the duration of the pandemic. This scheme was restricted to pregnant women, mothers with babies in custody, and those defined by NHS guidelines as *extremely vulnerable* to COVID-19 – and in March 2020 the Minister stated there were about 1,800 prisoners who met those guidelines. Few prisoners actually took up the Special Purpose ROTL scheme. The standard ROTL scheme, which in normal times had become a useful safety valve to relieve population pressure, had been run down and was eventually suspended. The End of Custody Temporary Release scheme was itself ended in August 2020, by which time just 275 prisoners had been released (*The Guardian*, 19.8.20).

HMPPS responded in other ways in an attempt to mitigate the effects of permanent lockdown at least for some prisoners. A Government update on 6 November 2020 reported that prisoners would still be able to see family and friends via one half-hour secure video call per month. More than 1,200 mobile handsets were also distributed with extra phone credit. But with so many prisoners experiencing the privations, duly recorded by the Chief Inspector and the National Audit Office, demand was certain to be much greater than the supply. Anecdotal reports on virtual visits have been poor owing to the limited facilities in some prisons and the fact that visits can be cut off if someone unsanctioned enters a room in a house.

However, in some ways, the prisons have coped much better than predicted. Some 143 deaths related to COVID-19 were reported between March 2020 and

March 2021. This was three times the rate for comparable age groups in the community but very much lower than the predicted worst-case scenario of up to 2,000 deaths. However, the rate of infection, unsurprisingly, was very high with over 4,000 new cases across the prison estate being recorded in January 2021 alone (Braithwaite et al. *Lancet*,16.3.21). It must have been frustrating for Phil Copple that Robert Buckland chose to ignore the clear advice from SAGE, to prioritise prisoners for vaccination. It was a decision that Anne Owers, Chair of prison Independent Monitoring Boards (IMBs), certainly found distressing. Interestingly, self-harm rates and assaults for males went down and have continued to be lower than in recent years, the former, perhaps, because lockdown removed some of the stressors normally associated with self-harm, and the latter through reduced opportunities.

Of course, COVID-19 has had an effect on staff as well as prisoners. The same *Lancet* paper quoted the Prison Officers' Association (POA) as referring to 20 COVID-19 deaths up to mid-January 2021 and that at that time 4,800 staff were absent. Official HMPPS statistics for 31 January 2021 provide a somewhat different picture with 32 staff deaths among prisons and youth custody staff, but with only 1,961 staff absent from work – still more than enough to raise anxiety levels for staff and their families. Enough also to have an influence on staff joining and leaving the service altogether. The recruitment drive, much trumpeted by Liz Truss and her successors, had gone into reverse, although there were enough officers in post to manage the restricted regimes. But surely not enough to run expanded regimes if and when it became time to resume them. It is also of note that the 1:6 ratio of keyworkers to residents of Truss's offender management in custody model (OMiC) had already risen to 1:10, and more tellingly, even prior to the pandemic, it was not operating as planned with one IMB reporting only 3 % of sessions taking place in 2019.

Probation, unification and COVID-19

Although the probation service was spared the accommodation problems that bedevilled the prison service, except perhaps in some approved premises, it was hit hard by the pandemic in other ways. Probation was given the job of monitoring all those to be released early from prison. However, as we have seen, very few were so released and it seems unlikely that the probation service could have coped with many more. The service was already overstretched with more than 600 vacancies in 2019 and workloads over target for almost two-thirds of probation officers. On 24 March 2020, the model for delivering probation supervision was changed dramatically to an 'exceptional delivery model'. All unpaid work was suspended as were most offender management programmes, and greater use was made of electronic monitoring. Digital supervision – via phone, Skype and messaging – quickly replaced face-to-face meetings for lower risk offenders. For higher risk offenders probation officers made doorstep home visits. In April 2020 Amy Rees, Director General of Probation, told the Justice Committee that around 2,000 staff were off work every day because of COVID-19 and there was obviously concern about how the backlog of offenders waiting to do unpaid work and other programmes could be cleared. Unsurprisingly morale remained low. The probation Inspectorate found that the 'exceptional delivery model' worked well for public protection arrangements but not so well for service users with complex needs. The backlog of the courts had a significant effect on all court-related probation work.

COVID-19 seems to have provided cover to dismantle the final elements of TR by bringing unpaid work and interventions back into the public domain as part of the reunification of probation services. The introduction of the new model for probation is scheduled to begin in June 2021. This is to be followed by a period of stabilisation and harmonisation, and a final phase in 2022, with a return to professional registration of probation staff and improved IT. There is much to be done, as indicated in the thematic review by HM Inspectorate of Probation to prepare for the unification of the probation service. But this will not be the National Probation Service (NPS) we previously knew with 42 boards that became 35 trusts working closely with the local community. Instead, it will be a much more centralised service, albeit with some 12 regional directors, some drawn from the now-defunct Community Rehabilitation Companies (CRCs). Fears of a two-tier system remain, in which former CRC personnel may be viewed as part of the 'failed' side of the TR experiment. The unified service will have a new operational model which speaks of 'target operating', working with 'individuals subject to supervision' not offenders, and a return to 'probation practitioners' rather than offender managers. It brings probation officers back into prisons, with a different community team taking over some seven and half months prior to release. It will, in our view, require very strong leadership to see these changes through smoothly, especially in the light of the need for a major staff recruitment drive, the demand for new training programmes, and the necessity to bind the wounds inflicted by TR. This we believe only adds weight to the argument for splitting HMPPS into two separate agencies. Given the numbers of vacancies, with some probation areas running at 35% below establishment levels for qualified probation officers, it remains to be seen whether probation will be spread too thinly, across prisons and the community, to meet its targets.

Lessons from the experience of COVID-19 and the government response

There may be some crumbs of comfort if there are any lessons that can be learned from the experience of COVID-19. Here are just a few possibilities.

Be prepared. Although the National Health Service (NHS) was spared the worst effects of the years of austerity the Government was quite unprepared for the pandemic despite having had good warning of the probability of one arising. Even well before the pandemic struck, the NHS was short of nurses, doctors and equipment, had ever-growing waiting lists for surgery, and faced insatiable demands for treatment at A and E departments as general practice declined in the community. The main focus of the Government's response was to ensure that the NHS was not overwhelmed. The MoJ, on the other hand, bore the full brunt of austerity, and like the NHS demand for prison and probation service outstripped supply. The costs of being unprepared have, we suppose, far exceeded what it would have cost to be adequately, or at least better, prepared. It may be that, in future, our politicians will be more inclined to fund our public services properly rather than demand more for less.

A better appreciation of what it means to be locked up. The experience of COVID-19 has been different for different groups of people, but large numbers have now been *locked down* for periods measured in months. For the more affluent this will have been in the relative comfort of their own homes. For the poor and disadvantaged this will have been an additional burden piled upon their already difficult situations. But for most this will have been their first experience of being locked down, with severe restrictions on their movements. All should be in a position to know something of what it must be like for prisoners to be *locked up* and for those on community sentences to be on tagging and curfew restrictions. A wise and honest Justice Secretary could use that experience to create a better understanding of the consequences of sending already troubled people to longer and longer custodial sentences, measured in tens, even scores, of years, and to promote a climate more in favour of community sentencing without the need to seek ever-tougher restrictions.

A better understanding of risks. Although information about the risks of falling victim to COVID-19 has sometimes been confusingly presented there is little doubt that the risks of death or serious long-term harm from COVID-19 are greater for some than those of becoming a victim of serious crime – and a focus on that has reversed the order of fears expressed by Morris and Hawkins. Yet even in the course of this pandemic Ministers (and sadly Opposition leaders) have been unable to resist playing up the actually relatively small risks of crime in search of political advantage. Just as good statistics are necessary to manage the risks from COVID-19 for different groups in the community, so wise and honest politicians would familiarise themselves with crime statistics and the real risks of crime compared to many other hazards and would ensure that the public is kept well informed.

The need to respect experts. During the pandemic we have got used to Ministers sharing a platform with experts. Admittedly the range of experts has been limited and some potential consequences have received more attention than others. But the general point remains: that whilst initially, the claims to being driven by the science seemed more like bluster, by the time of the second wave the Government became more cautious and stayed closer to the advice of the experts. Meanwhile, behind the scenes, scientists at Oxford and elsewhere devised the vaccines which may yet protect us from the virus. In criminal justice, Michael Gove once proclaimed that 'we have had enough of experts' although he mainly had economists in mind. In practice he sought out the advice of Martin Narey on sentencing policy although he 'swerved' the big issues. He also sought the advice of Judges John Samuels and David Fletcher on judicial monitoring and problem-solving courts but was moved on before he could do much about it. Sadly, too few Justice Secretaries have listened to their civil servants or experienced professionals responsible for operations. Had they done so, many mistakes could have been avoided.

No doubt there are many other lessons which could be learned from the handling of COVID-19, depending upon one's point of view. Would it be too much to hope that our politicians might take them on board, as well as those we have already offered in this guide to prisons and probation?

INDEX

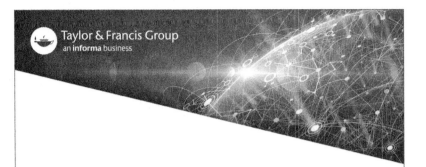

Printed in Great Britain
by Amazon